The Waygook Book

A Foreigner's Guide to South Korea

Matthew Caracciolo

Monday Creek Publishing LLC
mondaycreekpublishing.com

Copyright © 2018 Matthew Caracciolo
Copyright © 2018 Monday Creek Publishing. All rights reserved.
Monday Creek Publishing | Buchtel, Ohio 45716 | USA
www.mondaycreekpublishing.com
Kathy Bick, Editor

Cover photo courtesy Kelly Schinner. The name tag reads *Foreigner*.

Back cover photos courtesy Abbi Sauro.

1. Waygook Book, The   2. South Korea – Non-Fiction   3. Memoir

ISBN: 978-0-578-44981-4

For Maria, obviously.

Contents

Acknowledgements

For Christmas, when I was about five years old, I wanted one of those WWF Wrestling Buddies that you could punch in the face and throw against the wall and call names and do just about anything to. My mom wasn't about that, so instead I received a My Buddy doll, a smiling, tamer toy for a tamer sort of boy. I wasn't destined for hyper-masculinity, it seemed. I was to be the introspective, writer type. What I'm getting at is my mom is probably responsible for the book you hold in your hand.

Equally responsible is my dad, who before my short-lived WWF aspirations taught me to read using flash cards on our apartment floor. We'd put together sentences featuring Sesame Street characters and by kindergarten, I could more or less get through War and Peace.

I couldn't have written this book without the help of some stellar individuals. A big thank you is due to David, Kelly, Derek, Bethany, Jennifer, and Hallie for reading excerpts and offering feedback and reactions. A special thanks to Amy and Trent for our writing group meetings and their constructive criticisms. Thanks to Chuyoung for doing some translation work on the Gutenberg documentary.

Thanks to the Gu Crew, to Ji Young and Jang Mi and anyone else I shared life with in South Korea. You contributed to some of the best years of my life.

I'm deeply indebted to Gina and Monday Creek Publishing for taking a chance on a debut author.

Finally, the person most responsible for this book is Maria, whose love and support has pulled me out of insecurity and doubt to finish this project and get it published. Also, it was her idea to go to South Korea in the first place, so literally nothing in this book would have happened without her.

Prologue

In a hole in the ground, there lived a hobbit…

I am not a hobbit. I do not live in a hole in the ground. Yet, my goals in life couldn't be put plainer than when Bilbo Baggins, in *The Fellowship of the Ring*, tells the wizard Gandalf "I want to see mountains and find somewhere where I can finish my book."

The truth is, I identify a lot with Bilbo and all hobbits. I'm not all that tall. I have hairy feet. I approve of elevensies (a meal promptly at 11:00am). As an introvert, I'm also a bit of a homebody. I like routine. I like to schedule my meals ahead of time, and not be late for them. More than anything, though, I like to have certainty, which is what hobbits do best. They live in a quiet farming community, the Shire, living with the same neighbors they've always had, living in the same houses, and working the same jobs to the end of their days. They're certainly not the adventurous type. While on one hand that may sound boring, you never hear of a hobbit filing for unemployment, writing cover letters, or worrying about health insurance. Their station in life is secure.

Central Ohio reminds me of the Shire sometimes. Like the Shire, Ohio is not a place of mountain ranges or mighty rivers, but of woods and fields and 'good tilled earth.' It even rather looks like the Shire if you squint hard enough in the right corners. Aesthetics notwithstanding, it's where I grew up and it's where things make sense to me. Therefore it is where I most identify with as home.

This is the story of how this hobbit came back home to his Shire via South Korea.

There's an estimated 30,000 *waygook saram[1]*, or 'foreign people,' teaching English in South Korea, officially the Republic of Korea. Their reasons are as varied as their countries of origin. Some come to boost their ESL career. Others come to satisfy their wanderlust. A good many come because they need a job. I met a couple who came so that their Korean health insurance would pay

---

[1] As opposed to *waygookin* which is *foreigner*. Expats in South Korea often refer to themselves as *waygooks* even though this is grammatically incorrect.

for a pregnancy. If you're an American, then this will make complete sense to you. Me? I taught English in South Korea with my wife, Maria, because it was my best ticket back to Ohio, even though I knew practically nothing about it. After living there for two years, I know almost something about it now.

Before living there, I regarded South Korea as most Americans do: as the forgotten child of East Asia. This is simply because we haven't developed many stereotypes about the country or its citizens. We "know" a lot more about China and Japan. When we think of China we think of pandas, communism, Jackie Chan and General Tso's chicken (not a Chinese menu item, actually). Meanwhile, Japan has given us Godzilla, Pokémon, and sushi. We've seen movies with sumo wrestlers and samurai. We remember that we fought Japan hard in WWII, dropped atomic bombs on two of their cities, and that we've generally been friends ever since. Now how easy is it to generate a list of things associated with South Korea? Not very, at least to the untrained eye.

So what has Korea given us on the same level as Pikachu? A lot, actually. Samsung, the manufacturer of more smartphones than any other company in the world, is Korean. LG Electronics is Korean. Hyundai and Kia cars are Korean. In the span of three sentences, South Korea has influenced the way you communicate, watch TV, and commute. South Korea isn't only exporting things we need, but things we are beginning to like. Korean barbecue restaurants are opening every other day. Kimchi is gaining traction as a health food and even as a topping on tacos. Gradually, our attention is shifting to South Korea; we are adding its people and things to our cultural lexicon. After all, the Avengers cared enough about Seoul to destroy a small part of it in a car chase in the film *Avengers: Age of Ultron*. Busan received the same treatment in *Black Panther* three years later. You know you've got America's attention when your cities are the subject of our disaster movies. Meanwhile, South Korean culture is exploding in popularity throughout the rest of Asia in a movement known as the Hallyu Wave. Millions devour the country's TV Dramas, romantic comedies, and music. In some circles, these things are already popular in the United States.

But let's not reduce South Korea to pop culture references like we do China and Japan. It's an actual place, after all, full of actual people. The country is about the size of Indiana, but with the population of Texas, New York, and Indiana combined. 70% of the country is mountainous, so there's not much space for over 50 million people to pitch their tent, grow their food, and putt a few rounds. This makes South Korea one of the most crowded countries in the world. None of the country's mountains are particularly tall; the highest, Hallasan on Jeju Island, is only 6,400 feet – about as tall as the loftiest of the Appalachians. In fact, there is nothing jaw dropping about South Korean geography. There are taller, wider, deeper, hotter, colder, and wetter places just about everywhere else in the world. It may not make for riveting statistics, but it makes South Korea a pretty comfortable place to live. It's nestled safely in the temperate zone, with four distinct seasons plus a monsoon in the summer. Minus the monsoon, it's climate and geography are not unlike much of the eastern United States.

South Korea is also a lot wealthier and developed than you probably supposed, although this shouldn't come as a surprise with the likes of Samsung and Hyundai throwing their weight around. It wasn't always that way. In 1960, the country's per capita income was below Haiti's. Today, South Korea's economy is the 11th largest in the world, powered by the aforementioned manufacturing and technology juggernauts. Korea joined the OECD, or Organization for Economic Co-operation and Development, in 1996, which is an unofficial but widely accepted certification as an advanced, developed country. It doesn't barely pass muster either. South Korea is the only country in the OECD that was once an aid recipient but is now an aid donor. In 2016, the country's Human Development Index -- a composite score based on life expectancy, education and per capita income -- ranked the 19th highest in the world. By comparison, the United States was 10th, the United Kingdom 16th, France 21st and Italy 26th. Clearly, South Korea has been busy and we haven't noticed.

But don't think for a second that you have South Korea pegged already; it's a hard place to figure. I'm not going to tell you that it's a 'land of contrasts' (any country can be defined as such if you look hard enough) but I'll go one further: South Korea is downright contradictory. It is at once a collective hive of busy workers producing for the good of the mother country and a nation of individuals competing against each other for space and success. It's a country with one of the most highly-educated workforces in the world, yet a substantial percentage of the population believes that if you leave a fan on in a room with all the windows closed, you could suffocate. Korean culture places so much emphasis on appearances that job applications often require photographs along with resumes, yet you will never see a more drab landscape than a Korean metropolis. I've never been in a place more resistant to definition than South Korea. Really, the Koreans should be proud. This is not an easy achievement.

If you're reading this book, you likely fall into two camps: you are in some fashion interested in South Korea either because you're going or you've been, or you know me and I asked you to read it and you're being polite. Either way, you're likely to read this book with the desire to better understand South Korea. Full disclosure: I do not understand South Korea. I know some useful things about it, some places to go, and some food to eat. I know what it looks like to be an English teacher in a Korean public school. I will happily share all of this information in the pages ahead. However, there is no country on Earth, least of all South Korea, that can be summed up in a few hundred pages. Instead, my hope is that I paint a picture of the terrifying and rewarding experience of living abroad. Living in another country is a high risk/high reward activity, after all. The risk is that your heart may never be whole again, that some part of you will always be elsewhere and you will never again exist in one place. The reward is a modicum of perspective. For some, this price is too great. Better to be safe in a tree than lost in the woods. I understand, but I do not agree. In one year in a foreign country, preferably one that does not speak your language, you will learn more about yourself and your place in the world than 10 years at home. You'll feel smaller than you ever thought you could, but it's in this smallness as a foreigner, as a hobbit trying to get home, as a 'waygook,' that you learn two very important lessons: the hard truth that the world does not revolve around you or your tribe, and that one of the best things about homes is returning to them.

Like any honest attempt at retelling a true story, I've tweaked a few things. In the interest of privacy, I've changed the names of nearly everybody other than myself and Maria. It was also necessary to combine characters. Maria and I were fortunate to make good friends—practically family now—while in South Korea. Gail and

Phillip, as you will see, were present for nearly everything Maria and I experienced. That's because they represent four people apiece, all interchangeably along for this ride or that. As much as I'd like to describe who exactly was where when, frequent lists of four to eight people do not make for riveting prose. It will suffice to know that members of this family, under the pseudonyms of Gail and Phillip, were around and adding value to our lives. As far as the conversations go, they are as accurate as I can remember. Some of them were written down the day of, others condensed later. A handful are taken out of context and moved, word for word, to a different moment in time. All statistics and historical information are the result of research both online and at my local library and were accurate at the time of writing. All told, what follows is about 90% true. The news today should be so lucky.

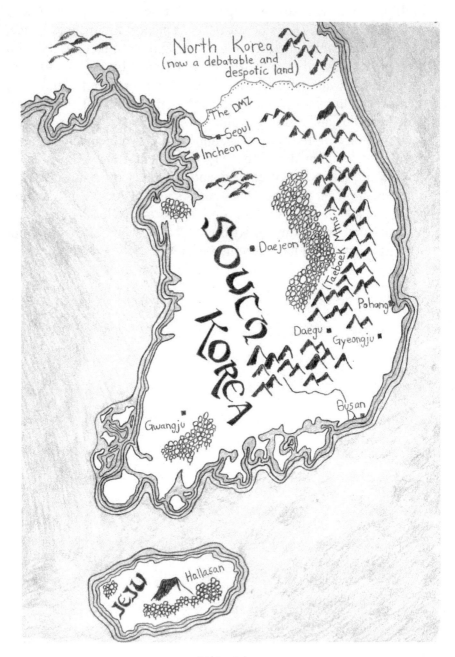

A thing I drew.

Leaving Chicago

That Time My Bike Was Stolen

I don't like Chicago. Actually, let me rephrase. I don't like *living* in Chicago. The city has fantastic architecture, world-class cultural amenities, and something masquerading as pizza called 'deep-dish,' but the thing about famous landmarks is that they cost a lot of money to see. On a daily, this-makes-life-better-or-easier sort of list, Lincoln Park is about it. I love that there is a free zoo that, if you're not paying attention, you may unwittingly wander into and bump into a rhinoceros. I love that the ponds are designed to be habitats for endangered and migratory birds. There's the lily pond, the harbors, the public art. It's all wonderful. What's best is the trail that extends the entire length of the park along Lake Michigan, on which I could ride my bike as far as my legs would carry me from my Lakeview apartment (so, to Oak Street Beach). I can't thank architect Daniel Burnham enough for his 1909 Chicago Plan, in which he laid out an expansive park along the water.

"The Lakefront by right belongs to the people," Burnham wrote. "Not a foot of its shores should be appropriated to the exclusion of the people."

And that's why I love Lincoln Park. It belongs to anybody. No matter what other stresses pestered me, I could leave them at home and spend a few hours amidst wildlife and greenery in the middle of a giant city. My bike was my free access to all these wonderful

1

things.

Until it wasn't.

It was a sunny day from what I could tell from our apartment window. Our place was a cave, facing an inner courtyard and receiving an hour or two of reliable natural light a day. It was August and I had finished a shift as an online writing tutor, one of my three jobs at the time. I taught basic composition at the College of Lake County, an hour and a half drive north on a good day. I was also a delivery driver during the winters at a soup restaurant, delivering hot soup to yuppies too rich to venture into the cold. I don't blame them. Chicago winters suck. Maria was at work at Pizza Persona, a sort of 'build your own' pizza joint, so the afternoon was mine. It was time for a bike ride through Lincoln Park. I changed into my gym shorts and my Ohio State freshman orientation shirt, still going strong as a workout shirt years after the fact. I put on my helmet, laced up my tennis shoes, and headed to the garage where I left my bike.

Our apartment building did not have a bike rack, so instead, people more or less piled their bikes against a wall in the building's garage. I always tried to place mine somewhat in the middle of the pile to be less conspicuous. I walked into the garage. There was the pile, but not my bike. I stood there frozen for a second, thinking. *Did I leave it somewhere? Did I ride my bike to Pizza Persona and take the bus back?* Further review of my last couple days proved that I had not. It should have been here.

I texted Maria. MY BIKE IS GONE. DO YOU KNOW WHERE IT IS? I walked back upstairs to our apartment.

She responded. NO. DID YOU LEAVE IT SOMEWHERE?

NO, I texted back. I THINK IT WAS STOLEN.

I'd never had something stolen from me before. It's an upsetting thing, spoiler alert. *Where's this thing I'm supposed to have? I've taken such good care of it. Somebody took it. Why would somebody do that?*

And then it dawned on me that my quick and easy access to Lincoln Park, my one free ticket to freedom and exercise, was taken from me, and that was a lot to handle at that moment.

Let's take a look at what 'that moment' was. I didn't grow up in Chicago. I was born and raised in Columbus, OH, a cheaper, not so crowded and very much smaller version of Chicago. Maria and I married two and a half weeks after graduating from The Ohio State

University and then moved to Chicago so I could pursue a master's degree in writing at DePaul University.

Nothing after that came easily. We came to the city with no money. We immediately took a job as a nanny/housekeeping team which took over our lives. Maria was working 14 hour days. I only got off easy with 10 hour days because I had classes at night. Five months later, apparently we sucked at our job and the family fired us. There was no warning, no real 'can you improve on this aspect of your job?' conversations, just 'we've decided to go in a different direction with our child care.' Maria was supposed to travel with them to Florida the next week. She was no longer needed. They'd already replaced us.

We had moved apartments to be close to them, which was a requirement for the position. Our original apartment's landlord wasn't too happy about that and tried to sue us. Even though we had legal help, it's unsettling to receive mail every day threatening a lawsuit. After getting fired, we both bounced around between part-time this and seasonal that. Maria worked as a temp, as an assistant for my aunt at her recruiting agency, as an assistant stage manager for a local theater, and as a wearer of many hats at another local theater until she landed the job at Pizza Persona. Even then, she still wore those hats at the latter theatre between shifts at the pizza place. As for myself, I was a temp as well for a few months. I also drove across the city to teach chess in schools, tutored at DePaul's writing center, and worked on a few eclectic freelance writing projects before settling into the two to three job shuffle I was currently in. We were constantly under-employed, making next to nothing, living in an expensive city, gaining weight, missing home, and starting to pay student loans for my graduate degree in writing which I had no time to use because I was too busy trying to earn enough money to live. And now my bike was gone, my one freely-available way to relieve stress and enjoy the city in which I found myself more-or-less imprisoned by underachievement. So that's what 'that moment' looked like, and it was too much for me. I wanted to go home.

Maria wasn't quite ready to go back to Columbus. She enjoyed Chicago more than I did and could see past the day-to-day struggles to appreciate the city for its liveliness, its diversity, and its beauty. I appreciated those things too, and there are aspects of urban life I picked up an appreciation for as a result of living there. I like walking places now and using public transportation, for instance. But she could see that I was deeply unhappy. There were much easier places to live, I'd remind her. And there were, like Columbus, where the majority of our friends and family still lived. When she came home from Pizza Persona that evening, I reminded her again. I made the case that we worked five jobs between the two of us so we could afford a one bedroom apartment. It wouldn't need to be so in Columbus.

"But if we go back to Columbus, we're going to stay there aren't we?" she said.

"Yeah, probably."

"I'm just not ready yet."

"What do you get here that you can't get in Columbus?" I posited. That was a stupid question.

"Free concerts at Millennium Park!" She had the answer in the barrel. "The museums. The buildings. The lake! I want to be near water."

"Yeah, well." I had answers in the barrel too. "Columbus' library is way better than Chicago's. And so is the zoo! And there's better ice cream."

"I know," she said.

I had her there. If there were three things Maria liked, it was libraries, zoos, and ice cream. Maria loves ice cream. I even used it in my marriage proposal, dangling the proposition of getting some to move her from Point A to Point B all the way to Point H or something like that. At last, she'd accumulated enough friends along the way and met me at the spot on Ohio State's campus where I first asked her to be my girlfriend. I proposed, we kissed, and then she said 'are we still getting ice cream?" We got ice cream, even though it was about 11am on a Sunday morning.

"There's more I want to do before we stay in one place," she sighed.

There was no use talking about it more that night. We played Mario Kart while I tried to forget about my stolen bike and Maria tried to forget about moving to Columbus. Autumn semester at College of Lake County was just starting, after all. It wasn't like I could give my two-week notice. We were there at least for another few months, and I'd have to find some other way to be happy about it. I had the feeling, however, that I was more like a circle and

Chicago was more like a square and ne'er the twain would fit.

Late on a Friday night, I went to bed but not to sleep. I tossed and turned but couldn't doze off. This wasn't unusual; it's often difficult for me to fall asleep. I can't shut off my brain. Maria eventually sat up.

"I'm going to go read in the living room," she said.

I felt bad. My turning and shuffling must have been keeping her awake too, I thought. She shut the door and I pulled the covers over my head, trying to get as comfortable as possible. My brain hacked through a thicket of self-doubt and frustration, wondering why I got a master's degree, studied English, wore blue instead of red that day. I put in my headphones and turned on some music to soothe me to sleep. Somewhere in the middle of John Mayer's "Heartbreak Warfare," a song only qualified to put people to sleep, I thought I heard a thud in the living room. *Probably just Maria*, I thought. I focused again on John Mayer. There were footsteps followed by a flushing toilet followed by more footsteps. Maria was doing something strangely noisy in the living room for two in the morning. I wasn't getting to sleep anytime soon (thanks for nothing, John) so I sat up, opened the door and walked into the brightness of the living room.

Four of my closest friends from Columbus were sitting on my sectional couch setting up sleeping bags on the floor. Two were college friends of ours and two were high school friends of mine. I looked at them and they looked at me and I realized I hadn't put any pants on.

"Dang, I was hoping you'd stay asleep!" laughed Maria. She picked up a piece of paper she'd placed in front of the door. She wrote *be right back!* on it in case I woke up and wondered where she was. "I went out to help them find a parking spot."

"What are you all doing in my living room?" I said, delighted but confused.

They explained that they had left Columbus after one of them, Joe, got off work. They were visiting for the weekend.

"Wow that's awesome," I said drowsily. "I should put on some pants."

My wonderful friends had driven from Columbus to Chicago through the night to surprise me in the morning. Unlike me, they were extremely tired and ready to get some sleep but decided to inform me of their dedication before turning in. Their story was that they didn't stop once on the trip, a story only plausible if you have a car like Joe's that looks like a piece of trash, is a piece of trash, but gets something like 700 miles to the gallon. They made good time, but at the expense of their bladders. When they arrived, all four were in desperate need of a bathroom. Their dilemma was that it'd be weird for me to wake up hearing Maria flush four times, so they agreed to wait to flush until the last person was finished. With that image in mind, we called it a night.

Maria and I were snug in bed again.

"What's the occasion?" I asked.

"I sent out a message on Facebook saying that you could really use some visitors right now," she explained. "They responded right away."

We kissed goodnight and she went to sleep. My wife's clandestine friend operation was another reminder that no matter where we lived, we were going to be okay so long as we were a team. To this day, I have never felt so loved in my life, both by my wife and my friends. Maria knew I wasn't feeling at home in Chicago, so she brought home to me.

A couple months after that incredible weekend, Maria sat on the couch with her computer in her lap. I sat at the desk, grading essays with a blue pen. Red pens are the worst.

"What do you think about teaching overseas?" she asked me. It was a completely new subject.

"Oh, uh...maybe? I haven't really thought about it."

"Where would you want to go?"

"Europe, I guess." That was the easiest answer. I'd never been to Europe and always wanted to go. Other than a church trip to Israel and a family vacation to Niagara Falls, I'd never been outside the country. "Maybe South America."

Maria explained that countries in Asia had the best benefits. South Korea paid for your flights, your housing, and a bonus for signing on for another year. She'd already been doing research.

"Ok, well we'll think about it," I said dismissively, trying to concentrate on grading the remaining essays.

Maria set her computer down and walked over to me. "I'm serious. Would you teach overseas?"

I set my pen down. "That's something that would take a lot of research. I have no time. If this is something you want to do, then you should find all the information."

She agreed to keep researching and let me finish grading.

Weeks marched by. My schedule was as busy as ever between my various jobs. I'd finish an online tutoring shift, grade a few papers, then rush out and deliver soup for a few hours. Delivering soup became my favorite of the three jobs: it didn't matter if my customers knew about dangling modifiers and they put cash in my hand. Maria slowly discovered new details about this program in Korea. EPIK, or English Program in Korea, looked more and more like the best option. Each week there was a new reason to consider moving to a new country, presumably South Korea, and teaching English.

"Korean food is cheap," she said, scrolling through a blog on food in Korea.

The weather changed in October and with it, my allergies. I got hit with a serious sinus infection.

"We'd get free health insurance in Korea," she said as I stood over the bathroom sink with a Neti Pot lodged in one nostril and warm, salty water pouring out the other. This was just before Obamacare was a thing, so we had no health insurance. Prescriptions for sinus infections included orange juice, cough drops, and happy thoughts.

"There's a lot of vacation time," she said, looking at the school calendar a few days after that. "Look at all the places we could go. We could go to New Zealand!"

I don't remember what I was doing at the time, but I stopped doing it. "We could do that, couldn't we," I mused. "It's got to be closer, right? Quick, look up some flights!" Maria did a quick search for flights to Auckland from Seoul compared to Columbus. They were a good thousand dollars cheaper.

I don't know if you could tell from the prologue, but now is as good a time as any to tell you something important: I like *The Lord of the Rings*. A lot. I like the movies. I like the books. I actually like the movies more than the books. Ever since I watched the trilogy in theaters, the number one place I wanted to go in the world by an outstanding margin was New Zealand, where they'd filmed the movies. I didn't just want to go, I needed to go, but given our pecuniary circumstances, I sullenly placed a trip to New Zealand into the 'when I'm old and have money' category. In front of us was an opportunity to go much sooner than that. With this new piece of information, everything came into perspective. Why on earth shouldn't we go somewhere for a year with a steady income, free apartment, health insurance, and the ability to go on vacation to New Zealand? It could be a new start, a reset button. Columbus could wait one more year. My sinus infection was gone, but now I was sick with the travel bug.

"Let's do it," I said.

"Let's do it?" Maria lit up.

"Let's do it!"

By Thanksgiving, we were announcing to friends and family that our intention was to teach overseas in South Korea. The reactions we received ranged from jealous excitement to confused surprise. Surely, we should be doing something like having babies, thought our mothers. And South Korea is, I guess you could put it, really far away. Is it even developed? Why did we want to go so far away? Aren't we scared of North Korea? We explained the perks and their reactions softened.

We'd made our biggest decision as a married couple. The next step was actually making it happen. A recruiting agency in Chicago named Greenheart Travel outlined the entire process and list of requirements on their website. This was not a short process. Before we could do anything, Maria needed to start on a Teaching English as a Foreign Language (TEFL) certificate. I was in the clear with my English degree. Then we needed to apply through Greenheart Travel first for their screening process. After we submitted the application, letters of recommendation, and a photo, we set up an interview with them on Skype. That was the easy part.

On top of the lengthy EPIK application that included mock lesson plans and an extensive report on our academic history spanning all the way back to kindergarten, we needed to send letters of recommendation, criminal background checks, copies of our bachelor's diplomas, original sealed transcripts, proof of teaching experience (if applicable), and our left foot all properly apostilled, notarized, and signed by Jesus himself. Since this was Maria's idea, and because she had more time, she took it upon herself to be responsible for organizing our documents and making sure we delivered everything on time. If we were to teach by the following August, we needed to get everything ready by March when the application window opened.

I don't know if you have ever needed anything apostilled, but before you can get something apostilled, you must get it notarized. Normally, getting something notarized isn't a big deal. You arrive, they stamp the thing, and you leave. Our nearest notary was the worst. His stamp, or stamping, was deficient twice, and we didn't discover this, twice, until the state department returned our documents with a note saying it wasn't properly done...twice. This ate up a lot of time. After explaining our frustration to a group of friends over dinner, one mentioned that she was a notary and could stamp our documents for us. We sent our stamped documents again. She got it right the first time.

Thank God she did. In January, Pizza Persona went out of business and Maria lost her job. Call it what you want: a sign from God, another tally in the 'why our time in Chicago sucked' list, another day in the business world. It was one more incentive to peace out and move to South Korea. Our future hinged on being accepted to teach.

I don't mean to ignore the very obvious solution to my problem -- that we could've just moved back home to Columbus. It's true that this was an option, but at the time it wasn't a very good one. Call it my Midwestern pride or my own persistent fear of failure, but I couldn't fathom returning to Columbus worse off than we'd left, with no jobs, no money, and no path. The idea of licking our wounds and returning with less than what we had when we left (and we left with about a thousand bucks) sounded awful. Also, my wife wasn't ready to go back yet. There was more she wanted to do before establishing roots somewhere, wherever that would be. What good is a home if your wife's not happy to be there?

Next on the list was an interview with EPIK itself. We went to a discount book store and bought a travel guide about Korea, memorizing the brief history of the country and some basic Korean words. It would be good to look engaged in the culture, advised our contacts at Greenheart Travel. There was no getting around the time difference, so our interview would be late in the evening.

The night of the interview, I laid on my bed with my suit on. Well, my suit coat and my boxers.

"Cam-sa-hab-nida," I mouthed, practicing what little Korean I'd learned. "Cam? Gam. Gam-sa-hab-ni-da. Cam-sabnida. Cam-samnida. Ann-yeong-ha-seo." I sat up, remembering that I didn't want my hair flattened or my suit coat wrinkled. I flipped through the travel book while clearing my throat and rolling my tongue; I wanted my words clear and my answers stellar and to the point. My suit pants laid on the floor while I debated if I should wear them or not. The answer was probably yes, but I sat there debating anyway. It's not like anybody would see my legs. I put them on anyway as Maria opened the door.

"It's your turn," she said, also dressed unusually nice for a late Tuesday night. I checked my tie once more in the mirror and walked into our living room, where a laptop sat on the coffee table. Skype was already opened, but nobody was connected on the other side. I sat on our sectional couch and waited for my appointment to show up. The clock in the bottom right corner said 11:42pm. My interview was scheduled for 11:45pm. In mid-yawn, the Skype song began to play. I let my yawn run its course, perked up my eyes, stretched my mouth, and clicked the camera button.

"Hello?" said a young Korean woman on my screen. "Are you Matthew?"

"Yes I am," I smiled. "Annyeong haseo!" *Hello.*
"Annyeong haseo!" the woman responded. "Your Korean pronunciation is very good!"

Here's where we would really find out. "Cam-samnida!" I said. *Thank you.*

"Excellent!" The woman was in a busy office somewhere in Seoul, sometime in the middle of the afternoon Seoul time.

The interview wasn't very interesting, with the typical questions designed to weed out people and look for intelligence. I finished my interview and closed the laptop. *She never would've seen my legs*, I thought. *I didn't need to put on pants.* It was past midnight and it was time to go to bed. I shut off all the lights, took off my suit, and joined Maria, who was playing on her phone, in bed.

"Do you think we did okay?" she asked.

"I think so."

"I think so too."

It was March now. Maria wrapped up her TEFL certificate and her volunteer hours at an Asian services center. There were a few more documents to collect as the application window loomed ahead. It was important to us that we didn't do this half-assed; if we were going to South Korea, we wanted to be first in line with our documents ready. Greenheart Travel was the one that would be sending our things to the Korean government, so the day after the window opened we took the Brown line to the Greenheart Travel office just north of the Loop. Our recruiter, whom we had interviewed with on Skype earlier, greeted us.

"Are you excited?" she smiled. "The hardest part is done!"

I have to admit, it was a relief to physically hand her our folders fat with documents and know that she would take it from there.

"You're going to love it," she said. "I lived in Daegu myself."

"So what's next?" I asked.

"Now you play the waiting game," she said. "The earliest you'll hear anything back is in May."

Two months is a perfect amount of time to stew over all the work you've done, wondering if there's anything you left out. Should I have said this one thing on that one question? Did I paint myself as a good applicant? It didn't take long for us to get anxious, almost depressed. On the rare occasion I didn't have somewhere to be, we'd walk to the lake from our apartment, sit in lawn chairs, and stare out into the blue abyss, wondering if they'd give us a 'yes' or a 'no.'

The answer, eventually, was yes for both of us. We got the first yes, as in 'yes, we received all necessary materials' in May. Our recruiter assured us that it would be highly unlikely for them to not accept us at this point, and that we needed to continue to be patient to learn our destination. I convinced Maria that we should get out of Chicago regardless, so in May we sub-let our apartment and dumped our stuff with some friends in Cincinnati. We'd stay with friends and my aunt in Evanston in the meantime.

A couple weeks later, I finished my last semester as an adjunct

English instructor and we drove out of Chicago. Driving south down the Dan Ryan highway, I didn't look back at the skyline once. It was an unsentimental exit for myself, although I knew Maria would miss it. Chicago had been an exciting time for us, that was for sure, a little too much excitement for this guy. Chicago was someone else's home, and that's fine, but it wasn't mine.

We were on track to go to South Korea, but until we heard about our destination, it felt like an unsure thing. We spent the summer visiting friends and family, taking advantage of their homes while we had none. It was quality time spent with people we loved: going backpacking, seeing concerts, racking up some major credit card debt. You know, responsible things to do when you're homeless, unemployed, and not 100% sure what you're doing or where you're going. In July, while we were in the Washington D.C. area staying with my parents, we found out that we would be going to Daegu the following month and that we should probably buy plane tickets. We decided it would be best to make our way to the West Coast and then fly from there. Imagine one of those Indiana Jones maps where the plane flies from one end of the map to the other with a line streaking behind it. Instead of a plane, our car that summer went from Washington D.C. to the Smoky Mountains for a family vacation, back up to Cincinnati for the funeral of Maria's grandfather, back to Tennessee where our family vacation was ongoing, back to Washington D.C., back to Cincinnati to repack all of our stuff for Korea, on to Oklahoma, then down to Texas, and then up to Seattle via plane to see some old friends and fly to our new home. On our last day in the states, we hiked in Mt. Rainier National Park on what couldn't be a lovelier day. The following morning, August 18, 2013, our plane departed for San Francisco, and then Incheon International Airport. We went to the currency exchange counter and converted the last thousand bucks to our name into Korean won. There was no turning back now. We were on our way to South Korea.

Orientation

That Time We Made Friends Over a Drug Test

The first person I saw coming out of the plane at Incheon International Airport was Robert De Niro. He'd been paid handsomely, I assume, to appear in a large poster promoting a tourist casino somewhere in the country. I would later see the same ad on about twelve other windows in the airport as well as billboards along the highway. In that way, De Niro was both an unexpected and repetitive welcome party to South Korea.

Our flight had been smooth, and I was delighted and relieved that, upon landing, South Korea turned out to be a real place that was willing to pay me money to speak English. Within a half an hour we were through customs and heading toward baggage claim, thankful for the ample English signage accompanied with Korean and Chinese. Even without it, Incheon International Airport is one of those airports that's so well designed that it's pretty easy to follow your nose. It was and still is one of the nicest airports I've ever visited. It's bright, it's efficient, and it's spotlessly clean. It didn't take long to realize that these three qualities were par for the course for most airports in East Asia and that it was American airports that were dark, inept, and dingy by comparison.

Baggage claimed, we called our hotel for a free pick-up. We'd thought it best to arrive a day before orientation in the event of a delayed flight, so we booked a hotel for one night near the airport. The man on the other end spoke some English and said our van would arrive in 20 minutes and that we should wait next to entrance 12. We found the nearest sliding door and exited the airport.

Woof. I hit a wall of humidity. Inside Incheon was busy, fresh, and clean. Outside Incheon was a thick and soupy monochromatic gray. The haze was so thick, the road leading away from Arrivals disappeared into a void. Our discomfort was exacerbated, of course, because we had with us our life's belongings for the next year in three bags apiece. By the time our van arrived, I was dripping in sweat. A middle-aged man jumped out of the driver seat and opened the trunk, apparently immune to the suffocating atmosphere. He shoved our bags into the back and ushered us to sit down inside. The haze thinned slightly as we drove away from the airport, but at this juncture, our first impression of South Korea was limited to our narrow visibility.

About 15 minutes from the airport is the little neighborhood of Unseo-dong. Technically part of the city of Incheon, Unseo sits on the same island as the airport, but is itself removed from other development on the island. It's a self-contained, almost fortress of a city; it's mid-rises, schools, churches, and supermarkets contrast with the nothingness surrounding it. Why anyone would want to live so close to the airport and so far away from the actual cities of Incheon and Seoul is beyond me, unless the inhabitants worked at the airport. It is a convenient place for hotels, however, and the van pulled up to ours, the appropriately named Cloud Hotel. We picked Cloud Hotel for two reasons: it was reasonably priced with good reviews and was located next door to a Dunkin Donuts. A real Korean breakfast could wait one more day.

We opened the door to our first Korean hotel room. It wasn't the smallest hotel room I'd ever stayed in, but it was close. Two small pairs of slippers sat waiting to be slipped in just outside the reach of the door; it was clear we were meant to take off our shoes and don the slippers lest we ruin the faux-hardwood floors. We ignored decorum for a minute as we dumped our heavy bags further into the room and then returned to the door. There was no way my feet would fit into the slippers, but I didn't expect to wear them anyway. It's not like I had far to walk. Otherwise, the room was pretty standard for a cheap hotel room in South Korea: bland wallpaper, rock hard bed and a small bathroom, but a serviceable place to spend a night.

The channel selection on the TV was, to no one's surprise, full of Korean options, mostly tearful Korean dramas or baseball. CNN was the only English option, so we left it on for background noise as we unpacked what we needed for the night. It was about 8:30pm and we were exhausted. I hadn't slept a wink on the 12-hour flight, which left San Francisco in the middle of the afternoon Pacific time. I thought, with the long hours of wakefulness and the additional fatigue of long distance traveling, that half past eight was a suitable time to call it a day and still wake up the following morning at a decent time. We turned off CNN and fell right to sleep.

———⟨≪◊≫⟩———

Koreans, in some form or another, have been studying English for over 100 years. In the 1880's, King Kojong permitted German advisor Paul George von Mollendorf to establish the first English academy in Korea to train interpreters. American missionaries weren't far behind and, along with providing medical care, taught English to locals. English education was primarily an exercise in grammatical regurgitation in writing up until the 1990's, when national and international language tests changed to focus on the more communicatively useful skills of listening and speaking. It had suddenly become clear that many Korean students, while adept at memorizing verb tenses and vocabulary, would be hopeless at interacting with a living, breathing native English speaker. As recently as 2004, South Korea's TOEFL (Test of English as a Foreign Language) scores were 93rd out of 147 countries.

South Korea had one more incentive to change the way it learned English: everyone else spoke it. After decades of unprecedented economic growth, the country emerged in the 1990's as a prosperous democracy that needed to speak more than just Korean to compete in an increasingly globalized economy. If Koreans couldn't speak or listen to English-speaking businessmen, then South Korea would not hold on to its newfound industrialization for long. Wealthy parents began sending their children to schools in the United States and other English-speaking countries in hopes that the linguistic and cultural immersion would improve their children's English. These 'wild geese families,' as they were called, became a national concern. All that money and brainpower was being spent elsewhere when it could be spent domestically. Something had to be done to improve English education in South Korea, so in 1995 the National Institute for International Education Development (NIIED) developed the EPIK program. Rather than go to where the English speakers are, the Korean government would bring the English speakers to Korea.

The program brought its first Native English Teachers – native English speakers from the United States, the United Kingdom, Ireland, Australia, New Zealand, and Canada (and later South Africa) – in 1997, when the government mandated that schools teach English beginning in the 3rd grade. There were very few Native English Teachers at first but the number steadily increased every year. Between 2000 and 2010, the number jumped from 146 to 8,546. It would take more than 10,000 to put at least one teacher in every public school, which was NIIED's ultimate goal. That way, every student could interact frequently with a native speaker without pissing their pants.

The EPIK program has been moderately successful. South Korea improved its TOEFL ranking from 93rd in 2004 to 82nd in 2006 and then 72nd in 2011. Today, the country's scores are slightly above the worldwide average. According to the EF English Proficiency Index, a not very scientific study where volunteers take a survey on the internet, South Korea ranks 27th in English proficiency: about on par with Italy and France, a good bit ahead of Japan, but nowhere near the Netherlands at number one. The Dutch have famously flawless English. They might as well live next door.

———

It was half past four in the morning when I decided I couldn't lay there in the dark anymore and needed to do something. Thus began our week-long battle with the awkward hours of jetlag. Maria was up soon after me, and together we admonished ourselves for going to sleep so early. We played cards on the bed, waiting for an acceptable hour to walk into Dunkin Donuts, Meanwhile, the world around us dozed in the early morning hours.

When the acceptable hour finally arrived, we made the quick jaunt to get some donuts and orange juice. Dunkin Donuts, is largely the same in South Korea as it is in America. They still do donuts – not fish tacos or anything like that -- which was the most important part. We packed up our stuff, said goodbye to the slippers, and took a van back to the airport where a charter bus would shuttle us to our EPIK orientation in Jeonju.

The city of Jeonju is a three-hour drive from the airport, so I made sure we were one of the first people on the bus and got a window seat. Fortunately, the haze gave way to blue sky as we distanced ourselves from Incheon. I'm one of those strange people that can entertain themselves for hours by looking out a window, especially if what's outside the window is something new. Halfway through the trip, all I'd seen of South Korea was high-rises, rice paddies, and mountains, but I drank it all in. By the time we rolled into Jeonju, I firmly concluded that 95% of the country consisted of high-rises, rice paddies, and mountains—a hypothesis that turned out to be accurate.

Jeonju itself is a medium-sized city and at the time was remarkable in its newness. The more Korean cities I visited, the more I realized Jeonju wasn't terribly remarkable. The monotony of the gray buildings was broken only by the gaudy neon of the noraebang (karaoke) establishments and fried chicken joints. The bus pulled into Jeonju University, which itself is a pleasant enough campus on a hill with concrete buildings. We stayed in the empty dorm where we were greeted by a gift bag of snacks and souvenirs, including a mug which I still own that says 'Jeonju University: Where Superstars are Made.'

Our orientation schedule went like this: wake up, eat a buffet breakfast, attend a few sessions led by current employees of EPIK, eat lunch, attend more sessions to learn about the job, eat a big dinner, and then try to stay awake longer than 8:30pm. Although the haze had stayed in Incheon, the humidity had not. Us westerners were desperately sweaty and light-headed in the stuffy classrooms, so the good people of EPIK provided refreshments throughout the day. Admirably, the university staff lent us some of their large fans.

Just as admirable was EPIK's ability to make almost every session unique, informative, and useful. One lecturer from Scotland went through a mock English class complete with songs and responses, with us as the students. His heavy Scottish brogue both mesmerized and baffled us. Another lecturer devoted her time slot to showing us the best resources for fun songs, activities, and PowerPoints. That woman was the patron saint of EPIK teachers.

And of course, there was the Korean language lessons led by two Korean college girls. They were excellent teachers, even if our pronunciation was terrible. Reading and writing in Korean, we learned, is not all that complicated. Hangul, the Korean alphabet, is a logical and simple alphabet that can be learned in a week. Once you know how to put the pieces together, you have the tools to write any word you want. Some sounds in English, though, are not easily replicated in the Korean language. I learned this the hard way when, at the beginning of one of our language lessons, we were instructed to find our name tags. In Korean, there are no sounds for the 'a' or 'th' sounds in the name 'Matthew.' Writing the closest estimation of my name in Hangul results in a word that sounds something like Metchu or Metyu, which is very close to the Korean word for beer: maekju. I sifted through the tags, wondering if this "Metyu" person was me. It was. Therefore, I spent my time in South Korea being called 'Metyu' by all but the better English speakers, wondering if their minds drifted to beer every time they spoke to me.

Each day, we went to bed and woke up the next morning a little later until we were finally waking up with the sun. We crammed our notebooks with useful tips and tidbits after every session, acquainting ourselves with the job we'd be performing and the country in which we'd be performing it.

"You'll have to teach English camps during the breaks," said one lecturer.

"Your relationship with your co-teacher is the most important aspect of your job," said another.

"Plans change at the last minute all the time," warned a woman with her Korean co-teacher in the room, who reluctantly nodded her head.

Like I mentioned before, the crop of teachers weren't only American. There was a large contingent of South Africans coming to teach, with smaller but noticeable clusters of British, Irish, Canadian, Australian and Kiwi persuasion. It was a treat to hear everybody's stories, what brought them to teach halfway across the world. Of course, at least half of the group was American. We were Millennials in 2013, after all, still finding ourselves after the financial crisis in 2008.

A requirement for every teacher entering the country was to pass a series of health exams. I was particularly worried about the blood test for Maria, who had a history of fainting when having blood taken. We sat in the front row of the university's auditorium. Ahead of us on the stage was a winding row of chairs leading to the booths where nurses were taking blood. Every few minutes, we'd shift over a few seats, inching closer to the test. My plan was to stay with Maria and keep her distracted with a conversation to avoid an embarrassing scene. As I brainstormed a topic that would keep her occupied, I noticed that the woman sitting next to Maria was also anxious.

"Ughhhhhhhh," she groaned to the guy on the other side of her. "I hate this."

"Are you a fainter?" asked Maria with a fake happiness to mask her nervousness.

"I have before," the woman replied. She spoke with what I thought at the time was a British accent.

"It's the worst, isn't it?" said Maria. And just like that, they were in the middle of a conversation about giving blood, which turned into a conversation about snacks, which turned into a conversation about Game of Thrones. Suddenly, I knew what topic to continue when Maria got her blood drawn.

The three of us continued talking as we scooted closer to the end of the line. Gail was from South Africa, it turned out, and although she was a couple years younger than us, she'd been a teacher before. She was the kind to use the word 'keen' a lot, as in she was 'keen' to not have her blood drawn. We liked her right away.

I approached the station with Maria. The nurses cautioned me to wait my turn, but I pointed to Maria and mimed her fainting, and they let me stay. I kept Maria occupied on the topic of our favorite characters in Westeros, which seemed to work well. The guy behind Gail did the same for her. His name turned out to be Phillip and he was from Boston. He was quick-witted and foul mouthed, but without the slightest tinge of a Boston accent. His pop culture reference game was strong. Again, we liked him immediately. After all four of us had given blood, we sat together in the auditorium seats munching on some provided snacks until we were ready to move on.

On the last night of orientation, EPIK held a closing ceremony inside a giant white tent. They'd prepared the most absurdly long buffet table I'd ever seen, but I did my darndest to try as much as I could. During the meal, one of the Korean volunteers for the week entertained us with a traditional fan dance. Following her was a larger group who danced to some K-pop song. In case you've never heard of K-pop, I can only describe it as 90's pop music on steroids. K-pop is primarily comprised of large groups of young men (or women) who, since childhood, have practiced gyrating in unison to an upbeat pop song with random English catchphrases in the lyrics. Members of these groups are talented dancers and sometimes just as talented singers. NSYNC, the quintessential 90's pop band, looks pedestrian in comparison. None of it appeals to me, but I appear to be in the minority. This is likely because I don't get nostalgic for 90's pop music the same way other people in my generation do. My relationship with most 90's music is "didn't Weird Al cover that in one of his polkas?" So I'm a terrible Millennial. Sue me. I still have a Creed album somewhere, for what it's worth.

At any rate, our 10-day orientation flew by quickly and I felt more prepared for our new life than I had beforehand. Call that a success.

A Hole in My Sock

That Time I Met the Principal

The next morning, we loaded our bags in trucks and then hopped on a bus to Daegu. Gail and Phillip were also headed to Daegu, so we saved them seats. Our bus was going to take us directly to a city-wide teacher meeting, where our co-teachers awaited us. It was then likely that our teachers would take us to our respective schools to meet our principals, so we were all dressed professionally. A good number of us were dressed in suits and ties, but it was a very hot day. I'd rather meet my new superiors dressed sort of nice and comfortable than super nice and dripping with sweat. Also, I didn't pack a suit. Khaki's, an oxford shirt, and a nice pair of shoes would have to suffice.

Of the mountains, rice paddies, and high-rises that comprise the vast majority of the country, the road between Jeonju and Daegu is primarily the first two. The highway meanders along valleys between forested mountains not unlike some mountain interstates in West Virginia or Tennessee. In fact, the southern, mountainy bits of South Korea look remarkably close to Appalachia. The mountains are roughly the same height and are covered by conifers and deciduous trees. Ignore the Korean signage on the highway and you could be on your way to Gatlinburg.

Our bus pulled into a rest stop in front of Maisan, or 'horse mountain.' The landmark is easy to recognize because its two steep and smooth peaks resemble a pair of horse ears. Allegedly, a hermit by the name of Lee Gap Young lived at the base of the mountain. Starting sometime in the late 19th century, he arrived at the mountain and began stacking rocks on top of each other to create stone pagodas. He wasn't a monk, and no one told him to build the pagodas, but he built nearly 120 of them, of which 80 are still around today. We did not have time to explore the surreal scene, as we were only scheduled for a 20 minute stop.

Eventually, the mountains spread and we came to a wide, hazy basin of farmland. Just beyond the farmland were the first in a series of high rise developments that marked the beginning of Daegu's suburbs. In what seemed like no time at all, we were surrounded by monotonous urban development.

The streetscape of Daegu is, like every other Korean city, boring. Identical high-rises march by like Leonardo DiCaprio's purgatory in *Inception*. The low-rise neighborhoods are the same monochromatic sprawl, with cartoonish fast food signs and neon that advertise noraebangs (karaoke cafes), cheap motels, and barbecue joints. It was through this ugliness the bus drove us to the center of town to a large, ultra-modern auditorium. We filtered into the building quietly and sat in the back of the auditorium, where our co-teachers were listening to a speaker. It was, of course, very dull for us, but it didn't look much better for the Korean teachers.

About a half hour later, the time came for us to be paired with our co-teachers, and they called us to the front one by one. I had zero expectations about my co-teacher. A smooth understanding of the English language was about all I hoped for, and good organization skills to make my expatriate life easier. An easygoing attitude would be nice. And a good sense of humor. Just someone to shoot the breeze with, you know? What I really needed was someone to teach me the local culture but meet me in the middle. I needed a friend, an ally, a mentor. Like I said, zero expectations.

What I got was Ji Young.

There are a lot of words that come to mind when I think of Ji Young, but starting with any of them would paint the wrong picture. For starters, she would turn out to be at once all of the above things and none of them. She was short, about my age, with long, black hair and heavy bangs covering her forehead. I bowed gently and recited my practiced '*manasaw bangop sibnida*' (nice to meet you). She laughed at my face, covering her mouth with her hand and tossing her hair. I waved goodbye to Maria, unsure when or where we would meet later that day, and followed Ji Young out of the auditorium.

We stepped into her gray Hyundai Accent. The first thing Ji Young did was play with her bangs in the mirror.

"*Dowa*," she whined. 'So hot.'

"I know," I replied. I'm a little shy, I admit. I don't know what to say to new people, especially when their English skills are a question mark and our only exchanges thus far involve laughing at my terrible Korean accent and whining about the temperature. She started the car, blasted the AC, and drove us out of the parking lot.

And then I was really in South Korea. There were no other newbies with me, not even my wife. It was only me and a Korean woman driving to a Korean school, where we were meeting more Koreans. Orientation peppered us with some Korean phrases that might be important in the context of meeting administrative superiors, so I tried to review them in my head. Ji Young and I made small talk in the meantime. My Hangul skills were still in its infancy, but as we drove past billboards and signs, I was able to pick out a few words.

"Does that sign say 'Daegu'?" I asked, pointing to a sign. I knew it did, but I wanted her to know that I knew.

"Oh! You know Korean?" gasped Ji Young.

"Just what they taught us at orientation."

I would learn soon enough that many Koreans were easily impressed by the most basic language skills. As patronizing as this could feel, it made me wonder more about the nature of previous expatriates. Were they lazy and didn't bother to learn the language? I'd been in Korea for at best 10 days and I could pronounce (if not comprehend) most of the signs I saw, and I'm not exactly an ace at learning languages. We arrived at a pink concrete building at the base of a large forested hill.

"This is our school," she said as she turned into the driveway.

Maecheon Elementary School is one of the oldest school buildings in the northern Daegu area. It has a main building flanked by two smaller but identical wings, and a newer gymnasium addition perpendicular to the whole thing. It's the kind of place where it's easy to get lost if you're not paying attention, since everything looks the same. Before we got out of the car, Ji Young checked her bangs in the rearview mirror one more time.

"Let's go," she said.

We got out of the car and the humidity hit me again. I was already sweating as we walked into the concrete, un-air-conditioned hallways. There wasn't much to look at—no large displays of student work or friendly signs. There was, however, a large trophy case of wrestling trophies.

Traditionally, Koreans spent a lot of time on the floor, especially at home. They sat on the floor to eat. They slept on the floor, kept warm by heated rocks underneath the wooden boards. Walking into somebody's house with your shoes on, then, would be the equivalent of walking onto their dining table or bed. It's just not done. Even though many modern homes in Korea have sofas and mattresses and chairs, people are still likely to sit on the floor. More traditional restaurants will have seating on the floor as well, and the rule is the same. Why this rule is extended to schools, where students sit in desks and faculty sit on computer chairs and nobody eats on the floor, I'm not sure, but I bring this up now because Ji Young told me to take off my shoes before entering the Vice Principal's office. This revealed a distressing reality: there was a hole in my sock.

My ears turned red and my heart pounded. Yes, in this culture of taking off your shoes in homes and at work, one does not gallivant around with a hole in the big toe. Lucky me, I grabbed one of the only pairs of socks I had with a hole in them, and I was about to meet the Vice-Principal. In a blur of panic, what little Korean I knew scattered to the distant corners of my brain. We stored our shoes in a shelf along the wall, where she pulled a pair of pink indoor slippers for herself. She did a quick look around the shelf for another pair. There wasn't one. I was to meet the head honchos in my socks. Ji Young slid the office door open. We bowed to the Vice-Principal, an older man whose untucked shirt and loquaciousness suggested a casual approach to school governance. I tried to glean what Ji Young and the Vice Principal were talking about, but didn't want to stare so I looked around the room, smiling. I read somewhere that Koreans don't put their hands in their pockets when in conversation – in fact, it's rude to do so -- so I played with my fingers until a use for them arose, praying that the Vice Principal didn't look at my feet. They continued to talk, but the conversation seemed strained. Ji Young laughed the same laugh as before, covering her mouth with her hand.

There seemed to be little to discuss so they stood up and bowed. I followed suit, and we left the room.

"Let's go meet the Principal," Ji Young laughed again. I realized she hadn't, in the strictest sense, laughed at my face when we first met. This was her nervous laugh. She was nervous to meet me and even more nervous to have to speak with the Vice Principal and especially the Principal.

Down the hall was an even larger office. We entered as the grandfatherly, almost Godfatherly perhaps, Principal sat at his desk beckoning us in. He stood to greet us. We shook hands the Korean way (left hand supporting the right wrist) and we repeated the ritual: Ji Young nervously making conversation, myself hoping the authoritative figure enjoyed the ceiling, and said authoritative figure probably wishing this strange foreigner would leave. The three of us shared an awkward moment of not knowing what to do next, broken by the Principal motioning that I should have a seat in one of the four lounge chairs in the middle of the room. They didn't cover sitting in orientation. Was I supposed to sit before he sits? Korea has a very reverent culture toward age and hierarchy, I knew that much. With his hand still extended toward the seat, I sat down. He offered me coffee. Unsure whether it was ruder to accept or deny the first offer, I accepted. Over on a side table he took a thin, yellow package, poured the powdery contents into a tiny paper cup and then poured hot water inside. He mixed the drink with the empty package and handed the cup to me. I thanked him and took a sip. It tasted good, I admit, but whatever the sugar-filled concoction was, it was not coffee. It was an exceedingly sweet brown beverage with a vague coffee taste. He took a seat opposite me, my foot now directly in his line of vision. What followed was a roughly 10 minute conversation about the pronunciation of the name 'Matthew,' throughout which I curled my toe in my sock so the skin wasn't noticeable. The conversation shifted to the Principal's name, and I spent about 10 minutes trying to pronounce it. I should have just given up. It likely would've ended the meeting sooner. However, without much warning, the principal and Ji Young stood, so I stood. We bowed once more, and Ji Young and I left the office.

Once we were down the hall, Ji Young whined. "I hate talking to the principal. So nervous." As we walked past a mirror in the hallway, she stopped to check her hair, and then we walked on. I breathed a sigh of relief. Either the hole in my sock went unnoticed, or the first three Koreans I met outside orientation were exceedingly polite.

We put our shoes back on, left the school and drove down the street to the apartment Maria and I would call home. The neighborhood was primarily composed of high-rise residential complexes—a dozen or so identical towers about 25 stories high connected by parking lots, landscaping, and playgrounds. Between two such complexes was a grid of much lower, grayer buildings with a sort of main street running down the northern end. From this main street, Ji Young turned the car down another street with a dead end, and then turned at the last possible turn—the edge of the neighborhood. She parked the car in front of one of the gray buildings. It was four stories tall, nearly all concrete, and had a glass sliding door at the front entrance. When we got out of the car, she pulled out a piece of paper and punched some numbers into the keypad. The door slid open and we headed up the third floor.

Upstairs, Maria and her co-teacher were already inside our apartment. Maria's co-teacher was quite a bit older than Ji Young, somewhere in the lower 40's I guessed, and her English was near fluent. Her hair went down to her shoulders in a sensible and motherly fashion.

My first reaction to our apartment was that there were stairs, which boded well. I had mentally prepared for a tiny apartment, perhaps no larger than a hotel room, so the fact that we'd be on two floors was a bit of a relief. My second reaction was that everything except the floor was wallpapered in a seasick green.

Ji Young agreed to take us shopping for basic kitchenware and appliances, so we said goodbye to Maria's co-teacher and the three of us hopped back into the car. The further we drove, the more Daegu looked the same: a checkerboard of high-rise residential complexes of varying luxury and stouter, interchangeably gray neighborhoods. We pulled into the underground parking garage of a department store called HomePlus. Ji Young backed into a tiny parking spot with skillful precision and we took the escalator to the ground floor. HomePlus, simply put, is the Korean version of Wal-Mart but stacked four stories high. It's a lasagna of groceries, cheap stuff, less cheap stuff, and restaurants. Before we even reached the grocery section, we passed a KFC, Baskin Robbins, book store, eye care center, and an enticing food court. Ji Young took out a 100 won coin and slid it into a shopping cart handle, which unlocked it by pushing a chain out.

We did not bring enough cash for such a large store, and I felt bad that Ji Young had to meander through the aisles with us as we discussed priorities and bought things with which to fill our apartment. We were broke in two countries, with no American cash, credit cards nearly maxed out, and, we hoped, enough Korean won to get us through a month. We'd received a terrible exchange rate for our won at the airport; our $1000 in American dollars was now worth roughly the equivalent of $800. Even at Korean Wal-Mart, buying new things for an apartment adds up. We bought the cheapest plates we could find, which were these flimsy plastic things that were one step above picnic plates. We bought some pots and pans and silverware. A microwave would have to wait, but we did grab a toaster. We spent 10 minutes debating which fan to buy: a small, portable guy or a large floor fan. Meanwhile, Ji Young politely looked at sale items and pretended that she might consider buying something. When we finally took our cart to the checkout line, though, she was empty handed. The lady at the register began ringing up our items and it soon became apparent that our math wasn't right. We didn't have enough money to purchase everything. We told her to take off the bowls, some food, and other items that we could do without for a week. We managed to bring the total down to what cash we brought with us, and took our things back to the car. Ji Young dropped us off at our apartment, made sure we got back in, and drove off.

Back inside the apartment, Maria and I explored our new apartment more thoroughly. The room on the first floor was an unusual confluence of a living room dining room closet with a fridge. It had a small table big enough for two, possibly three people to sit around. A small TV sat on top of a diminutive entertainment center. A wardrobe and some shelving were built under the stairs, and a second stand-alone wardrobe stood on the opposite wall next to the refrigerator.

The kitchen was, and this is being generous, incomplete. It was separated from the rest of the floor by a sliding door, as if it had been a balcony in another lifetime. It had a small sink and gas range and the slimmest of counter spaces. A couple tall shelves would have to fit all our food and dishes. I say 'all' like we had a lot, but we unloaded our lackluster haul from HomePlus and the cabinets still had plenty of space. I don't know which was sadder, that we had such little kitchen space or that we hadn't even filled what little space there was. In the kitchen was also the washing machine. Maria's co-teacher had written some instructions on how to use it, as the machine's buttons were all in Korean, and taped them to the wall.

Our bathroom would take some getting used to. It was tiny, for one. A notch in the outer wall held a showerhead in place, perched over the entire bathroom as if it were the shower itself. This was 100% the case, meaning if we took a shower, everything in the bathroom would get wet. A drain behind the sink ensured that the room wouldn't flood every morning after we washed ourselves.

As we walked up our stairs, I couldn't help but notice the shoddy construction methods used by the interior decorators. Our wallpaper, ugly as it was, was held in place between the walls and ceiling with thumb tacks. In a hidden corner of the second floor above the stairs, the wallpaper was already peeling off. The second floor was much roomier than the first, with a single room sprawling over our entire first floor and over the neighbors below. Beneath the southern window, two single beds stood apart. The rest of the space was completely empty and featured only two outlets. We opened the tinted windows to see what our views were. On the north side was our street and the surrounding gray high rise condominiums. A large, red neon cross from the steeple of the local Presbyterian church gave the view some color. To our south, Mt. Ap framed the rest of the city of Daegu. It was a hazy day, but the view would be quite nice on clear days. Directly behind our apartment, however, was some sort of scrap metal dump.

I sat down on one of the single beds. The mattress was rock hard. Also, the bed frame was not attached in any way and fell to the floor. What held the mattresses up were what appeared to be plastic shelving units. We made two decisions immediately. One, we pushed the beds together to make a king-size bed. Two, we slid the pieces of the frame under the bed, since they served zero purpose.

We returned to our living room dining room closet and began the task of putting things where they go. We hauled the TV up to the second floor to create a living room/bedroom hybrid. Goodness knows we had to do something with that extra space on the second floor. We unzipped our suitcases, which more or less burst in relief. I claimed the wardrobe next to the refrigerator and Maria took the other. All in all, I can't say we liked our new apartment very much. Its inadequacies were minor but numerous, and there were a lot of quirks that would need getting used to. And that was just our home. The next day was our first day on the job, and time would only tell what oddities that would bring. We were broke, we were on our own, and all the farther away from home, wherever that was anymore. We unpacked if only to keep from crying.

A New Job

That Time I Didn't Know My Blood Type

Our bedroom, with its five windows, was very bright in the morning and I was awake before my alarm went off at seven. I can pull covers over my head easily enough, but that wasn't the issue. Trucks had been honking and their drivers yelling since around 5 o'clock. I never did figure out what the business across the street did, but whatever it was attracted a lot of inconsiderate truck drivers every morning. I thanked God that we'd come to our senses at HomePlus and bought the floor fan. It was the only thing keeping the bedroom livable, what with the unyielding humidity. We had the air conditioning on, but the unit was downstairs and the air didn't seem to reach the second floor. In all, it wasn't a great first night.

I pulled myself out of bed and headed downstairs for a shower. Immediately, I was hit with a wall of cool air. The first floor was a good 20 degrees cooler than the second, proving the air conditioner worked just fine, but not for the second floor. I walked into the bathroom with my change of clothes, looking for a place where they'd keep dry. Nothing came to mind, so I tossed the clothes out to the living room and took my shower. In seconds, every square inch of the bathroom was soaked. I hadn't thought about the toilet seat, but whoever used the toilet next would either need to spend a lot of time drying the seat or sit with a wet butt. Neither was an attractive proposition. Maria needed to take a shower too, so I decided to let her worry about it and get dressed.

A frigid breeze hit my body hard as soon as I opened the door. The air conditioner unit, right outside the bathroom door below the ceiling, was still on full blast. My wet body was not prepared for the change of seasons and I threw on my clothes as quickly as possible. Who, pray tell, was in charge of deciding where to put the air conditioning unit, and why did they choose in front of the bathroom door? Did anybody think about the layout of this apartment at all? All evidence pointed to the contrary.

We were told to dress to impress for our first day, perhaps our first week of school. With no suit, a tie would have to do. After Maria finished her shower, I rolled up my pants to keep them dry above my ankles, wiped the condensation from the mirror, and tied my tie. I buttoned the top button of my dress shirt, my neck snugly reminding me that I'd gained weight since I bought the shirt. Too much pizza in Chicago, I guess.

The walk to my school was an easy one, about 15 minutes down a straight, busy road. Because of the humidity, however, and my dress pants and long-sleeved shirt buttoned up to my neck, I was dripping with sweat by the time I walked into my office at the school. Ji Young was already there, busy with paperwork and writing emails. We shared an unused classroom that seconded as a breakroom for the classroom teachers. Our desks sat side by side in the far corner. Our backs faced the door so that if somebody walked in, we had to turn around to see who it was. This happened with annoying frequency. Kids would walk in, mumble 'annyeong haseo' to announce their presence, and begin sweeping the floors or collecting our large water bottles in the fridge to refill in the cafeteria's water fountain. Teachers also stumbled in every few minutes, speaking with Ji Young about something or getting the kettle started for some instant coffee. I had no idea what was expected of me other than that I would introduce myself with a PowerPoint I'd made. EPIK contracts are funny in that people can either join for the start of a school year or halfway through. I came halfway into the year, so even though it was August, everyone was halfway through their school year already and was well into their groove. Ji Young eventually pulled herself away from the computer.

"Let's go meet Hyun Soo," she said standing up. Other than Ji Young, Hyun Soo would be my other co-teacher. Together, the three of us comprised the entire English department for the school, which by mandate starts English classes at 3rd grade and goes up to 6th grade. In this way, English is like gym or art or music, a class outside the homeroom. I followed her out of the office and into the adjacent classroom, where a skinny, 30-something man got up from his desk, smiled warmly and shook my hand.

"Good to meet you," he said. His accent was a bit thicker than Ji Young's, but his English seemed competent. That was about all the introduction we had time for at the moment, because school was about to begin. Ji Young and I rushed down to her classroom, which was not in what I would have deemed the English department, but down the hallway, across the central building, and at the end of a long hallway in the far building. Why her classroom wasn't alongside our office and Hyun Soo's classroom, I have no idea.

Ji Young's classroom was perhaps the dullest in the school, and it wasn't for lack of trying. She had student work displayed on pin boards in front of colorful paper. There were friendly stickers on the wall with easy English words like colors and animals. Every other inch, though, was a desolate gray. The lighting, even though there was a row of large windows in the back, couldn't reach a level above 'cell-block dim.' The tile floor, despite being cleaned daily by students, was filthy past redemption. Despite Ji Young's best efforts, her room seemed to absorb light and happiness.

"Our office is South Korea," she said to me as she turned the computer on. She pointed to the projector above the desks, which in minutes would be occupied by children, and told me to turn it on. "Our classroom is in North Korea." She pushed a switch on the wall and the projector screen unspooled over the whiteboard. I jabbed the "on" button of the projector above me with my finger and within seconds the computer's desktop was visible on the screen. Without missing a beat, our first class of third graders entered the room. They chatted amicably with one another then, one or two at a time, saw the white guy in the room.

"Uwaa!" they all seemed to say in exactly the same inflection, the Korean equivalent of 'wow.' I had nothing to say back to them other than 'hello.' They took their seats and I smiled at them and Ji Young obliviously sat on the computer typing away at emails. I pretended to be engaged in whatever Ji Young was doing as if it pertained to me. Meanwhile, the kids didn't even feign to pretend they weren't talking about the new white guy in the room.

Eventually, she pulled a PowerPoint slide of six or seven vocabulary words and the kids began furiously scribbling in their notebooks. They'd finish writing, put their hands on top of their heads to signal their completion, and lean into their neighbors to whisper something while looking my way. Their clothing was much the same as what kids their age wear in America -- shorts, colorful socks, t-shirts with superhero logos -- save for many of the boys' shorts that covered three fourths of their legs. Within a minute, every child's hands were on their heads and their eyes were on me.

"So you read the words one at a time," instructed Ji Young, "and the kids repeat after you. Then pick some kid to read them again."

Time waits for no vocab, I supposed, and introductions would have to come later. In my best teacher voice, I read off the words one at a time and the children repeated the words in unison. I spoke with clarity, authority, and volume. The kids did the same, and I thought for a hot minute that I might be naturally good at my job. Once we reached the end of the list, hands shot up to volunteer and I chose one at random, not knowing a single child's name. The little boy, who was sitting up front, stood up and read the words, nearly screaming them, and the other kids did likewise. Once he was finished he sat down and the students awaited whatever came next.

Ji Young stood up and addressed the students in Korean. I had no idea what she was saying, obviously, so I stood there trying to look as professional as I'd sounded when I read the vocabulary words, like I belonged in a classroom. I didn't know what to do with my hands, so I played with my knuckles again to avoid slipping them back into my pockets. Amidst the Korean, I heard the word 'Metyu Teacher' thrown in there and all eyes skirted to me. She kept going, they kept looking at me, and I kept smiling. Finally, she stopped, pulled up my PowerPoint presentation and told me to begin.

In my PowerPoint, I tried to cover the basics, that I'm from the United States, that I like movies and games, and that my wife is also a teacher. On the word 'America,' a boy in the front 'uwaa'd' and said "Captain America!"

"Yes," I replied pointing to myself. "Captain America." I included pictures of Columbus and Chicago and things they were famous for. The kids got to see Maria, my sister, and my parents. It was a pretty all-encompassing but succinct introduction. All the while, Ji Young translated since they were third graders and didn't have a clue what I was saying. After the PowerPoint, I opened the floor for questions. Most hands shot in the air. I picked the ones belonging to the kids that looked the most patient.

A little girl asked her question and Ji Young translated. "How tall are you?"

I don't know my height in centimeters, so I told them 5'7 and they didn't have a clue what that meant.

Another boy in the front asked his question and Ji Young translated, looking disapprovingly at the boy. "How much do you weigh?"

I mocked a stern look, with my fists on my hips, and then moved on to the next question.

"What's your blood type?"

"My blood type?!" I said. "I don't know."

"You don't know your blood type?" asked Ji Young.

"It's not something I memorize."

"Everyone knows their blood type."

The kids, and Ji Young a little too, gave me this look like I'd said I didn't know my name. Blood type is just something Koreans keep in mind a lot. There are even personality quirks attributed to blood type, so they ask your blood type like they ask your zodiac sign. I guess I'd have to remain an enigma. An overweight, white mystery. We killed the questions at that point and resumed regular classroom activities. Everyone opened their textbooks and I more or less followed along and repeated English words when asked.

The fourth graders in the next class recited their daily vocabulary words with slightly less gusto than the third graders. Their English was a little better, although Ji Young still translated everything I said. Their eyes looked at me politely and engagingly until I finished speaking, at which point they shifted to Ji Young for the meaning of my speech. During the designated question time, I again received the blood type question, but Ji Young told them that Americans don't bother to memorize their blood types because they're morons.

The fifth graders were the first to understand at least some of what I was saying. I'd explain something in my PowerPoint and a few kids in the class would go 'ahh' understandingly and nod in approval. They liked that I liked games. I would have to go through all this tomorrow and the next day until I'd seen all the classes, but already I could tell that 5th grade would be my favorite. They were clever enough at English to understand the basics of what I was saying and engage with me, but not old enough to think I was lame. This class in particular was also exceedingly polite and good-tempered. We would have a good time.

After the fifth graders left, it was time for lunch. I followed Ji Young down the stairs, waiting for her to check her hair in every mirror along the way, until we reached the ground floor. We walked past the busy cafeteria and into a lounge where trays of food sat on a table for the teachers. Again, I followed Ji Young's lead, grabbing a tray and ensuring that my portions were roughly similar to hers. There were a handful of other teachers in the room still eating at nearby tables, and I didn't want to make a bad impression about my eating habits. There was a brown stew of some kind with sprouts and tiny bits of what appeared to be beef, some bulgogi in red sauce, a large pot of sticky rice, what appeared to be grass in some spicy sauce, and kimchi. I ate everything but the grass, which tasted exactly how it looked. My chopsticks skills were nascent but not incompetent, and some of the teachers marveled at my use of them. We exchanged greetings as Ji Young explained that I was the new Native English Teacher and they smiled and said "nice to meet you" and I responded with "nice to meet you " in Korean. Again, I won points for speaking in Korean. The teachers left and it was only Ji Young and I, and not a moment too soon. My hand was cramping from the chopsticks and my form deteriorated. I could barely pick up the last pieces of bulgogi.

"You look like a child," Ji Young giggled.

"Thanks," I muttered. Back in the hallway outside the cafeteria, we took our trays and leftover food to the waste line. A small line of stragglers from the cafeteria formed and we separated our food waste, trash, cutlery and the tray itself in a sloppy, but methodical line. Ji Young had one more class for the day, but my schedule dictated that I join Hyun Soo for his afternoon sixth grade class. She checked her hair in each mirror as we ascended back up the stairs to her classroom, where we parted ways.

Already, I was fast becoming a celebrity in the building. It didn't take a genius to figure out that the only reason for my sudden popularity was the fact that I was the only non-Korean person in the school. Students I'd just met hours ago waved or shouted 'Metyu

Teacher, hi!' or gave a quick bow. Accompanying them were students I'd not met yet, and some of them shared in their friends' enthusiasm.

The first and second graders were a different story. Having never spent time with a Native English Teacher unless they took private lessons, the youngsters thought this new white guy in the building was fascinating. By third grade, most kids develop some tact. These youngsters had no qualms about pointing or following or touching my hairy arms.

"*Waygook saram yogi-oh*," said one diminutive boy to himself as we passed each other in the hallway. *There's a foreigner here*, he said. I hadn't noticed, kid. Thanks for keeping me informed.

After sitting at my desk for a couple minutes, hoping that nobody would come in unless accompanied by Ji Young, I made the arduous four second trip from my desk to Hyun Soo's room. Immediately upon entering the room, I was greeted with a unanimous 'uwaa!' Hyun Soo, at work at his computer, acknowledged me as the thing that made them go 'uwaa!' then turned back to the computer screen, typing away. Nearly the entire class was already seated; their eyes followed me as I walked closer to Hyun Soo. Their 'uwaa!' was not the curious, innocent 'uwaa!' of the adorable younger grades. Theirs was an appraising, 'get a load of this chump' kind of 'uwaa!' These were middle schoolers trapped in the last hours of elementary school. Sixth grade is the last elementary grade in South Korea, and it's one year too many if you ask me. This particular bunch, halfway through their school year with one foot out the door toward Maria's middle school, was already checked out. Their 'uwaa!' was a dare to pique their interests six months before they took a hike.

Hyun Soo finally rose from his desk. In his left hand was a clipboard, and in his right was a pointer stick with a cartoonish hand at the end. He spoke and the kids fell silent, that is, except for one. A chubby boy with long bangs hanging over his eyes was still turned to his neighbor behind him. Hyun Soo struck the desk with the pointer wand and the boy startled back to facing forward. From there, Hyun Soo delivered a speech not unlike Ji Young's, one where I eventually heard my name pronounced 'Metyu Teacher.' At last, Hyun Soo looked at me calmly and said "you have a presentation?"

"I do." I brandished my flash drive and Hyun Soo invited me to the computer to plug it in. The room stayed silent as the kids, patiently or not, awaited my presentation to flash before them on the screen. Once it did, I proceeded with my introduction to a mildly attentive crowd. Hyun Soo provided translation much in the same fashion as Ji Young did in the morning. None of my personality quirks or hobbies described in the PowerPoint seemed to interest the kids much, or perhaps they didn't care that I had an interest in those things. At last, I opened the floor for questions. I chose the least surly looking boy.

"How much do you weigh?" he said in slow English.

Hyun Soo glared at the boy and admonished him in Korean. "Sorry. It's a common question in Korea."

"I understand."

Hyun Soo handed me a flimsy paper with a list of words and phrases and asked me to say them aloud and have the students repeat them. Again, I put my Anthony Hopkins pants on and attempted to say each word and phrase, simple as they were, with authority and professionalism. I'd bark out a word and the kids would bark back with diminishing enthusiasm as we went down the page. That was the extent of my responsibilities for the day as Hyun Soo instructed the students to open their textbooks. Together, they went through the exercises in the book and corresponding CD-ROM and I stood there ready to exert my professional opinion or display my skill at speaking English. It was a dull business, but I did finally have a chance to sneak a glance at the room itself. Despite the coldness of the learning environment, Hyun Soo's room looked much more like a school room than Ji Young's. The floor, like most rooms in the school, was charming but old hardwood. The walls were a playful orange with brick wallpaper. Landmarks from primarily the western world, such as the Parthenon or the White House, decorated the shades keeping out the hot summer sun. Paper cut-outs of jack-o-lanterns mysteriously hung across the ceiling in August. For all intents and purposes, the room checked off all the elementary school room requirements, and then some. The room itself was quite long, perhaps the length of two classrooms without a wall in between. In the back half of the room was a long, green bookshelf of children's books separating the student area from what I would later discover to be a smattering of random things: a small refrigerator, dusty textbooks, and an old piano.

With my classes finished for the day, I retreated to my desk and pretended to be busy until Ji Young popped in.

"We have to go to a meeting," she said, scampering across the room to her desk chair. She pulled open a drawer and checked her bangs in a hand mirror, swiping an errant bang with her finger. "Hul," she said, taking a look at the time. "We're late." I had no idea what 'hul' meant, but I liked it right away. Together, we scurried down to the ground floor to the Vice Principal's office. The large room, about the size of Hyun Soo's classroom, was half meeting space and half administrative office. The Vice Principal's desk stood at one end, flanked on each side by another desk, and on the other end a cluster of assistants crouched behind computers at their own desks. In between were two long tables and two shorter ones, with most seats already filled by teachers. I spotted two seats together, but Ji Young blazed past them. Coming to her senses, she turned around and pointed to one of the free seats.

"Sit here," she said. Puzzled, I pulled the chair out while Ji Young took what I supposed was her assigned seat. I gave a quick bow and 'annyeong haseo' to the three other teachers at my table, polite but noticeably on guard with a stranger in their territory, and slid into my seat. Luckily, there wasn't much time for chit chat. The Principal began to speak.

I didn't understand much of anything anybody said that day, but I didn't understand a single word from the Principal. Whether it was his age or his accent or his speaking style, I had a difficult time picking out even the most basic words. His voice was raspy, to begin with. Before, when Ji Young had introduced me to the man, he'd spoken softly and kindly. Now, addressing 40 some people, he spoke with an almost dictatorial tone, loud and brash. Every so often, he'd interrupt his sentence with an elongated raspy syllable, a 'bahhh!' that sounded half clearing his throat and half thinking out loud. He droned on for quite some time. I didn't want to be rude and get out my phone, so I sat back in my chair and soaked in the drab rectangle that was the Vice Principal's office. Never in my life have I so carefully studied the intricacies of a printer, the subtle roundness of a keyboard, the smooth contours of a laminator.

The meeting finished as suddenly as it began, with teachers scooting out of their chairs and filtering out. I followed Ji Young out of the room.

"Do you have plans tomorrow night?" she asked.

"No."

"There's a teacher dinner tomorrow night. I'll drive us."

They'd warned us about teacher dinners in orientation. At their most benign, teacher dinners are voluntary but secretly mandatory evening get-togethers at a restaurant prized by the Principal. More often than not, the night may start that way but carry on with heavy drinking and karaoke, two things I don't really put on my list of hobbies. I didn't have any ready excuses to not go, so I was stuck.

It was 4:30. Quitting time. After we shut off our computers and gathered our things, Ji Young locked the door and hid the key in a shoe sitting on the slipper shelf in the hallway. We walked out together and said our goodbyes. One day down. Hundreds to go.

The following day went much the same. Excessive honking and shouting from the street below woke me as much as my alarm. This morning, there was another noise too. Somebody was making an announcement with a loud speaker from a truck. It sounded stern, authoritarian, and important. Whatever he was saying, he was saying it again and again and again as he drove through the neighborhood. We were concerned, for a minute, that something serious like an invasion or air strike from North Korea was imminent and we were being told to seek shelter. We didn't get any calls from our co-teachers, so we assumed that the announcement, disconcerting as it sounded, was nothing important and that everything was normal. We went about the rest of our morning as if nothing was unusual.

Maria came up with the genius idea of keeping the toilet seat up while showering to keep it dry. That was our first major work-around in our quirky apartment, aside from pushing the beds together. We established early on that post-shower privacy wasn't really going to be a thing in our apartment. One of us would have to dress for the day while the other ate breakfast at the table. Such is life when your bathroom is attached to the living room dining room closet. Because of the humidity, I made an executive decision to keep my sleeves rolled up. I still wore the tie, so I was still drenched in sweat when I walked into the school moments later.

At school, my introduction presentations went about the same as before, with 'uwaa's' and impertinent questions and general awkwardness. The sixth graders were, perhaps, a touch less grouchy than the group before, but no more amused. Since these students followed the same lesson plan as the class before, my responsibility was the same: say English words. At 4:30, Ji Young locked up the office with the shoe key again and we went to her car.

"What kind of restaurant are we going to?" I asked as she sped out of the parking lot.

"Oh, I don't know," she whined. "I've never been there." This conversation summed up much of what my life would be like in South Korea: a clueless foreigner who had no choice but to go with the flow, providing his Korean counterpart knew what the flow was. She punched in the address in the car's GPS and within seconds our car appeared on a moving map of the city. "The Vice Principal got a promotion. He's moving to a different school. That's why there's a teacher dinner."

It was odd to me that the Vice Principal got a promotion in the middle of the school year, but then again, I was just starting in the middle of the school year.

"I feel sorry for you," she added unexpectedly.

"Why do you feel sorry for me?"

"The Principal wants you to come to the teacher meetings," she explained. "It's a waste of time. You don't speak Korean."

I didn't disagree, but I wasn't in any position to refuse the Principal.

"He just talks and says nothing," she said.

"Well maybe I should feel bad for you," I replied.

"A waste of both of our times."

The restaurant ended up being on the other side of town. The city was starting to give way to the mountains when Ji Young pulled into a parking lot in front of a big square building. I never got a sense of what the rest of the restaurant looked like, but the school had reserved a private banquet space upstairs with two long tables and space enough for dancing, if the need arose. It was a simply-decorated room, and bright. Hyun Soo was already seated and ushered us to sit next to him.

"Do you enjoy duck?" he asked a little robotically.

"I, uh…I don't know," I replied.

"It's the specialty here," he said. I'd never had duck. Ji Young bowed and they said hello politely in Korean. The Principal walked to the front of the room with a microphone and began addressing the crowd. Knowing that the teachers were only marginally more interested in what he had to say than I was did more to make me feel part of the group than any of my introductions.

"The Principal is going to introduce you," whispered Ji Young.

"What? Do I have to do something?"

"Just say something. It doesn't matter."

"In what language?!"

And with that, I heard 'Metyu' for the 19th time that day. The Principal gestured at me and I felt the eyes of the room shift my way. He was still speaking, so I kept my eyes locked on him and awaited what I hoped to be an obvious cue. Sure enough, everyone began to clap and Ji Young whispered that I should stand.

"Annyeong haseo," I said, bowing. "Cha neun Metyu imnida. Cha neun Mi Gook saram imnida. Manasaw bangop simnida." *Hello. My name is Matthew. I'm an American. It's nice to meet you.* Not exactly Winston Churchill, but it was all I had and it was grammatically correct. Also, if it's what they taught me to say at orientation, I had to hope it was the correct form of politeness. A sentence in Korean changes depending on the formality required. This 'imnida' ending was, to my knowledge, a formal way to address a crowd of superiors. Even if it was incorrect, attempting to speak the local language goes a long way. The faculty was visibly impressed that I could at least say four complete, if simple sentences in Korean. They applauded and I sat down as the Principal continued his speech.

"The Principal is pleased that you are already studying Korean," said Ji Young, confirming my theory. The Vice Principal was then invited to stand next to the Principal. Two female teachers presented the Vice Principal with a plaque to thank him for his time at the school. He held the plaque for some time as the Principal talked on. Eventually, the Vice Principal was permitted to speak. His speech was humble and, unlike the Principal's, short.

At last, it was time to eat, and servers trotted out with trolleys of food and drinks. For every four or five people, there was a selection of soju, Sprite, and Fanta. Hyun Soo wasted no time in pouring a shot for Ji Young and I and enlisting Ji Young to pour his. You never pour your own in South Korea.

"Do you like soju?" he asked, never minding the fact that it was already poured and I was going to have to drink it anyway.

"I've never had it," I said, which was untrue. I tried some after orientation one night and hated it. It tastes like something I should use to clean my drain. We raised our shot glasses.

"We say 'geon bae,'" Hyun Soo explained.

"Geon bae!" I said. Both of them turned to their sides to drink. It's impolite to kick back your shot in full view of your neighbors, so they turn to the side and do it in semi-privacy. Sitting in between them, I wasn't sure which side to turn to, so I played the ignorant foreigner card and drank my shot facing forward. My punishment for cultural insensitivity was the burning sensation of soju racing down my throat.

The barbecued duck meat, it turned out, was wonderfully fatty and melt-in-your-mouth soft. It was my first favorite Korean food. There was also rice, of course, along with an exciting assortment of banchon, or side dishes. Most Korean sit-down restaurants provide a plethora of side dishes to accompany whatever you order. Kimchi is typically one of the side dishes, but also egg in some format, peanuts, and a variety of vegetables. I needn't worry about starving in South Korea with food like this.

Ji Young disappeared for a while to talk with other teachers, so Hyun Soo and I got to know one another. I hadn't had a real opportunity to speak with Hyun Soo, so I'd assumed his English was on par with Ji Young's. While serviceable enough for conversation, I found myself speaking slowly, choosing simpler words or phrases, and repeating myself more often. It was the beginning of a transformation in the way I spoke on a regular basis. Somehow, we got to the topic of celebrity doppelgangers.

"I've been told I look like Russell Crowe," said Hyun Soo. "What do you think?"

I pulled up a picture of a younger Russell Crowe on my phone and held it up to compare to Hyun Soo's face. Shia LeBeouf could more easily pass as Mel Brooks.

"Oh yeah, a little," I said. Truly, it had nothing to do with their different races. Almost immediately, I started picking out faces amongst the students and faculty that reminded me of other people. One teacher in particular looked a lot like Lisa Kudrow. Ji Young reminded me of a previous co-worker, notably a white person. A fourth grader bore an uncomfortable resemblance, both in appearance and personality, to myself at that age.

"What about you?" he said. "Who do you look like?"

"I've been told Steve Carell and Ben Affleck in the same day, so I really have no idea."

Ji Young returned with a giant black folder and dropped it in front of me on the table.

"You should pick a karaoke song," she said, smiling. This was part of the plan all along. Get the foreigner to sing karaoke. I don't mind singing. As part of a group, I rather like it. As a solo performance in front of strangers, my interest level is on par with sticking my face in a hornet's nest. In the spirit of doing new things and not disappointing potential new friends, I flipped through the book to look for a song. All the English songs were in the very back. I don't sing karaoke often, so I don't have my 'song' that I can lean on at any time. Also, there wasn't a ton of options that I knew to begin with. I chose 'Starlight' by Muse because I knew it better than most of the songs on the list. Ji Young took the book and disappeared again.

"Do you like karaoke?" asked Hyun Soo.

It didn't matter what I said next. I'd have to sing anyway. "Sometimes," I lied.

"Good. You're first." He led me to the front of the room next to the karaoke machine, where Ji Young was pointing out the song to another teacher. Hyun Soo produced a microphone from somewhere and handed it to me. The Principal pulled two tambourines from a box and handed them to Ji Young and Hyun Soo. I would not be alone after all.

The rousing guitar and drums of Muse filled the banquet hall, followed by the piano melody. Both my parents are music teachers, so I'm not completely hopeless at singing, but it's not something I do on the regular. I hoped to God that 'Starlight' was in an appropriate chord for me. It wasn't. Immediately, I realized Matthew Bellamy sings much higher than I do. This should have been obvious, given that half of Muse's songs from the album *Black Holes and Revelations* sound like Queen's forgotten record. I had to pick high or low and I chose low, a gravely, embarrassing low unyieldingly amplified in the microphone. I refused to make eye contact with anybody, but I could tell Ji Young and Hyun Soo were trying to keep positive with energetic tambourine playing. The Principal, having never left the front of the room, accompanied me with some air guitar. At last, the chorus came around and I could sing with more ease. I thought maybe, just maybe, I'd get through the song without embarrassing myself. Maybe I'd make it in this new country, this new job, with this new cast of characters. So far, all I'd done in South Korea was go with the flow. It was time that the flow went with me.

But the chorus was over, and I was back to an unbecomingly low second verse.

Colorful Daegu

That Time I was 'Dongchimed' in Public

Daegu is South Korea's third largest metropolitan area by population, but something like its 59th most important city. It has been a regional capital and market town for centuries, but the same could be said about Lincoln, Nebraska. In *A Brief History of Korea*, Daegu gets one mention in its entire heft, and that is to say that it was a fairly unimportant town until the railroad came through. It's a bit of a pariah among its metropolitan peers, with no glittering coasts like Busan, little cultural significance compared to Seoul or Gwangju, no major industries like Incheon or Ulsan (Samsung, founded here in 1938, has long since moved to plusher zip codes), and few historical treasures that help mid-sized cities like Jeonju punch above their weight. As the largest inland city in the country, its transportation network does an excellent job of getting people to other places that aren't Daegu. The city does have mountains, but so does the rest of the country, and Daegu's aren't especially tall or romantic. This part of South Korea is the most conservative and it's not unusual for Koreans from elsewhere to have difficulty connecting with the perceived backwardness of locals. This is all to say that no one has an especially high opinion of Daegu and Daegu doesn't have an especially high opinion of itself.

You would think such a city would be terrible, but that's not the case. With no expectations from outside or within, Daegu is content to be itself, whatever that self turns out to be. It's cheaper to live in than Seoul or Busan, and has plenty of good food. It's large enough to have anything a foreigner would need: excellent movie theaters, tons of shopping, a Costco. The diversions, such as they are, aren't highlights of the country but certainly satisfy the needs of the locals. It's an overlooked but pleasant place that has seen better times, not unlike Ohio.

If Daegu is famous for one thing, it's for being hot. The city sits in a cauldron of humidity between Mt. Palgong and Mt. Ap. The humid subtropical climate, then, is reportedly perfect for growing two things: apples and beautiful, if hot-tempered women. Women from Daegu routinely win beauty pageants and are often featured in desirable K-Pop groups. The men don't do so bad themselves.

Of course, I'd been in the city only a few days and knew none of this. At the time, Daegu was an unexplored monster outside our southern window. Directly beneath that same window, starting around eight in the morning on our first Saturday, the scrap metal dump came to life. Maria and I awoke to the mechanical symphony of an excavator, or some such loud machine, grabbing a heap of garbage and dropping it into a different heap. I sat up and shut the window and tried to get back to sleep, but it was no use. I was awake.

For our first weekend in Daegu, Ji Young graciously offered to show us around downtown. Her apartment was close to ours, so we agreed to meet at a nearby bus stop. Our walk to the stop was our first real opportunity to see our new neighborhood of Maecheon. The sun was shining, perfect for a mid-morning stroll through our new digs. Maecheon is largely a lower-middle class area. "Not poor, but not rich" is the best description I ever pulled out of Ji Young. It's split in two by an inconsequential stream, above which a monorail track follows the same path through the subdivisions. Daegu was in the midst of constructing a third, above-ground metro line that would connect with their two below-ground ones. A station sat promisingly across the street from my school, but remained unopened. On our side of the stream was the low-rise apartment blocks that we lived in, adjacent to a pleasant high-rise development. On the other side were two more high-rise developments nearly identical to the first, along with Maria's middle school and Maecheon High School side by side. Wedged in between these high-rises was a small park with a badminton court and a playful fountain. It was too early to be filled with jumping children, but an old woman in a comically-large visor paid us no heed as we walked by. Connecting all this was a busy three-lane road, along which on either end sat retail stacked three or four stories tall. Chain coffee shops and self-serve bakeries, cell phone stores, convenience stores, and a handful of cheap eateries lined the ground floors while doctor's offices and private academies got the better views from the upper levels. Next to the high school sat a post office and behind it was a sizeable grocery store. At that particular intersection, another middle-aged woman in a large visor sat on the ground behind red bowls of enticing apples and tangerines. In all, Maecheon had everything a neighborhood needed neatly framed between two low mountain ridges.

Ji Young met us at the bus stop as promised and within minutes we hopped on board a crowded bus. There was nowhere to sit, but we found an area where the three of us could stand together. In Chicago, it wasn't unusual to step into a crowded bus, but there seemed to be a threshold that the driver was unwilling to cross. You could call this a legal requirement. This driver seemed to view it as a challenge to see how many people he could stuff into his bus. At every stop, three people would get off and seven would get on. Ji Young had probably accounted for this as she chose a spot toward the back of the bus, where standing passengers are less likely to crush themselves into a sardine-like state of familiarity. While anybody and everybody rode the bus, there seemed to be a disproportionate number of *adjummas*.

Let's take a moment to talk about adjummas. Adjummas are, by definition, older married women, but the word's daily use has nothing to do with marital status. When referring to adjummas, people usually mean a woman over the age of 40 who adheres to a certain aesthetic. They're easy to spot – they often wear clashing hiking clothes or flowery blouses and a visor with a bill that a welder might find useful. They have short, permed hair and an even shorter tolerance for nonsense. Adjummas, found solitary or in groups, are the sturdiest people I know, with elbows of steel and equally hard glares. They use those elbows to make their way through crowds, say on a bus or train. Even their male counterparts, adjeossi's, give them a wide berth. If you find yourself in the direct path of an adjumma, stay calm. They are perfectly wonderful people. Keep your arms tucked at your sides, be wary of sharp elbows plowing a path, and smile. They may smile back, or melt you with their eyes.

The cityscape between Maecheon and downtown was, I'm sorry to say, bleaker than the one getting to the auditorium. The entire city, it seemed, was devoted to maintaining a gray palate which flies in the face of the city's slogan, "Colorful Daegu." Dingy motels dominated the area around Buk-gu bus station. Along the wide sidewalks (and some not so wide), more people set up make-shift market stands with their produce. Discount clothes retailers wheeled out racks of bright hiking shirts and pants, the same sort worn by the folks perusing the merchandise. The stores began repeating themselves, the same Paris Baguette and Tous Les Jours bakeries, Sk Telecom phone stores, and too many fried chicken franchises to name. To practice my Hangul, I did my best to read signage as we whizzed past.

"Suh-puh-ghe-ti," I read aloud, pronouncing the Hangul syllables one at a time. "Oh, that place serves spaghetti."

On our left, opposite a bus stop, a gray cube masquerading as a building was labeled 'Fashion Shopping Mall.' Above the words, something resembling Santa Claus was giving the thumbs up to a snowman with a top hat, but no thorax. I had questions.

"Is that place any good?" I asked Ji Young.

"No," she said firmly. "Only old people go there."

I could see what she meant. In front of the entrance were more stalls of clothes and shoes and only people above 50 seemed to be stopping in front of them. The bus left the depressing mall and we were the happier for it. Soon after, the bus took a turn and, apparently, so did the city. We were back in the realm of high-rise developments, nice ones by the look of them, and multi-level department stores. The sidewalks grew more crowded, and there was music coming from the street. At last, Ji Young told us to get off the bus. Ji Young took Maria's arm and the three of us moseyed into the city.

Downtown Daegu is a treat if you like mazes and few discernable landmarks. Most of the buildings are like the retail buildings back in Maecheon -- concrete sandwiches with few enough stories to count on one hand – but infinitely more packed together and crowded with people. Every building has another intriguing hole in the wall selling grilled food or phone cases or designer clothing. With every turn down a side street are more

Korean barbecue joints, bars, clubs, apparel stores, fast food, and cafes. There are a fistful of McDonalds, KFC's, and Starbucks thrown into the mix. Handsome looking movie theaters deserved a later second look. The entire streetscape is complemented by enough neon to make Las Vegas go 'hey, what are you trying to pull?" It's a lot to take in.

And the noise. Never mind that there were thousands of people walking around the roads that were sometimes pedestrian only and sometimes not. Every other shop or restaurant, it seemed, found the need to pump music into the street to lure customers. Out of one barbecue restaurant, of all songs, came Bloodhound Gang's "The Bad Touch," an overall unlikely song to play around children, who may ask what 'do it like they do on the Discovery Channel' means.

This side of Daegu was arguably more cosmopolitan than Maecheon. Here the restaurants served Italian, Thai, Japanese, and American cuisines as likely as they served Korean. A Mexican place or two even made it into the mix, as did a Turkish kebab joint. I noticed something else in downtown Daegu that I hadn't seen elsewhere yet—people that looked like me. Amidst the throngs of chattering women, the couples entangled in each other's DNA, and fashion connoisseurs with skirts higher than the Rockies were sprinkled the Americans, Brits, and other nationalities that I'd forgotten lived here too. Some chatted with friends as they let their feet lead them to their destinations. Others, like Maria and I, took everything in with our mouths ajar. If I made eye contact with a Westerner, I made a point to say hello, and they usually did the same.

"Do you know him?" Ji Young asked after one such instance.

"No," I replied.

"Why did you say hello?"

"I don't know." Because he looked like me, and for a moment I wanted to share a moment of solidarity with someone who, perhaps as unusually as myself, found themselves a minority. It wouldn't be the last time I said hello to someone I didn't know; sometimes, it felt like a good reason to go downtown.

Soon after we settled into our apartment, we reconnected with Gail and Phillip. Gail had been placed in a university neighborhood on the northeast side of town – geographically not far from us, but

25 minutes away by bus. Phillip was clear down on the southwest side within walking distance to a metro station. That didn't help us much, seeing how our monorail wasn't operational. Gail had spotted an advertisement for an event called the "Sharing Life Festival" that was geared toward foreigners. There would be a photo scavenger hunt, she told us, with prizes. None of us had plans because none of us knew anyone, so the four of us met in Gukchaebosong Memorial Park a block or two east of the downtown labyrinth.

It was another sunny Saturday – there didn't seem to be a scarcity of them. Hundreds of foreigners had decided to come to the park, where a stage was set up in a basketball court. While stragglers arrived, a band with traditional Korean instruments played music, including a soulful cover of "Hey Jude." At last, the event organizers handed out sheets with scavenger hunt instructions and the foreigners scattered into the city in groups. Some of the items on the list included booths where volunteers would assist us in some traditional Korean activity. Others required us to find Koreans off the street. Helpfully, the sheet came prepared with Korean translations. There appeared to be a high density of activities in the park, and they were worth a lot of points, so we headed that way. Each booth had us do something different, such as bow in the traditional Korean way, write Chinese characters, or wear Hanbok, traditional and colorful Korean clothing. One station required us to juggle *jegi*, a sort of hacky sack with a tail, at least five times with our feet before we could score the points.

After exhausting the park's options, we decided to pursue the items that required Korean volunteers. We asked a group of adjummas to do the Can-can with us. At first they were unsure, but one brave volunteer started and the rest joined in. We had to find a couple in matching clothes, which in Korea is not hard to do. We were making excellent progress to the point that we were forced to pursue the more awkward photos. One item required us to take a picture of a Korean person 'dongchim-ing' a member of our group. A dongchim, or 'poop needle,' is an elementary school trick where one folds their hands together in a gun-like fashion, sneaks behind a person, and shoots their sturdy index fingers up a person's butthole. Horror stories of students dongchim-ing their Native English Teachers surfaced every now and then. As a newbie that hadn't gained the respect or authority of his students yet, I lived in constant fear of the dongchim.

Unlike the Can-can, which is a perfectly reasonable thing to ask someone to do, people were not interested in helping us with the dongchim. It was also tricky finding the right person to ask. We had to find someone young enough to find the proposition amusing, but old enough to not take it too far. Someone with some semblance of class, but not too much class. We eventually cornered a couple about our age, in matching blue shirts and black bottoms, no less, into helping us out. We handed the scavenger hunt sheet to the guy, who would likely do the honors, and pointed to the item in question. He handed us the sheet and shook his head. We pleaded, trying to explain that he didn't actually need to stick his fingers in any of our buttholes. We just needed a picture pretending. Neither of their English was that good, but they seemed to get the idea. Reluctantly, with some bullying from us and some encouragement from his girlfriend, the man assumed the position. As if proposing, he went down on one knee and folded his hands in preparation to dongchim. I don't know if we drew imaginary straws or what, but somehow the duty of being fake dongchim-ed fell on me. So, I stood with my butt facing our poor friend's face and Gail took a picture.

In the end, our team won second place in the scavenger hunt. Our prize was a bag of silly Korean socks with superheroes and dozing kittens and other beguiling characters that would decorate our feet. I remind Gail and Phillip whenever possible that our victory rested on the dongchim picture. I believe it still exists somewhere, perhaps in a furnace.

By November, I'd established a relationship as a freelance writer for the Daegu Compass, the local English-language magazine that featured articles on food, events, and travel within the Daegu area and South Korea as a whole. They soon sent me on assignments within the city, allowing me to experience what Daegu had to offer in tourist activities and services. Many of these assignments revolved around the medical tourism industry, which the city was aggressively trying to promote. They took me to neighborhoods that, on the surface, appeared rough and neglected, especially compared to the bright and buzzy downtown only blocks away. However, in a city as parched for recognition as Daegu, these are the places that give the city character, that reward the patient pedestrian with a glimpse of the city as it is: an industrial backwater searching for a new identity.

Part of this identity that the city tries to foster is one of more historical importance. To write a piece on one of the city's few cultural treasures, I spent an afternoon wandering the streets of Yangnyeongsi. Just across Jungang-dae Road, the Yangnyeongsi Medicine Market couldn't be a more opposite neighbor to the downtown glamour and clamor. The decidedly quieter alleys feature medicinal herb stores, restful tea shops, and purveyors of strange, but timeworn cures for every ailment. Stumbling into the area's shops, you're more likely to find the root of some gnarly mountain bush or a set of antlers than a $100 pair of jeans.

The neighborhood sits under Dongsan Cheongna Hill, a small bluff overlooking the city that long harbored Christian missionaries and the medical services they provided. The March First Independence Movement Road, a generous name for a series of stairs, leads to the top. On one side is the large and stately Jeil Presbyterian Church, the first Presbyterian congregation in the city. The church's wide façade, with its two towers and spires, commands a watchful presence over central Daegu. On either side on top of the hill are old houses (now a missionary museum) built by American missionaries at the turn of the century that delightfully combine elements of Western and Korean architecture.

At the foot of the hill sits the green-roofed Gyesan Catholic Cathedral built in 1902. It was a Sunday, right around lunchtime, and I didn't want to disturb a worship service, but smiling people in suits and dresses streamed out of the front door and church appeared to be over. I found an unlocked side door and took a peek inside. The bare, white walls and gray brick appealed to a somewhat French aesthetic. Indeed, I discovered later that the building was designed by a French priest named Paul Rober Achill. The colorful stained glass windows depicted saints, draped in Hanbok, martyred during the Joseon dynasty. Having grown up attending traditional Lutheran churches, stained glass windows depicting non-white people in Eastern clothing was a jarring, but welcome reminder of the Church's breadth across the world.

Even with only a couple months under our belt, I got the feeling that there are really two South Koreas. There's the old Korea with its Hanbok dresses, Pansori music, and adjummas in hiking clothes and there's the new Korea with K-Pop, Samsung smartphones, and plastic surgery. Between them is Seomun Market. Neither touristy nor inaccessible, Seomun Market is where to find the Korea of now, a place not particularly concerned about looking behind or ahead. Old, young, and families mix comfortably here in a country where generations sometimes appear to come from different planets. It's huge, it's busy, and it was one of the easiest places in Daegu to take a moment and consider how far from home I'd come.

Seomun Market, together with the nearby Yangnyeongsi Medicine Market, long ago solidified Daegu's status as a market town and crossroads. Its roots began in the late Joseon Dynasty period, during the last years of which the market became one of the three largest in Korea. The name 'Seomun,' or 'west gate,' refers to its location outside the western gate of Daegu's fortress walls, demolished by the Japanese in 1907. Today, the area sits just west of downtown Daegu.

The market really starts to buzz after lunchtime on the weekends, when well-rested families make their way to the market in search of, well, anything. The over 4000 stalls are divided across six 'districts' that roughly focus on different products. One can find almost anything in the market, including plenty of seafood, produce, designer bags, hiking gear, shoes, toys, and crafts, but the market is especially known as a place to browse for textiles and clothing. Prices are often cheaper than conventional stores, and some stall owners may be willing to haggle prices. Exploring inside the buildings as well as outside is essential in grasping the enormity and variety of the place. It's a bustling, crowded, and strictly Korean labyrinth.

Maria and I took several trips to Seomun Market, usually in search of fun socks. For whatever reason, thin socks with pop culture characters or fun designs are ubiquitous in South Korea. Copyright laws be damned, these socks could feature superheroes, Disney characters, K-Pop singers, or anything else someone might want dancing above their toes. They were also easy gifts for people back home, so occasionally we made the trek to Seomun Market in search of a section that had the city's best selection of socks. Because of the similarity of the buildings and the claustrophobic grid inside, we only found the sock stand of choice about 50% of the time.

But that's part of the allure of a trip to Seomun Market: getting hopelessly turned around. I'm not one for conspiracy theories, but it feels like the stalls change and start selling new things the longer you stay. You swear you've been down this thoroughfare before, past the linens, but now they've got pig intestines for sale. Had I passed this backpack shop before? All I can say is don't go in a hurry because you're going to leave upset.

If the trip is looking like a failure, best find some food to make up for the loss of time. *Beondegi,* or baked silkworm larvae, are a staple at the market. They're served in, what else, paper cups, and are a bit of a divisive issue in Korea, like candy corn. About half the population loves them. The other half thinks they're vile. I tried one once. They're mushy and taste foul and get stuck in your teeth – not unlike candy corn -- but they're something uniquely Korean to try nonetheless.

There are far less disgusting things to eat around. *Hoddeok*, a steaming, doughy pancake stuffed with brown sugar and sunflower seeds, is heavenly. Even better, it costs about a dollar. *Kalguksoo*, a simple but hearty noodle soup, is widely available within the market and is also a popular dish. In the cold winter months, nothing sounds finer than to pull up a stool at a kalguksoo stand, and there's no finer place to do that than Seomun Market.

In 1938, Lee Byung-chull started a trading company in Daegu's Ingyo-dong district, today most known for an ugly but vital strip of machinery shops known as 'tool alley.' The business, called Samsung Trading Company, started in a simple wooden structure. 40 employees worked the front office, made noodles, and procured goods for export. Located near the Seoul-Busan rail line, Samsung Trading Company expanded rapidly into new ventures and moved to Seoul after seven years of booming business in Daegu. The original building was demolished long ago, but the location is easy enough to find at the Dalseong Park bus stop. An outdoor memorial includes a small replica of the building, as well as an impression of the facade carved into a large wall.

In stark contrast to the memorial's implications of wealth and power are the endless rows of tool shops in the immediate area to the east called Bukseongno. The first time I set foot in the neighborhood, I thought I might have finally discovered Daegu's seedy side of town. The streets themselves were largely deserted, and most shops were shuttered for the day, or decade by the looks of them. What shops were open looked more like garages that hadn't been organized or swept in at least as long. Looking down the straight road, I saw a lot of lifeless concrete and tin buildings. Surely, I must have come during off hours. Otherwise, this was a set for a post-apocalyptic zombie flick. This was where murderers came to murder. The weather that day, cloudy and blustery, did little to soften the impression. I kept walking: my assignment about the neighborhood that birthed Samsung told me I must.

Within these drab corridors are some absolute gems, I'm happy to report. Homey and quiet Samduk Sanghoe café sits in a renovated Japanese colonial house. The wood framework and spartan, white walls are unmistakably Japanese, making the café easy to spot amid the dross described above. In the second floor seating, I had the option of sipping my café mocha on the floor in a traditional Japanese setting. I haven't been much good at sitting on the floor with any kind of dignified posture since the 5th grade, so I settled with a table and chairs.

About a block from the café is the Bukseongno Tools Museum, another Japanese build. Inside the building are somewhat disorganized displays of antiquated tools, donated by long-time shopkeepers of the area. It was said that, if need be, the shopkeepers of the neighborhood could build a tank; such was the depth of materials and tools in Bukseongno. Luckily, this need was never exploited by the Japanese. To represent this idea, an old artillery piece is on display inside the museum, empty on the cold day I went.

Closer to Daegu Station, a once featureless parking lot was transformed into a colorful mural display. I never did find out who painted those murals, but whoever did had a time doing it; they occupy entire side walls of two and three story buildings. They're delightfully odd as well. A pale deer with enormous antlers stands on a moon and watches people as they pass through the street. Next to that mural is another mural of a man's face accompanied with the word 'demolished.' I have no explanation to offer.

The real stars of 'tool alley' don't appear until about 6pm, when a handful of hardy cooks and their employees strike up red tents and sell bulgogi and bowls of udon late into the night. A staff member of the Daegu Compass, a bookish Korean girl with thick, lens-less glasses, explained that these tents aren't strictly legal, that the owners don't have the proper permits or pay taxes on their businesses or some such questionable behavior. She took Maria and I to one of the tents, reportedly the best one. It sat in a parking lot that, hours earlier, was empty when we'd passed. Now, a giant red tent with a grill at the end beckoned hungry people in. We'd passed a few other tents on the way to this one, their owners calling at us and offering a table. Our friend insisted on this one. There was no real entrance, just an open flap closest to the street.

The décor inside was makeshift like the restaurant itself: hastily set up plastic chairs and tables large enough for four, maybe five people to crowd around. We chose a table and ordered a large portion of bulgogi -- or 'fired meat' in Korean -- bowls of udon and some drinks. Now, at this point in my life, I hadn't made it a habit to eat street food on plastic seats in a tent of questionable legality, but this meal changed everything. The bite-sized twists of beef were grilled to perfection, the udon soup piping hot and peppery. Clearly, I'd been eating at the wrong restaurants. The total came to something absurdly cheap as well. Food this good had to be illegal. What was the catch, I thought. If the cops show up, am I expected to grab some chairs and run? On a later date, Maria and I ended up taking Gail and Phillip and their reactions were the same. Who in their right minds would expect to find Daegu's best food in a red tent behind a tool shed? It shouldn't come as a surprise. Daegu, after all, is practically the red tent of South Korea.

Becoming Metyu Teacher

That Time Someone Spoke English and I Didn't Know It

As much as I wanted to control my surroundings, I was stuck in the flow of 'follow and react' for a long time. There wasn't much of a choice. I didn't know the students and the students didn't know me, and we didn't know each other's language. I smiled and bowed at fellow faculty members, but most didn't know English so I kept a self-imposed distance to avoid awkward situations. For the first couple months, I only had a vague idea of what was going on and relied on Ji Young or Hyun Soo to pull me through. I needed to meet more coworkers to pull me through.

It didn't take long to discover that Ji Young was a flighty individual. One had the sense that she was always winging it, and that she was not especially good at winging things. She was also not very punctual. More often than not, I'd show up in the morning and find the office locked. Luckily, I knew all about the shoe key. I'd spend the next half an hour settling in, typing up some PowerPoints that might be useful for an upcoming lesson, or perusing the internet. It was a good time to scour Waygook.com for anything useful. Waygook.com is a resource for English speakers in Korea, with forums and advice on anything from food to travel to dating Koreans. More importantly, an entire section is devoted to educational resources, organized by textbook. If in a pinch, it was simply a matter of locating the textbook and chapter and downloading materials uploaded by other teachers. There's a lot of garbage, but sifting through the noise to find the perfect PowerPoint game saved the day on more than a few occasions.

After a while, Ji Young would shuffle in with her heels about five minutes before class began. She'd kick them off at her desk and slide her feet into her slippers, completely exasperated.

"Metyu," she'd whimper. "Sorry I'm late."

"It's fine," I'd reply. I would've preferred to spend the previous half an hour discussing the plan for the day, but five minutes is good too. I'd tried establishing a routine of asking the day before, but Ji Young wasn't the sort to plan that far in advance. The best I could do was equip myself with PowerPoint presentations on vocabulary and a game or two.

"So what are we doing today?" she'd ask me.

"Where are we in the textbook?"

Ji Young would find the appropriate textbook out of a stack on her desk and flip to where she deemed was the next lesson. "Here."

Usually, I'd remembered correctly where we were in the textbook and the materials I'd collected matched. Sometimes, I was wrong, and I then had three minutes to come up with something else.

The morning bell would ring. "*Hul,*" Ji Young would say. I never learned the actual meaning of 'hul,' but it's said the way we say "oh my God.' It was always used with the same inflection as well, with the 'l' lingering in a deeply satisfying exhale. I added it to my lexicon. "Do you have a game or something?" she'd ask.

And thus was the extent of the majority of our lesson planning. It's not the system I would've preferred, since I was at the mercy of a plan to make it look like I knew what I was doing, but it got the job done about 80% of the time. Also, I was in no position to tell Ji Young how to do her job. With class about to start, we'd rush across the school to her classroom, sometimes with the first period's students right behind us.

I stopped wearing a tie to work after about three days, when Ji Young took pity on my poor, sweaty soul and said something along the lines of "you don't have to wear that and look terrible." My comfort level rose dramatically once I began wearing typical business casual clothing. Also, the humidity finally broke in late September and the climate was warm, but comfortable. Maria and I had very little money left until our first paycheck, but we decided it was important enough to buy work shoes for school. By work shoes, of course, I mean leather slippers. For two years, I wore leather flip flops with socks to work.

With each day, I grew slowly more comfortable in the class routine, and Ji Young and I developed a halfway decent partnership. I knew where to find the vocabulary PowerPoints on Ji Young's desktop in case she wasn't available. The students showed up and jotted down the English vocabulary and their Korean meanings and put their hands on their head. We'd take turns saying the English words and then move onto the textbook lesson. With the remaining time, we'd play a game. On many, many days, my role as Native English Teacher looked more like an overly-enthusiastic game show host. The kids enjoyed themselves, anyway, and so did I. Through these games, the kids slowly grew accustomed to me. I began to form relationships with them, the younger ones quicker than the older ones. Unfortunately, Korean names are, syllabically speaking, easily exchangeable and difficult to memorize. Min Ji, Ji Min, Hyun Ji, Ji Young, Ah Young, Young Jin, Jin Woo, Jun Ho, Tae Min. It was a nightmare. I felt like a terrible human being for not knowing my students' names. In the first few months, when discussing students with Ji Young, all I had were physical descriptions and personality quirks to go off of. I remembered faces well and could tell you which class they belonged to, but even a few months into the job I perhaps had less than 10 names memorized. By the time I left Korea, I at best had memorized half my students' names.

Besides games, there were lots of videos and songs. Ji Young and I often used YouTube either as motivation in the beginning of class or as a time waster at the end. This is one area in which Ji Young was exemplary. She had an entire library of videos, either saved in her browser favorites or in her brain, to use when she needed. I learned the songs as fast as possible so I could sing vigorously and thus inspire the students to do the same.

The songs, of course, were designed to be repetitive and easy to remember since they were meant to illustrate some facet of the English language. The only problem with these songs being fetchingly simple is that they got stuck in my head. The worst offender was a song called 'Whose Puppy is it?" and it goes like this:

Whose is it? Whose is it? Whose is it? Whose puppy is it?

It's mine. It's my puppy. It's yours. It's your puppy.
It's his. It's his puppy. It's hers. It's her puppy.
It's ours. It's our puppy. It's theirs. It's their puppy.
Whose puppy is it? Whose puppy is it?

The obvious point of the song is for kids to practice their pronouns, and practice they did. I didn't give a damn whose puppy it was, but the song was stuck in my head all the time. There is likely some circle of hell that plays the song on a loop, and you never get to know whose puppy it is. To make matters worse, the song was stuck in Ji Young's head too. We'd walk down the hallway after class, the song safely, for the time being, outside my thoughts, and I'd hear Ji Young mumbling to herself "it's mine. It's my puppy..." and I'd be in the fold once more. There was no refuge from the infectious song. If any of my former students are reading this, I'd like you to know that I sacrificed a not inconsiderable percentage of my sanity so that you could learn your pronouns. You're welcome.

Hyun Soo's classes were less fun. Every day, the students repeated the English words I read from the chapter sheet. If Hyun Soo ever needed anything from the textbook's CD-ROM repeated, I was the guy. My one additional task was to start the class with an introductory routine. I'd ask the kids how they were doing, and they'd grunt that they were sleepy, or fine, or whatever. I'd ask them what day it was and they'd moan, or shout if Hyun Soo provoked them, "today is Monday, yesterday was Sunday and tomorrow will be Tuesday." Riveting stuff. If time allowed, I'd open up with some conversation—what I did on the weekend, what movie I watched recently, etc. Sometimes, this generated questions or engagement. Usually, it generated blank stares. On a few occasions, I approached Hyun Soo with some ideas, either a game on Waygook.com or an idea for one myself. Hyun Soo was content to stick with the textbook. If I brought up an interesting video in conversation, Hyun Soo waved it off. I played such a small role in that classroom.

If Ji Young was flighty, Hyun Soo was intransigent. Although not unfriendly, he kept a more professional distance that permeated the classroom; he wasn't especially chummy with students or other faculty members. I attempted a few more times to suggest activities I could lead, but he was married to the textbook. I gave up and relegated myself to a dull, but ultimately easy job in his classroom as the talking parrot. As a conciliatory gesture, he often offered me snacks or drinks, the latter usually in the form of disgusting energy shots that he must've relied on to get through the day. In his defense, he was a very busy man. Teachers often assume additional responsibilities for the school, usually in the form of paperwork. Hyun Soo's responsibilities never appeared to end. He was hunched over his computer every time I entered the room, or else running some errand in which case I either could attempt small talk with the students or stand in silence. Neither was very preferable, at least not with 6th graders.

I was in danger of resenting Hyun Soo for his boring classes. Luckily for Hyun Soo, we found common ground over our love for movies. In general, I got the sense that he was unhappy with his life. He worked long hours. He had a baby at home. He was tired in the way Koreans are often tired; disillusioned with the expectations of the Korean workplace and familial obligations. He'd checked off all the boxes he was supposed to only to find more boxes. The one topic of conversation that would perk him up was movies. Ji Young was a contract teacher like myself, but worked between two schools. This meant that there were some days, and lunches in particular, that I would spend more time with Hyun Soo. On several occasions, we were the last teachers to leave the lounge, discussing our favorite movies and our opinions on the latest films over empty lunch trays. He was well versed in action movies and was nostalgic for the ultra-violent, take-no-prisoner explosion fests of the 80's. Eventually, though, he'd remember some paperwork he needed to finish by the end of the day and we'd leave. His spirits lifted, if only for a moment, we'd return to the English hallway. He'd disappear into his classroom and I'd disappear into my office and things would go back to the way they were.

The office became a refuge, real or imagined, from the unfamiliar that lay just outside the sliding doors. After a morning of being in the spotlight as the only non-Korean in the near vicinity, it was a relief to sit at my desk and hide behind headphones. Also, as an introvert, the office was the only place that I could seek relative solitude. The only problem was that it wasn't exactly quiet. The border of my refuge was semipermeable; anybody could walk in. Anybody that did had a specific reason to do so and if I couldn't help them they'd be on their way. One such person that popped his head in from time to time was the new Vice Principal. If I had to take a stab at his age, I'd have guessed he was in his mid-50's. He wasn't all that tall, but wore a scowl and a suit most of the time. Word around the school, according to Ji Young, was that he was a good Vice Principal. I had nothing to base that assumption on. Other than his popping in, looking for Ji Young, seeing that Ji Young wasn't there but that the foreigner was there, receiving the awkward bow from said foreigner and then leaving as quickly as possible, our interactions were pretty limited.

With Ji Young around, the room was decidedly busier. Teachers would come in on business, or students for help or reprimanding. A few weeks in, I was sitting at my desk in the dozy afternoon hours after class but before I could go home. I can't recall exactly what I was doing. I'd like to tell you I was industriously preparing some class activity weeks in advance. More than likely, I was on YouTube.

Into the scene stomped an upset 6th grade girl. She immediately plopped herself next to Ji Young. With long hair half over her eyes, big, dark glasses, and an oversized plaid shirt, she was the incarnation of teenage angst. I had no idea what the problem was, but no matter the language, it's easy to tell when a child is in trouble and must explain themselves. The student told her side of whatever story needed telling, but would occasionally look my way. I pretended to not notice and clicked on an open PowerPoint window to pretend I was making something. The looks grew longer until finally she paused her story and said "*annyeong haseo*."

"Hello," I replied, unsure of the pretense.

"Ha!" she exclaimed, vindicated in some way. She continued to prattle on with her story, faster than before. I continued to type random words into my PowerPoint, with no particular theme. This lesson would cover colors, rooms in the house, and the complete cast of *The Avengers*. A small glance confirmed that I was once again the object of the room's attention.

"*Hwa jang shil!*" the student declared.

"What about a bathroom?" I responded, as one does when someone shouts 'bathroom' at you. Once again whatever theory needed proving was proven and the conversation went onward, perhaps for another 10 minutes. Eventually, I decided to be productive and type something useful into the PowerPoint slide.

When the student finished her story, and when Ji Young said what needed saying, the student went to exit the room, but turned around and said goodbye to me in Korean.

"Good bye!" I said, proud that I knew what she said.

"Ha!" she pointed, and then stormed off.

"What was that all about?" I asked Ji Young.

"I wanted her to tell me about an argument she had with another student, but she didn't want anybody to hear," she explained. "She said 'but Matthew Teacher is here' and I told her you don't understand anything. Thanks for proving me wrong."

Had the girl chosen nearly anything else to say, I would've given her a blank stare and disproven her theory. As it was, she chose the first three things anyone should learn from any new language.

With Hyun Soo busy and Ji Young gone 40% of the time, I began to grow lonely at work. The first few months of any job can be lonely. You're not part of the 'in' crowd, if there is one. You're not sure who to mingle with. You're not even sure what side of your personality to use. It's like sixth grade all over again, but with actual sixth graders running around. When you don't know the language, you're almost certainly never going to be in any 'in' crowd, and mingling is determined by how much of a middle ground you can find. My Hangul reading and writing was coming along, but my vocabulary was shit and I had a difficult time listening and comprehending. It's embarrassing not to know the native tongue, especially when you come from a country that really values people knowing theirs. At that point, I was completely at the mercy of my coworkers' English abilities.

Between third and fourth period every morning was a 30-minute recess called Happy Time. I don't mean it was called something in Korean that translated to Happy Time. I mean there must've been a meeting at some point in which they came up with the phrase Happy Time to describe the half an hour break in the mornings. Every morning during Happy Time' a clique of fifth grade teachers came into the office, fired up the kettle, and gathered around the table to snack on whatever somebody brought that day: cookies, fruit, cake on occasion. They always invited me to join them, and I obliged, fulfilling my duty to eat or drink whatever they offered me. Then I'd silently sit at the table and half pretend to be engaged with the conversation. I'd pull out my phone and play a game of spades, remaining a part of the group by proximity only. One teacher in particular, a tall guy a few years older than myself, did most of the offering. I'd assumed this was because his English was decent, although I learned later that his English wasn't even the best of the bunch. Perhaps he was the most curious, and liked to make conversation. Instead of allowing me to remain on the periphery, he began to ask me questions.

"What is the weather like in your hometown?" he asked on an unusually warm day for October.

"Same," I'd say, trying to keep my English simple. "A little colder." I didn't have the language abilities in Korean to elucidate that Korea's topography and climate is very similar to that of North Carolina's or Tennessee's, where summers are humid and disgusting but winters are mild. In fact, Daegu and Knoxville both lie on the 35th parallel. So I went with 'same.'

Day after day, 'Happy Time' after 'Happy Time,' the fifth grade teachers would filter in one at a time, get the coffee going, invite me to sit with them, and this teacher would ask basic questions, attempting to carry a conversation.

"What is the most popular sport in America?" he wondered. This one was a bit easier to respond to. I held my hand high parallel to the floor and said 'football' and stepping down to indicate rank said 'baseball, basketball, hockey.' I held my hand low over the table. "Soccer." I lifted my hand like an elevator. "But growing."

"Ah, growing," he nodded in recognition.

The questions gradually became deeper, as we discussed politics or cultural differences. Both our natural curiosities got the best of us as we exchanged tidbits of information.

"What religion are you?" I asked one day, since we were already on the topic of religion.

He thought about the word for a second. "Catholic. You?"

"Christian," I replied. "I grew up Lutheran."

"What?"

"Lutheran. You know, Martin Luther?"

I got a blank stare. I said the name one more time and added "in Germany." A light switched on and we were on the same page, though he had no idea there was a denomination named after the man. Or maybe he did and, as a Catholic, wanted a change in subject.

With the ever-deepening topics we covered daily, we got to the point in our relationship where it was much too late and embarrassing to ask what his name was. I asked Ji Young one day after the teachers left the room. "What's that teacher's name?"

"The tall one?"

"Yeah."

"Ji Ho."

Ji Ho. That wouldn't be too hard to remember. The next day, I made a point of greeting him with his name. Ji Ho and I became fast friends, discussing everything from politics to jazz music to apple varieties. He became a go-to reference for Korean vocabulary, cultural customs, and history, even though his English language skills were limited. Our conversations were stilted, laced with basic vocabulary and long pauses. Occasionally I'd try to respond in Korean, even if it was just the word 'yes,' out of respect. He put so much effort in speaking with me, it was the least I could do to throw some Korean into the mix.

I looked forward to our conversations, sipping on the brown, coffee-ish sugar water that constituted the instant coffee selection in my school and every school I ever visited. It was the same coffee the Principal had offered me on our first meeting, exclusively poured, from some unspoken law, into tiny paper cups. Even worse, it was common for teachers to only fill the cups about halfway, creating a water to sugar ratio that could only be described as 'apocalyptically diabetic.' Ji Ho would hand me a cup, and I'd top it off when he wasn't looking. When I think about that coffee, I can't help but think of all the sugar I consumed and paper cups I threw away. Mostly, though, I remember drinking it with Ji Ho and making my first Korean friend.

There was only one problem I had with Ji Ho, and that was his students. Since Ji Ho taught fifth grade, I saw his class twice a week. Ji Young and I consistently ranked them as the absolute worst class in the school. They didn't listen, they didn't shut up, and they didn't score well on any exams. They were rude to me, they were rude to Ji Young, and we hated them. There were, at most, four or five decent kids in the class that I felt bad for because their English learning experience paled in comparison to other classes. At least once a week, Ji Young halted the lesson in its tracks and lectured the kids, meaning we almost never played games or did anything fun with them, which probably exacerbated the problem. Why should they enjoy English if they didn't do anything fun and were admonished every five minutes?

The worst of the crop were the wrestling kids. *Ssireum* is a form of Korean wrestling that is a point of pride for many schools in the country, even down to elementary schools. Kids arrive at school early to train, leave classes to train, and even stay after school to train. Meanwhile, their test scores fall behind that of their classmates, and in the case of seemingly unimportant topics like English, many simply give up. Some of these students keep their frustrations silent, avoiding eye contact and never volunteering answers because they don't know any. Instead, the ssireum students in Ji Ho's class were loud and obnoxious, happy to be the class clowns and remind everyone that they didn't know a thing and were okay with it. They were the ringleaders of Ji Ho's easily distracted class, and all was lost as soon as their tiny attention spans ran dry.

What made the situation more difficult was that the class generally behaved for Ji Ho, so negative reports from Ji Young were usually disregarded. This put me in an uncomfortable spot between my two closest allies in the school at this point.

"Don't talk to me about Ji Ho," said Ji Young if I happened to mention him. So I didn't. Meanwhile, Ji Ho seemed to ignore Ji Young whenever she was around. So much for an entourage.

On top of regular classes, it's expected that Native English Teachers teach after school classes independent from regular teachers. These English clubs are for students who want to practice their English, or for students whose parents want them to practice their English, or for students who don't have anywhere to go before their parents come home so they might as well sit in Metyu Teacher's class and get some candy. I was at liberty to teach just about anything I wanted so long as it helped students read, write, speak, or listen to my language better. Mostly, I played games. I built my own Apples to Apples deck with simple words. It completely defeated the purpose when a student would hold up a card and ask me what it was, but so be it. Later, getting a bit cheekier, I designed an appropriately wholesome Cards Against Humanity deck (based off an existing template from Waygook.com) with which students could finish sentences with silly words. We had a good time.

One day, I was practicing words for body parts with my third and fourth grade after school class. I pointed to a body part on myself and they shouted what it was.

I pointed to my head.

"Head!"

I pointed to my arm.

"Arm!"

I patted my stomach.

"Fat," the only student to answer said. He corrected himself. "Uh, stomach."

That was enough for one day, so I sent the kids off and prepared to go home myself. While I was glad to be done with students for the day, I was mostly enjoying the fact that, at last, temperatures had firmly dropped to a breezy, comfortable Autumn and I wasn't drenched in sweat. I waved farewell to Ji Young back at the office.

"Wait, Matthew," Ji Young said. "We have to plan for our evaluation."

I was less than two months into the job and it was already time for Ji Young and I's first evaluation as a team. They told us in orientation that this was something that would happen, but that didn't change the fact that it came up quickly and I didn't want to do it. It would involve a representative from the school district, Hyun Soo, and possibly the Vice Principal or Principal sitting in on one of our classes. In addition, a panel of my fellow Native English Teachers would sit in and offer feedback. I sat back down.

"What do you think we should do?" I said, hoping she had a plan. "Any ideas?"

She whined. "No. What do you think?"

"We should make a video," I suggested. Editing videos is a favorite diversion of mine. She liked that idea. We agreed that I would develop the activities while she worked on the lesson plan, which needed to be in Korean and English. I returned to my office desk and whipped up a script for the video, which would involve Ji Young and I walking around town and deciding what food we wanted to eat. It was a thrilling screenplay, really, but the target language for the students to learn included 'what do you want to eat?', 'do you like (name a food)?' and 'yes I do' or 'no I don't.' Not exactly ingredients for a Shakespearean tragedy. I sent the script to Ji Young, who probably didn't look at it but approved it anyway. We decided to film the next afternoon after work.

At 4:30pm, when Ji Young agreed to meet me at the front of the school, the front of the school was empty. There was nowhere to sit, so I looked at my phone to convince anyone passing by that I meant to be there, that I hadn't forgotten where my apartment was. A handful of students walked by and waved sheepishly, going home after whatever after-school activities their parents enrolled them in. I smiled and said 'see you later,' since I didn't yet have a rapport with any of my students. For all I knew, they might not even be my students. About 10 minutes later, Ji Young walked up to me speaking with another female teacher who I'd never met. She was a bit taller than Ji Young, with hair to her shoulders framing a pretty face.

"This is Jang Mi," said Ji Young. "She is going to help us film."

We exchanged 'hello's, I in her language and she in mine, both of us scoring easy manners points for speaking in each other's language. Ji Young laughed at the awkwardness.

"What's so funny?" I asked.

"Nothing," she said, covering her laughing mouth with her hand. "I just never hear you speak Korean."

"It's something I do here," I said. "From time to time." I was eager to get this over with, so I motioned toward the crosswalk where we waited for a walk signal. The two of them continued to talk in Korean, although the more I listened the more I realized the conversation was mostly Ji Young talking and Jang Mi listening and nodding. Occasionally Jang Mi would fit in a sentence between Ji Young's rants about whatever she was ranting about. "Should we talk about the video?" I interrupted.

"Yeah, so…," Ji Young trailed off. She used a mirror app on her phone to check her bangs. "What are we doing?"

I handed her a copy of the script with her lines highlighted. "Did you memorize any of your lines?"

"No."

"Do you know a good place we can film?"

"No."

"So we don't know where we're going?"

She laughed. At least we were on the same page on how absurdly unprepared she was. "Well, there's a street by my apartment with a bunch of restaurants," I suggested.

"Okay, we'll follow you." I couldn't help but notice that I, a resident of Korea for all of two months, was leading two ladies who had spent their entire lives there. As I led them across the intersection and down to the street I had in mind, Ji Young continued to ramble and Jang Mi continued to listen. It was soon clear by Ji Young's tone that Jang Mi was her sounding board for all her anxieties and problems. She was her gossip partner, her confidant, and a patient one at that. We passed an entire apartment complex before Jang Mi said a full sentence.

Meanwhile, in the front of the parade, I felt a little tossed aside. I suppose I did a little of the tossing myself, walking 10 steps ahead of the pair of them. I'm a fast walker, I can't help it. I eventually evened out my pace, surrendering to the notion that we weren't going anywhere or doing anything quickly that evening. Let me tell you, what a joy it is to set a slow pace, looking over your shoulder to remain part of a group, while the rest of your company is engaged in a conversation in a different language.

We walked to the other side of Maecheon, past the sidewalk fruit stalls, the post office, the cheap diners busy with uniformed students laughing with their hands covering their mouths. They were likely Maria's kids, or high schoolers. Both are required to wear uniforms to school. Elementary kids are still free to wear whatever. Twenty lonely minutes later, we turned the corner to the street I had in mind. I'd imagined the road had sidewalks wider than two feet across. We'd have to film in the street. One side of the street was the back of the retail shops we'd passed; the other side was a grab bag of generic barbeque restaurants and bars. It wasn't the most cinematic of landscapes, but it would do.

Ji Young and I rehearsed our lines on the corner while Jang Mi waited patiently. I felt bad that this woman was taking time out of her evening to help with a silly project. It gave me even more incentive to hurry. With our lines semi-memorized, we walked to the slim sidewalk on the restaurant side of the street.

"Ok," I said, putting my directorial hat on, "so tell Jang Mi she is going to walk backwards with the phone and film us walking toward her."

I looked at Jang Mi, who looked at Ji Young. Ji Young said something in Korean. Jang Mi nodded her head.

"Tell her to hit the record button, wait two seconds, then say 'action!'" I looked at Jang Mi again, who again looked at Ji Young, who again said something in Korean, to which Jang Mi again nodded in affirmation. She positioned herself a few feet in front of us and held up my phone. She tapped the record button and, as instructed, said 'action' two seconds later.

In the first try, Jang Mi was a little too far away and it was difficult to hear us. In the second, a truck advertising something with a song through a loudspeaker drove by. We got it on the third try. Next, we needed to film the following scene where, in the scenario, I ate too much of the pizza I said I wanted to eat. We retraced our steps and headed to the front of the high school which had a lovely bench for which to sit on and feign a stomachache. To avoid playing the part of the distant foreigner, I decided to let the two of them lead the way to the high school. This proved disastrous, as Ji Young continued wherever she left off in whatever story she was whining about before. And they walked incredibly slowly. But at least I was part of the group, albeit a silent and frustrated part.

Luckily, the school wasn't far and we arrived while I was still in my 20's. Again, I showed Jang Mi where I wanted her to stand with the phone and film us. I took my place on the bench and held my pretend food baby. Jang Mi said action.

"How much pizza did you eat?" said Ji Young, walking up to me.

"Seven pieces," I groaned, holding up seven fingers. And that was it. First try.

"Is that it?" said Ji Young, tossing her hair.

"Yeah, I think so," I said.

"So we can go?"

"Yeah. Thank you!"

I turned to Jang Mi. "Thank you for helping us film. It was a big help."

In the middle of my pivot to Ji Young to translate, Jang Mi said "you're welcome. Any time."

I bit my tongue for a second, and then I looked at Ji Young. It would be one of the few times that we were on exactly the same wavelength.

"She understands everything you say," said Ji Young. "She's just slow at speaking English."

Jang Mi nodded in agreement. "It was nice to meet you."

I smiled sheepishly. "It was nice to meet you too."

And that was how I met Jang Mi, who I would later learn taught third grade. They waved goodbye and walked the opposite direction from my apartment. As I walked home, I did a quick review of everything I said in the last hour or so, hoping I didn't embarrass myself. It was a reminder that the English level of every person I encountered was a complete mystery and that I couldn't assume that the level was zero.

I saw Jang Mi now and then at school. Her classroom was at the opposite end of the hallway as Ji Young's, so often I'd be walking from my end and Jang Mi would walk from hers and we'd meet in the middle and say hello. We'd exchange small talk for about a hallway's length, after which she'd go in whichever direction she was heading and I'd go in mine, likely back to my office. That was, for a while, the extent of our relationship, but it was good to be on "Hi Metyu" terms with another human being that wasn't a student.

No Place Like Home

That Time a Whale was at the Nativity

Koreans don't celebrate Thanksgiving, but that doesn't keep Americans in the country from trying. In Daegu, folks with access to the Camp Walker commissary buy a bunch of turkeys and then sell them at a premium to the poor louts on the outside. Anxious for a Thanksgiving meal, a large group of teachers decided to split the cost of a cooked turkey, something egregious like $100, and pitch in with potatoes, stuffing, and all the necessary standards. Since our apartment was larger than most, we offered to host.

There was only one place in Daegu that was likely to have everything we needed for our feast, and that was Costco. The four of us, Gail and Phillip being present, stepped off a city bus in front of the massive white and red box. With the first floor reserved for the parking lot, already this location differed from others I'd visited. To get to the shopping, a series of long, flat escalators dumped us in front of the cafeteria on the bottommost level. Two giant floors of shopping, as wide and tall as any warehouse, were stacked one on top of the other and underground. In the event of a zombie apocalypse, it would be an ideal place to hole up provided some padlocks and a cache of firearms.

We were hard up for some authentic American food, so we eagerly stood in line for Costco's pizza and hot dogs. With such greasy treats in hand, we walked to the seating area only to find that every table was taken. Families huddled around whole pizzas, sharing one 500 won soda between six straws. We stood by the wall, decorated with pictures of other Costco locations like a parent decorates the front hallway with senior pictures, and waited for a table to become available. Every time, we were much too slow. The moment a father stood up, another father carrying a bulgogi pizza moved in with a family in tow. If we were going to sit for this dinner, we were going to have to be rude. Indeed, as a mother and her son cleaned their table, we surrounded them and the table until it was ours to claim. Had another party intervened, we were prepared to punch.

As if the Costco cafeteria isn't cheap enough, Koreans have devised a way to add a side dish with no extra cost. The mother picked up a large, half eaten heap of curious salad that seemed to be on everyone's table. Indeed, everyone had built an onion relish mustard mix courtesy of the complimentary condiment station. Later, when I returned to the soda fountain for a refill, I watched a father hungrily churn the onion dispenser until a pile of white shavings filled his plate. While you won't find the dish on my table, I won't fault the Koreans for being thrifty.

Our visit, of course, wasn't only to eat junk food. We'd come for Thanksgiving fare. The selection in the shopping area –both levels-- was largely the same as anywhere else. We found our apple pie without any problems. We purchased a rotisserie chicken to supplement the turkey, now too small to accommodate the growing number of people coming to the dinner. There was mashed potato mix, instant stuffing boxes, the whole shebang. The trip was a massive success.

Over the course of our stay in Daegu, we made many trips to Costco, and they all went about the same. It turned into a routine: throw out feelers for a shopping trip, hoping someone with a membership wanted to go; compete for space in the cafeteria with pizza and hot dogs in hand while families munched on free condiments; grab the last shopping cart and split it between the party; split the cost of items that were too large and expensive for one of us, and then take taxis home. We often stole each other's memberships; the poor employees were too bewildered to question us. Our cheekiness gave us a sense of ownership, like we'd found a small portal to the Western world and this was our terrain. We Americans were back in the land of bulk food, red meat, and 700 calorie pastries.

Of course, it wasn't only Americans who joined in our Thanksgiving festivities. Our South African and Irish friends were curious to celebrate an American Thanksgiving. That is, to eat turkey. We really did have a feast. People brought desserts and side dishes not customarily found on Thanksgiving tables. Gail brought a milk tart dessert that ought to be a regular on Thanksgiving tables. Upstairs, I had an old Ohio State game playing on my laptop for seasonally appropriate background noise.

At school, I decided to take the opportunity to teach students about Thanksgiving. Thanksgiving is one of those holidays that would've been much easier to explain in 1950 than in the 21st century. I didn't really want to get bogged down in colonial history and the oppression of Native Americans with a bunch of elementary school children who just wanted to learn the word 'cranberry sauce,' so I mostly focused on modern traditions like watching football and eating way too much food. My mom, by request, sent pictures of our most recent family Thanksgiving get together and I put them on a PowerPoint for everyone to see. I come from a very large, very loving family, so our holidays can be massive undertakings. For Thanksgiving in particular, we usually have enough people to play a game of football before it's time to eat. Additionally, Ohio State and Michigan typically play on the Saturday after Thanksgiving, so at least half of us are wearing scarlet and gray jerseys, hoodies, and other clothes in support of the team. I showed pictures of us filling our trays from a large spread of meat and potatoes, of us playing cards, taking naps, and watching football.

Afterwards in the office, Ji Young wanted another look at the pictures.

"Why is everyone wearing that costume?" she asked.

I was confused for a second, but then I realized she was talking about the jerseys. I explained that people in Ohio, myself included, go all out for The Ohio State Buckeyes and that there was a game that day.

"Who organizes all that?"

I explained that anyone wearing Ohio State apparel in the pictures did so of their own volition. She continued to marvel at the pictures, at everyone's smiling faces, at all the wonderful food.

"It seems like you all know how to enjoy life more," she said.

"When we meet as families, we just talk about small things."

I admit I was at a loss for words at that moment. Was this some cultural difference? Could Americans have better family dynamics than Koreans? It depends on the family, I suppose. There are plenty of dysfunctional families in America. There are wonderfully close families in Korea. I got the sense, though, that none of my coworkers enjoyed holidays with their families. Hyun Soo looked at family holidays as an obligation. Ji Young didn't get along with her parents that well. Jang Mi, I believed, enjoyed a closer relationship with her parents, but they lived in Busan, an hour and a half away. In Korean terms, that's far.

Rather than some generic cultural difference, though, I think her comment cemented two things for me. I assured her that my family is quite unique that we are so large yet so close. I didn't want her to assume that all families have the luxury of gathering every Thanksgiving to play a game, eat a giant lunch, and watch a football game together. Second, if a friend from out of the country came to America and asked to go to one event that represented myself, my culture, and my home, I think I would take that friend to my family's Thanksgiving.

That epiphany is why, at work on Thanksgiving Day, for the first time since we'd arrived in South Korea, I was devastatingly homesick.

Christmas was even worse. I'm not sure what to make of Christmas in Korea, because I'm not sure what Koreans make of Christmas. The day is important enough to get the day off from work, if you work somewhere that recognizes bank holidays. Everything else is still open, so it's popular to go shopping or out to eat, particularly on romantic dates. Christmas, then, is something between Valentine's Day and Labor Day to most South Koreans, even though about one third of the country is Christian.

By late November, downtown Daegu was decked out in Christmas lights and displays. Our trips downtown were frequent, what with the restaurants and movie theaters all within walking distance of each other, and its central location and all. Once or twice a week, we'd venture down to the board game café--an oversized living room overlooking a busy downtown street--to spend a few hours knocking back exceedingly sweet café mochas while playing

Settlers of Catan, Ticket to Ride, or some such diversion in board form. The owner, a frowning 30-something guy, recognized us soon enough, but we were never quite sure if he liked us. For one, he was always frowning. However, on the rare occasion that we couldn't decide what to play, he'd quietly walk to the game shelf and plop a recommendation at our table. His suggestions were always spot on.

On the nights that we walked to the board game café, Mariah Carey's 'All I Want for Christmas Is You' became the song most likely heard from stores blaring music. An early Christmas present to foreigners in Daegu, though, was a new H&M in the heart of downtown. Besides being stylish, H&M was heralded for one much more important reason: they carried Western sizes. It's a bit discouraging when you only fit into what Koreans call 'extra-large.' At H&M, that same shirt could be a medium. Also, H&M was inexpensive, unlike the designer boutiques or luxury department stores that charge $60 for a T-shirt. Yes, Christmas had indeed come early for foreigners. Our only concern was that it would go out of business. Retail in downtown Daegu had a habit of disappearing, making landmarks even harder to use to get around. Your favorite Italian restaurant could start selling shoes at the drop of a hat.

We were delighted to hear that Daegu was hosting a Christmas festival downtown the weekend before Christmas, starting with a parade. On the day of, Maria and I found a spot along the route and awaited the festivities. We'd made it just in time; already, we could hear the parade on its way. The first float to pass was of a whale, on top of which was, obviously, Snow White waving at the crowd. Following them were floats of cottages and other, more passably Christmas things, with people dressed in red and white waving and shouting 'Merry Christmas!' Mary and Joseph, with a merry band of Judean characters in tow, waved from a float. A small marching band played appropriate Christmas songs. On the last float of the parade, rather than Santa Claus, was some sort of Christmas Queen on top of her noble steed, a rhinoceros.

The parade lead folks to Gukchaebosong Memorial Park. The crowd circled around a small stage, on which was the marching band and parade characters. The marching band led everyone in the singing of Christmas carols, including the most upbeat and loud version of Silent Night I've ever heard. A very skinny Santa made his appearance, hauling a sack behind his back. Someone dressed as an angel came to sing 'O Come, All Ye Faithful.' *Okay*, I thought. *We're getting back on track after that whale business.*

Then the pageant began. A very morose Mary and Joseph slowly walked a lap around the circle, holding a doll in swaddling clothes. I'm sure Christ's earthly parents weren't exactly skipping through Bethlehem after they were denied at the inns, but I imagine a scene with a bit more urgency, or at the very least, without the sort of background music you might hear at a Halloween costume store. After what felt like a century, the shepherds made the same lap accompanied by the same eerie soundtrack. Once all the biblical characters had made the passage, Snow White stood in the center and sang 'O Holy Night.' The Three Musketeers, of all people, stood in two lines and held their swords in the air, making way for the Christmas Queen, or whatever she was. She sang a duet with Snow White.

Throughout this eclectic Christmas pageant, costumed characters roamed about the crowd and took pictures with children. Included in the bunch were two kangaroos. Why kangaroos at the manger scene? You tell me. To recap, present at the birth of our Lord and Savior was a whale, a rhinoceros, Snow White, the Three Musketeers, the Christmas Queen, and a pair of kangaroos. Bethlehem, it turns out, wasn't so much a backwater as it was a comic convention. I saw a lot of odd things in South Korea, but none of them were as random, as defiant to explanation as the Christmas Festival.

Knowing we had Christmas day off, we began to make plans. We'd heard of a Christmas Tree festival in Busan, an hour and a half southeast of Daegu on the coast, and thought that would be a festive way to spend the day. In Busan, there is also the Shinsegae Centum City Department Store, the largest department store in the world. What better way to spend Christmas, given the options, than to splurge at a department store and then wander amongst thousands of twinkling Christmas displays? Gail and Phillip were up for it as well, so we ordered our train tickets. Late on a brisk Christmas morning, we boarded at Daegu Station and took the train to Busan.

By the time our train pulled into Busan Station, we were all hungry. The original idea, on this 'treat yourself' kind of day, was to find somewhere exciting to eat. Perhaps some decent American food to keep homesickness at bay. Rather than take the time to reach a more fashionable end of town, we decided we were hungry enough to eat at the station's cafeteria. So, rather than a heaping plate of steak and potatoes or some such American dish, we ate passable *bibimbop*, a spicy bowl of mixed rice and vegetables, on some metal chairs in a cafeteria.

The Centum City department store, it turns out, would've been a much better choice. On the bottom level was a gigantic food court with every specialty imaginable. Ice cream, baked goods, pizza, pasta, and more sat waiting to be purchased by hungry foreigners looking to make a day of their increasingly non-traditional Christmas. No longer hungry for a meal, we purchased some appetizing cupcakes for later.

I'm a bit murky on what constitutes a department store and a mall in South Korea. Centum City is billed as the world's largest of the former, but for all intents and purposes looks much more like the latter. You don't walk into the enormous, modern building and exit having only walked through one store. There are corridors like any shopping mall has, and separate companies. There's even an H&M. There's an ice skating rink, a spa, a movie theater, a playground on the roof. And, I was disappointed to see, they were all swarmed with people having a holly, jolly Christmas. The price tags throughout the building were much too high to even consider treating ourselves. Our Christmas was in danger of failing.

If we learned one thing that day, it was to take romantic Korean holidays seriously. The subway to Nampo station, the closest stop to the Christmas Tree festival, was completely filled with singles, couples, families, old people, young people, circus clowns, noted figures from antiquity, the entire 1979 Pittsburgh Steelers roster, both houses of Congress, and everyone that ever existed at any point in time. It was unbelievably crowded. I've never been one to claim claustrophobia, but I was about to develop it fast. When the doors opened and spewed out a fourth of the world's population, a bottleneck formed immediately at the foot of the escalator. Even worse than that bottleneck was the one at the top. There was only so much space until the turnstiles, and people weren't getting through them fast enough. The escalator delivered us from below, but there wasn't a square inch to move to, and there were more people coming behind us. It was dangerous, actually, how crowded it was.

Above ground was better, for a time, but once we entered the main pedestrian street, we returned to the shoulder-to-shoulder masses that had arrived to look at Christmas lights. There was no real walking involved, only a shuffle here, a shove there. This was not the way to enjoy Christmas decorations. And you know what? They weren't that great. They would be perfectly festive and welcome displays on a normal evening stroll, but they weren't worth travelling and standing in a sea of humanity for. There weren't many restaurants on this road either, and the ones that were there looked average and busy beyond hyperbole, with lines stretching into the throngs in the streets. We were getting hungry, though, so we kept our eyes open for that restaurant that would satisfy our 'treat yourself' mantra but be quiet enough to have a table available or a short wait. Obviously, that restaurant never materialized. Forced to make a choice, we wandered into a bar called 'Millers Time' for the sheer reason that it was mostly empty. The place was more of an appetizer bar, without a full menu. We took a table near the window to watch the crowds shuffle by. A waiter came and we ordered some cheap beer and subpar fried chicken and at least enjoyed the fact that there was oxygen to breathe and space to breathe it in. That was about all there was to celebrate on, up to that point, my least favorite Christmas Day of my life.

Back on the train to Daegu, we opened our cupcakes from the department store, the one 'treat yourself' purchase we'd made throughout the entire day. Even though I don't drink coffee at night, I'd bought a cup to enjoy with my cupcake. I might've regretted it later, lying in bed unable to sleep, but I was determined to make at least one impulsive, immediately gratifying decision that day. Silently, as the train rolled out of the station, I stuffed my face with cupcake and savored five minutes of Christmas.

Christmas that year was on a Wednesday, which meant that everyone was back to work on Thursday. The Korean school calendar is unique in that Christmas is a separate entity from winter vacation, which doesn't come until sometime in January.

Thus far in our stay, I'd avoided getting sick. That January, though, I went to work one day with my stomach feeling weird. The feeling didn't subside in my first couple classes, and by Happy Time, I was sure there was going to be vomit in my near future. I had a free period afterwards, so I sat at my desk waiting either for the deed to be done or for the feeling to go away. Next door, in Hyun Soo's room, students were singing 'Let it Go' from Disney's *Frozen* in some rare free time in his class.

I'm forever grateful to the movie *Frozen*. There are blockbusters, and then there are blockbusters. *Frozen*, in South Korea as in the rest of the world, was the latter. The country took to *Frozen* in a way I would never see replicated. At the time of its release, it was the second highest grossing foreign movie in the country's history, bested only by *Avatar*. Kids loved every song, even the second-tier ones like 'Do You Want to Build a Snowman?' They knew the words too, and it was no wonder. Walking downtown, the same stores that pumped Bloodhound Gang were now pumping any *Frozen* song they could get their hands on. After the movie was released, if we had any free time in class, the easiest video to show was a sing-a-long of 'Let it Go.' As soon as students, no matter the age, saw the swirling snow and heard the piano intro, they knew exactly what was coming and cheered. They sang their heart out. It was a gift from Disney to the Native English Teachers of South Korea, who, at the end of their ropes at the school year's end, needed something to get the kids out of their hair for three and a half minutes.

I have a more personal reason to be thankful for *Frozen*, specifically the song 'Let it Go.' It was during the sing-along next door when my head got the dizzy feeling that you only get when vomit is going to geyser out of your stomach. I flung open the bathroom door, feet from the classroom, and kneeled in front of the toilet. The kids took to the chorus with gusto, the best-timed crescendo of my life. 'Let it go!' they sang, and so I did.

Visiting a Frenemy

That Time We Went to Japan

For our first adventure out of the country, Maria and I chose to visit a friend living outside Tokyo. Teachers in South Korea have long summer and winter breaks and often travel internationally. It's hard not to, with so many choices nearby and discount airlines to fly you there. When asked by my coworkers what I would do for winter break, I explained that I was going to visit a friend in Japan. The interest level in my vacation instantly plummeted.

Like all good frenemies, there isn't a single thing Japan and South Korea agree on.

"The Dokdo islands are ours," say the Koreans.

"I don't think so," say the Japanese.

"All that water is called the East Sea."

"I'm pretty sure it's called the Sea of Japan."

"The dress is white."

"The dress is blue."

And on, and on and on. There's nothing the two countries do better than antagonize each other. At best, it's a friendly jab at their long, intertwined histories. At worst, it's racism and nationalism used as tools to ignore history.

It's not quite clear when Korea and Japan began their feud, but it was probably soon after names were exchanged. Neither side is blameless, really. For hundreds of years, pirates from either side harassed coastal villages. In 1274 and again in 1281, the Mongols, under the leadership of Kublai Khan, conscripted a Korean fleet to sail in concert with theirs to Japan and invade the country. The second fleet, in particular, was a massive undertaking, with some 4,000 ships carrying 140,000 men. It was an amphibious invasion the likes of which not seen again until the D-Day invasion of Normandy. On both occasions, the ships drowned in a storm, giving birth to the Japanese legend of the 'divine wind,' or Kamikaze.

The relationship soured in the 16th century. At this time, Japan was marked by chaos and warfare. Various warlords clashed for power throughout the islands, with eventual victor Toyotomi Hideyoshi unifying the country under his rule near the end of the century. Not content to sit on his spoils, Hideyoshi set his sights on China as the beginning of a new Japanese empire. Korea, he thought, would serve nicely as a forward operating base. In 1591, he sent a letter to the Joseon dynasty in Korea requesting safe access to mainland China. The Koreans, more culturally and economically linked to China than they were to Japan, were insulted by the idea that they'd betray the Chinese for these "dwarfs," the Korean pejorative for the Japanese. They sent an ambassador to Japan with their answer.

While in Japan, the Korean ambassador took a glance at their island neighbor's military might with an official delegation. He returned to the council in Korea and confirmed that Japan was not a threat. Korea needn't worry about an invasion. The deputy ambassador, who had stolen away from the delegation, thought otherwise. He saw Japan's newly acquired weapons from Europeans, among them muzzle-loading firearms. Their fighting skills, perfected after years of fighting amongst each other, were fearsome. Korea must make preparations for war, he said. The council liked the ambassador's answer better and disregarded the deputy ambassador. Nothing was done to prepare the military for an invasion.

Whereas Japan was a violent and unstable region in the 16th century, Korea was enjoying 200 years of peace. The time period was marked by significant cultural advances, but practically nobody had real combat experience. The Japanese took note and swiftly invaded. In May 1592, they landed a massive force near Busan and reached Seoul within weeks.

Things looked bad for Korea. The royal family fled to China, where they pleaded for help. The Chinese recognized that it would be better to fight on somebody else's farm rather than their own, and organized a military force to restore balance to the engagement. They reached the Korean peninsula and, with a reorganized Korean force, succeeded in helping the Japanese destroy the countryside in battle.

The war would be locked in stalemate for several more years, but out of the endless warfare rose two legendary battles that would live on in the hearts of Koreans. The first is the siege of Jinju. In 1592, Korea scored one of its few initial victories when the outmatched defenders of the fortress in Jinju repelled a large Japanese force. The Japanese would return a year later and, with the help of explosives, breach the wall and overtake the fortress. In the ensuing massacre, every defender was killed. This second battle in particular takes on an Alamo-type call of remembrance amongst Koreans, who commemorate the battle with an annual lantern festival in the city. The fortress, rebuilt several times over the centuries, still stands on a modest bluff overlooking the Nam River. Lanterns depicting defending soldiers line the outer walls and on the land inside. On the river, artists take more liberty in what constitutes an appropriate lantern. Such anachronistic subjects floating on the river include the Statue of Liberty, Noah's Ark, and Spider-Man.

The suffering out of the Imjin War, as the war with Japan is called, gave rise to heroic figures such as Admiral Yi Sunsin. If Korea had one capable sector of its military, it was the navy. Under the leadership of Admiral Yi, Korea's navy, along with China's, cut off Japan's resupply routes across Korea's southern and western coasts. Yi knew the waters well and his strategies led to decisive victories. It didn't hurt that he employed his 'turtle ships,' bulky, iron-clad warships that were impervious to fire arrows and made mincemeat out of wooden ships. Yi's navy consistently faced and defeated insurmountable odds. Their victories, in retrospect, sound as silly as the odds they faced. In the Battle of Myeongnyang, Yi's 13 ships defeated a Japanese fleet of 130. Total losses for the Japanese were at least 30 ships completely destroyed and half the soldiers killed or drowned. Total losses on the Korean side amounted to two killed on Yi's flagship, another eight drowned elsewhere, and a lost hat.

Together, these two instances remind Koreans of when they

really stuck it to their larger, more powerful neighbors. Both are heavily celebrated even though the Imjin War devastated the country and left millions of Koreans killed. The Japanese army finally retreated to their archipelago in 1598.

The two countries maintained their bad blood until it got especially ugly in the 20th century, when Japan annexed Korea as a colony. While periods of Japan's dominion over the Korean peninsula were marked by relative autonomy and modern development, the later part that coincides with Japan's imperial expansion and WWII are what people choose to remember, and I don't blame them. Japan governed every aspect of the colony and established policies to extinguish Korean culture and replace it with that of Japan's. They demolished temples and palaces. Koreans were forced to surrender their native surnames and adopt Japanese ones instead. Even though their country was annexed, Koreans were not granted Japanese citizenship. They were a lower-class people with few rights, a marginalized culture, and restricted means of commerce. In short, Koreans were stripped of their home.

None of this riles up Koreans as much as the issue of comfort women. In the 1930's, as Japan conquered Manchuria, it became a common, deplorable practice after taking cities such as Shanghai or Nanking for the soldiers to rape the local women. To reestablish military discipline and to prevent the spread of disease, the Japanese army established the 'comfort corps,' a permanent group of women on hand to provide sexual services for the men. Throughout WWII, the Japanese army conscripted women of their conquered lands either through coercion, kidnapping, or finding existing prostitutes. Chinese, Filipinas, Burmese, and even Dutch women (from Dutch Indonesia) were absorbed into this service, but none more so than Koreans. There were perhaps as many as 200,000 Korean comfort women. When the war ended, they returned to their homeland only to be shamed by their families. As such, many kept their "service" a secret.

In the 1980's, these women held their tongues no longer. They demanded an apology from Japan, who denied that comfort women were ever a thing. The testimonies and documentation piled up and Japan officially apologized in 1993.

South Korea has never been satisfied with this apology and perhaps rightly so. Japanese textbooks often skim this brutal part of their history, so there are many deniers (imagine, then, holocaust deniers in Germany and what sort of reaction they might elicit from, say, Israel). South Korea looks at Germany as an example of how to atone for your sins and wonders why Japan can't do the same. Japan feels they've done so. Nevertheless, protestors in Seoul and government officials press the issue annually. In 2015, Japanese Prime Minister Shinzo Abe issued another official apology for their actions and set up a reparation fund for surviving comfort women. He called this act the 'final and irreversible solution."

Nothing seems to be final or irreversible for Koreans when it comes to this issue. In 2017, fresh protests continued the quest for, to be honest, I'm not quite sure what. There are only a few dozen surviving comfort women. Their extended families, of course, continue their legacy and keep their mothers' or grandmothers' stories close to their hearts, but there will likely be little else done in the name of comfort women. I'm not sure what else can be done. It seems cruel to tell people to 'get over it,' but I'm not the first to suggest that emotions as much as facts can fuel a grudge.

Park Yu-Ha, a professor of Japanese language and literature at Seoul's Sejong University, wrote a book titled *Comfort Women of the Empire* in which, through interviews of survivors and research of Japanese military documents, she points out that the narrative isn't always quite straightforward. Some women were given labor contracts for their services. Rather than abducted by the Japanese military, some of the women were trafficked by Korean men or unscrupulous or desperate family members. These facts don't necessarily make the situation better, but it does put a damper on the "Korea equals good, Japan equals bad" narrative. Park has, of course, been branded a traitor and apologist for suggesting a middle-of-the line truth.

Today, South Korea and Japan are de facto allies through the United States against China and North Korea, although both have plenty of reason to team up without the nudging of the Americans. Both have similar economies. Both value democracy and freedom of speech. Both are highly educated and respected civilizations throughout the world. On a regular, day to day basis, Koreans and Japanese get along fine. They do business together. They visit each other on the weekends. They even jointly hosted the 2002 World Cup. They are more alike than they'd like to admit. Just don't mention the Dokdo islands, or comfort women, or anything political or historical ever.

We followed this advice starting minute one out of Haneda airport. We boarded a bus that would take us to Kiryu Station, halfway to my friend Evan's house in Gunma. His work schedule was rigid and he was unable to meet us in Tokyo, so he sent us detailed instructions, with maps and everything, on how to go halfway across Honshu to his house. It was all very exciting, like we were following a treasure map.

Tokyo, in case you hadn't heard, is very large. It doesn't end. It's possible I'm still there, over four years later, trying to find my way out of the suburbs. It took at least an hour to pass the Tokyo Skytree, a giant wand pointing to space. After the center of the city is a sprawling constellation of satellite cities and towns that have coalesced to become the largest urban area in the world. Nearly 38 million people live in an area the size of Yellowstone National Park.

While Maria and I had settled in the third largest city in South Korea, I couldn't help but feel Evan had been marooned in some forgotten corner of Japan. We were still on the bus when city surrendered to intermittent rice fields and vegetable patches. Farmland surrounded blocks of country houses like a sea surrounds an archipelago, a pattern that doesn't really exist in the American landscape. A bright sunset highlighted the nearby mountain ranges and solitary volcanoes that run up the spine of Honshu. The bus stopped twice, letting people off at indistinguishable stations. Evan had made it clear that ours was the last stop. About three hours from the airport, the bus pulled into a quiet parking lot next to a train station. The driver said something that sounded final and resolute, and all the remaining passengers, which weren't many, stood up and exited. We followed suit as we walked up to what I was glad to see was Kiryu station.

Evan, leaving no detail unremarked, had graciously provided the Japanese text for our destination along with its English approximation. That didn't help, though, when the train that pulled up didn't display the destination on its exterior. Japanese trains, much like Korean trains, are invariably punctual. The train that had pulled up was about five minutes earlier than our scheduled train. Did that mean this was our train and that it would leave in five minutes' time? Or did that mean we should wait until a train showed up at exactly the time on the table? Maria waved down a friendly-looking woman and pointed to the Japanese version of Iwajuku, the station Evan had marked as his. Then she pointed at the train. The woman shook her head and then boarded. We sat down on a bench as the train inched away, hoping the woman wasn't a practical joker. Sure enough, in five minutes, another train showed up. We repeated the pointing and shrugging with a businessman who nodded and pointed to the newly arrived train. This was the train to Iwajuku.

The sun drowned beneath the mountains and all was dark when we arrived at our station about 45 minutes later. Our last step of the journey was on foot from Iwajuku station to the house. It was dark, and cold, but there were plenty of street lights and we had Evan's map along with detailed visual cues and instructions. Step one was to cross the bridge over the tracks and a major highway. We hauled our luggage down crumbling sidewalks and across the busy bridge. Our first right was at a pink dentist's office. We knew it was a dentist office because of a grinning tooth mascot on the sign. Thanks to Evan's clues and straightforward roads, we navigated through the quiet neighborhood and fields to Evan's unlocked front door with no problems.

Inside, Evan had left sticky notes everywhere. 'Put your shoes here.' 'Here are some snacks.' That sort of thing. The one place he forgot to put a note was the toilet which, as Japanese toilets go, is more or less a spaceship and not a latrine. Of the 30 or so buttons, I chose about 12 wrong ones. I texted him on Facebook, "HOW DO I MAKE THE POOP GO AWAY?" He responded that he was leaving school that moment. I eventually found the correct button. Rather than telling Maria which one it was, I decided not to rob her of the experience.

The house was an old, traditional style house with sliding doors, hardwood floors and no central heat. A space heater sat in the living room, so that's where we stayed until Evan showed up about a half hour later. He changed from his suit into something more comfortable and took us to an Australian-themed burger bar for dinner.

There's not a lot to do in Gunma, but I think we covered it well. We walked to the nearby self-serve bakery and with tongs selected our packaged pastries for upcoming meals. Evan did not own a car, which is too bad because I've rarely seen such polite drivers. Once, not one but two taxis approached an intersection and waited for us, standing on the sidewalk, to cross the street before they continued. No taxi drivers in any other country, let alone two in one go, have done this for me. As such, Gunma was a pleasant place to take a walk, even in January. We walked to the local archeology museum which featured an entire mammoth skeleton excavated from the area. Before we'd arrived in Japan, Evan had described an electronics store with an aisle of used game consoles sold for absurdly cheap prices. We, of course, made a trek out that way and bought a green Nintendo 64 for $18. It still works to this day. When Evan was at work, Maria and I took the train to the nearby city of Maebashi. We strolled along the river and marveled at the cleanliness and orderliness of it all. Everything was organized. Everything was structured. Even the gardens are fastidiously man-made. It doesn't take long to understand that Japanese take nothing by chance. Coming from Korea, which sees itself in a similar manner but to an outsider can feel completely opposite, it was a breath of fresh air.

Early on a Saturday morning, the three of us took a Shinkansen train back to Tokyo for the weekend. Riding on a bullet train is much like riding a plane that never takes off. It's a remarkably comfortable and efficient way of getting from A to B. Why America hasn't built these things yet is a question worth getting angry about. Evan's Japanese fiancée met us at the station in Tokyo. Together, they showed us what Tokyo had to offer. Like their country, their tour was organized perfectly and not a moment was wasted. We walked across the Shibuya intersection, a pentagon of pedestrian crossings dubbed the world's busiest intersection. As much fun as crossing was admiring the hundreds of people doing the same from the adjacent Starbucks. We walked through Harajuku, the street that is either heaven or hell depending on who you ask. It's the famed street of cosplayers and nerd culture, where people walk around in meticulously curated costumes depicting their favorite pop culture characters. In daylight, it was rather tame. We spent the entire following day at Tokyo DisneySea, probably the most original Disney theme park I've been to with the biggest cast of C-list Disney characters. Rather than Goofy or Donald or the latest princess, we took our pictures with Max (Goofy's son), Marie from *The Aristocats*, and Jose Carioca from *The Three Caballeros*.

Evan was required to report back to work on Monday, so he took a very late train back on Sunday night. It was just Maria and I again, only now we were in the world's largest city and there was less English signage than even Daegu at times. Rather than spending too much time on the city's extensive train and subway network, we thought we'd just wander Ueno Park and its cultural offerings. This was a good plan until we got to the park and established that nearly everything was closed on Mondays. The Tokyo National Museum was closed. The zoo was closed. We did find a contemporary art museum with some galleries open, so in the interest of seeing something and getting out of the cold, we perused the rooms and gave perhaps a bit more attention to contemporary art than we typically would. Still, it was only contemporary art, and it was more fun to be bored outside, so we left.

I only mention this aimless meandering because it was in this delirious frustration of bad planning that we came across perhaps the funniest thing I've ever seen with my own eyes. Outside the art museum was a busker doing what, on some planet, someone could call magic tricks. Why he'd chosen a January Monday in Ueno Park to do his busking is an excellent question and one for which I don't have an answer. Somehow, this man had attracted a crowd of about 15 or so and decided it was time to do his best trick. He rummaged through his chest of props and took out a single latex glove which he then stretched over his head until it covered his nose. With clasped hands around the glove he proceeded to exhale through his nose repeatedly to inflate the glove around his face like a balloon. Of course, such a commonplace activity couldn't be done standing straight. He pranced around and made a big show of it, kicking and dancing in circles. It was in this moment that his foot went a little too astray and landed on a skateboard he'd used in a previous trick. He crashed into all his props, and nobody did a thing. At the time, I honestly had no idea what to do about the situation. Here was a grown man with an inflated latex glove around his face who'd slipped on a skateboard and fell in the most comic fashion on the ground and nobody cared. He was clearly okay, because he immediately got up, replaced the latex glove, and did it all again. He danced, he grunted, the glove inflated, and several feet from his pile of props, the glove burst. Around his head was now the ring of the glove along with a few errant pieces of latex. We clapped politely and then left. I hadn't laughed at any of it. My mind hadn't processed anything. It wasn't until hours later in a shopping mall's food court that Maria showed me the video of the man falling on the skateboard and I realized the complete absurdity of what I'd seen. We watched it at least 20 times. I've never laughed so hard in my life. The people in the food court probably thought I was insane. I might have been.

The next morning, we returned to South Korea. I admit at the time we stepped back into Daegu and thought back to Japan with longing thoughts. Couldn't Korea keep the streets a little cleaner? Obey traffic laws a bit better? Stand in lines? Japan was, with South Korea, in the running for us to teach English in, but the more I thought about it, the more I understood that Korea was the right choice. It was cheaper to get around, for one. The Shinkansen bullet trains not only feel like a flight, but are priced like one too. Also, Hangul was much easier to get the hang of than any of Japan's three alphabets. I liked the food better. Still, any time our friends made a trip to Japan, they'd come back with the same look on their face: if only South Korea was a little more like Japan. Don't tell anyone I said that.

Pilgrimages to Seoul

That Time I Went to Mos Eisley

Let's throw around some numbers. The Seoul Capital Area accounts for half of South Korea's 50 million or so people, half of the country's economic output, and about 12% of the country's total land area. South Korea's primary international airport is in Incheon and is destined to be one of the world's ten busiest by 2020. The region's 200 twisty miles of metro system reach as far south as Asan, 54 miles away in a straight line, and they're building more routes. To read Seoul's subway map is to read a plate of spaghetti. All this is to say that Seoul is absolutely massive and if you spend any time at all in South Korea, you will likely spend some of it in this behemoth. It's almost impossible not to.

We traveled to Seoul on multiple occasions. I've lost count, but I can safely remember at least five separate instances. There's always an excuse to go there, it seems, and for foreigners living in other parts of the country, a pilgrimage to Seoul can feel a bit like going home. Here they have Mexican restaurants, several of them, and they serve Mexican food. There are non-Koreans in numbers, either residents or tourists. The level of English the locals speak is typically higher than elsewhere. English teachers in Seoul know all this and have gathered a reputation for being snobbish about their city of choice. If you're going to live in Korea, they might ask you, why would you consider anywhere other than here? I admit I gave the question a hard think once or twice. It's easier to be a foreigner in Seoul than anywhere else in the country. Your people are here, your food is here, your airport to wondrous adventures is here. But, I suppose, it's the same rationale for people that live in, say, New York or Los Angeles. 'Why live in those middle parts of the country,' they might ask. 'There's nothing there.' There is, in fact, and the same is true for South Korea. Still, I don't deny I could've used one or two of Seoul's restaurants in Daegu.

In Seoul, you can learn a lot about a person by which side of the Han River they prefer to spend time. South of the Han River lies Gangnam, the ritzy neighborhood immortalized in Psy's infectious ditty, "Gangnam Style." Everything in Gangnam is expensive, so you either go there because you can afford things or because you want to be seen with people that can afford things. Block upon block of designer stores lure the richest in Korea to buy status symbols. Accordingly, Gangnam and the surrounding posh neighborhoods have many of the city's most popular bars and clubs that often attract Korean celebrities. In short, if you prefer to spend your time watching rich people spend money, go south of the river. At no time have I indicated in this book that this is my jam, so you'll keenly observe that I spent nearly all my time in Seoul north of the river. There are trendy shopping areas north of the Han, to be sure, but in general the attractions in this part of town have more history, character, or cultural relevance.

Any trip to Seoul should include a palace. Gyeongbokgung, the largest in the country, is a good choice. Its' main gate sits prominently at the end of a grand plaza, on the other side of which is a grand statue of King Sejong keeping watch over the central business district. Maria and I chose to visit Gyeongbokgung on a pleasantly wintry January day during our first trip to Seoul. We expected to find food outside the nearest metro station to the palace's entrance, but could only find a 7-Eleven. Thus, our lunch was a handful of cheap onigiri, Japanese rice and seaweed snacks that are popular to find at convenient stores. We ate our unsatisfying lunch on cold cement landscaping outside the 7-Eleven. Meanwhile, a crowd grew around the palace gate, so we finished the onigiri and crossed the street. Two groups of costumed soldiers, one in red robes and the other in blue, performed a changing of the guard ceremony. Strange hats, wide-brimmed with two long feathers pointing scissorlike at the sky, sat fastened to each man's head. The men finished their performance and we were allowed through the gate into the first plaza.

Palaces in South Korea often follow a similar pattern of gate, large courtyard surrounded by covered walkways, second gate, and larger courtyard with a throne room. Gyeongbokgung's throne room, Geunjeongjeon Hall, stands atop a stone platform. The ceiling is high and decorative, the wooden beams are a deep and majestic red, and the throne itself is suitably tall and ornate. It's not difficult to imagine many high-browed conversations and edicts taking place in the hall, once the center of Korean government. Surrounding the hall and its' granite courtyard is a series of smaller courtyards framed with covered walkways, living quarters, offices and servant buildings. It can be fun, or tiresome depending on your mood, to get lost in the maze of courtyards and walls. The crowds do thin as you descend further into the details. While taking a peek inside the throne room was a bit of a hassle, nobody is clamoring to look inside the servant's chambers. The color scheme of it all follows the typical Joseon dynasty palate of red and green, so buildings tended to look the same the longer we stuck around. We eventually found our way out of the labyrinth and into the back of the complex, where the kings of old constructed an artificial pond and a pavilion to entertain notable guests.

Most of Gyeongbokgung's hundreds of buildings, unfortunately, are not from antiquity. The palace, built in 1395, was destroyed by none other than the Japanese during their 16th century invasion. For over 250 years, the complex lay in ruins until 1867 when it was rebuilt by the Prince Regent. He oversaw the reconstruction of over 300 buildings within the palace grounds. Then, in 1910, the Japanese invaded the country and occupied the palace grounds. Ownership of the land transferred to the Japanese who by 1915 had demolished 90% of the reconstructed buildings under the pretense of using the land for an exhibition celebrating their rule in Korea. Following the exhibition, they tore down nearly all that was left and, in what historians commonly refer to as 'a dick move,' built their colonial headquarters directly in front of Geunjeongjeon Hall. There it stayed until 1995, when it was finally demolished. Only a handful of the buildings, including Geunjeongjeon Hall, are original from the 1867 reconstruction.

Restoration of the palace didn't start until the 1980's and is ongoing. Only half of the 19th century complex has been rebuilt, and the government doesn't expect the rest to be complete for another 20 years. In the meantime, Gyeongbokgung's return has been an important symbol of reestablishing autonomy and justice to South Korea.

Lest you think the royal family toiled in the streets for nearly 300 years, there are a total of five 'gung's in Seoul ('gung,' pronounced 'goong,' is short for 'palace'). Down the street a stretch from Gyeongbokgung is the smaller but beautiful Changdeokgung. The layout of the two palaces is very similar, so I will not go into detail describing what has already nearly been described. Changdeokgung is 30% original, well-preserved compared to Gyeongbokgung. The signature difference between the two is that Changdeokgung's sprawling grounds give way to gardens and the hilly topography rather than imposing itself with an urban layout as Gyeongbokgung does. This smaller, more intimate palace is as popular for its natural beauty as it is for its' place in royal history. As such, it is a UNESCO World Heritage Site while the larger palace is not.

Because of the natural setting and age of many of the buildings, Changdeokgung takes on a much more timeless quality than Gyeongbokgung, especially as you head further back into the 'secret gardens' of the royal family. It didn't hurt that, on the day Maria and I went, a humid, August mist gave the grounds an eerie, ethereal personality. Large, gangly trees surround the gardens and mask the metropolis nearby. Gyeongbokgung, with its scale and openness, keeps downtown Seoul firmly in view. One of the buildings, the name of which I unfortunately cannot find again, survives from its construction in 1776, a playful reminder that while American colonists were having daddy issues with the British monarchy, the Korean royal family was taking a turnabout the gardens.

To the southwest of Changdeokgung's main gate is a charming and busy shopping neighborhood called Insadong. From the busy road connecting the two palaces, the main drag heads south into a dense corridor of traditional Korean restaurants, artsy boutiques and galleries. A tangle of inviting alleys deviate from the crowded road, leading wanderers to cozy tea shops or antique stores. I had my hand on an old abacus at such a store, considering for a few minutes that an old abacus was something I needed. I thankfully remembered that it wasn't. While it's not difficult to find souvenirs in terms of t-shirts and magnets and mugs throughout the country, it can be annoying to look for souvenirs with any kind of cultural relevance, something to say, 'look at this piece of Korean culture that I thought was special and wanted to remember.' Insadong is the place to look for those sorts of souvenirs. Maria and I decided we wanted something to take home with us that had our last name written in Hangul. Insadong has a handful of calligraphy shops where one can buy brushes and appropriate paper. One at a time, we approached a shop and asked whoever was working if they took commissions. Two or three said no until we ended up in one that said yes. We handed the gentleman working there our last name spelled in Hangul, along with a scroll we'd picked out, and we watched as he took a brush and carefully painted the name on the scroll. It hangs in our dining room to this day.

If your favorite sort of cultural experience is best defined as 'indoors, preferably free,' then Seoul offers two excellent museums free of charge which are both north of the river. The War Memorial of Korea is both a touching tribute to the lives lost in the Korean War and an educational journey through the country's wars throughout history. The Korean War exhibit is, unsurprisingly, a highlight. The artifacts and displays do a memorable job of showing how overmatched South Korea was in the beginning of the war, and how the United Nations saved them from the brink. I will never forget one display depicting a South Korean fighter pilot dropping a bomb over the side of the plane with his hands, completely eyeballing his target. Such was the disparity between the two countries' fighting capabilities.

Another excellent choice is the enormous National Museum of Korea. Primarily an art museum, the building curates a large collection of paintings, sculptures, and other artifacts of Korean antiquity. The building itself is imposing and grandeur, offering a sense of stability on a peninsula that has seen anything but in the last century. A large outdoor atrium separates the building into two sections: the permanent stuff and the traveling stuff. We went for the permanent stuff first.

In Western art museums, you may tire of seeing Jesus, Mary, or a handful of other typical subjects of old art. Walking on a guided tour in the National Museum of Korea, I realized that the museum's collection largely revolves around Buddha in any one of several poses. The collection was impressive, of course, but I can only marvel at artful depictions of the same guy for so long. Luckily, the tour was only an hour long and we were free to look for the not Buddha related things. The calligraphy was gorgeous, as was a ten-level pagoda in the main hallway.

The traveling exhibits in Korea's art and history museums were always surprising. Once, in a small museum inside Gyeongbokgung, Maria and I stumbled upon a visiting exhibit about the Habsburg monarchy. I wouldn't in a thousand tries have guessed that a museum in Seoul might have an exhibit on the Habsburgs. Americans hardly study the Habsburgs as it is, so I myopically hadn't considered that South Koreans might also know who the Habsburgs were. Less obscure but no less surprising was the National Museum's visiting exhibit on Pompeii. The National Museum itself is free, but the Pompeii exhibit cost something like $20 a person. Since we weren't going to make it to Italy any time soon, we forked over the money and waited in line to see mosaics, ceramics, and casts of Pompeiians who suffocated in their homes. Cheerful.

You may be reading this section thinking that you'd rather I'd spent more time in the southern half of Seoul so I could talk at more length about the nightclubs, shopping, and plastic surgery. None of the aforementioned sites seem remotely interesting to you, and you've concluded that I have the vacation interests and expectations of a 70-year old librarian with an acute sleep disorder. Before you pass final judgement on me, let me tell you about my favorite place in Seoul, Itaewon.

Any trip to Seoul for foreigners living in the country begins and ends in the neighborhood of Itaewon. It's a bit rough around the edges, having suffered for decades from a debilitating and accurate reputation as a seedy red-light district. Even these days, this is not one of those glittering high-rise neighborhoods with landscaping and playgrounds. This is a low, gritty, graffiti-filled tangle of narrow roads and alleys perched on top of a hill, but it grows on you. It sits directly east of Yongsan Garrison, the largest garrison of American soldiers in the country. As with most neighborhoods next to military bases, the primary business is to serve the military community. This used to mean prostitution, but today mostly means shops with knock-off leather goods, jerseys, and other counterfeit goods a bored, homesick American might want to spend money on. There's the best English bookstore to my knowledge in the country. A nearby grocery store sells Americans their hard to find comforts from home such as candy, cereal, and snacks. They charge a premium for them too. Worse, they buy a good amount of their stuff from Costco outside the city and then upcharge everything. There are, of course, also lots of bars. Koreans looking to meet foreigners and vice versa cram the clubs and bars down the main stretch. At night, the atmosphere can get a little bro-ey.

There were two things that kept me coming to Itaewon. The first is my guesthouse of choice. When a group of us were planning a trip to Seoul, we were looking for a place to stay and I happened upon a listing for this place on AirBnb. The price was right, it looked nice, and it was in Itaewon (in the middle of the city), so I booked it for our group. When it came time to find the place once we were in Itaewon, I got some dubious looks from the group as we hauled our luggage up a hill, up a steeper hill, and farther and farther away from the main drag. A portal somewhere must connect directly to Pakistan as there were few Koreans around but a large number of South Asians. A crowd formed outside a white and blue mosque as a prayer service was either starting or ending. We kept on down the road, which grew emptier and dirtier, until we came to a sign: Haus Guesthouse. A spunky Korean woman with short hair tucked behind her ears greeted us in near perfect English and introduced herself. Ha Young, it turned out, used to work for a large corporation in Ulsan when she realized that she didn't feel like working for a large corporation in Ulsan, so she quit. She saved money to travel to Europe, but instead spent the money on some property and opened a guesthouse in Seoul. It was a short, but refreshing story in a country where people feel they have a duty to work the most stressful, highest-paying job they can find.

Haus Guesthouse is everything a guesthouse should be: clean, cheap, and small. There are about eight rooms, so there are only so many people you have to meet. If people aren't your thing, then consider that Ha Young had also acquired a bunch of kittens that were in need of petting. Breakfast is included, and you can eat it on the rooftop which looks over the entire city, or at least it does when the hazy sky allows it. Throughout our time in Korea, we ended up staying there three or four times. I felt exotic, having a go-to place to stay in a foreign city.

The second thing that brought me back to Itaewon was the food. Holy smokes, is there good food in Itaewon. Restaurants followed the taste buds of the servicemen and opened burger shacks, pizza joints, and other places an American might enjoy. It didn't take long for other non-Koreans to gravitate toward the neighborhood's amenities, and Itaewon gained a reputation as the international hub of Seoul. South Asians in particular came in numbers. There were enough Muslims in the area, either from Bangladesh, Pakistan, Indonesia or elsewhere, to merit building the aforementioned Seoul Central Mosque in 1976, the only one in town. The surrounding streets, including the one we had taken to Haus Guesthouse, feature shops and restaurants that cater to a Halal diet. Thus, Itaewon is an excellent place to find Middle Eastern food. Actually, it's an excellent place to find just about any kind of food. There's Vietnamese, Thai, Greek, Italian, American barbecue, and Mexican. The best Mexican choice, Vatos, fuses typical Mexican dishes with Korean ingredients. Their chili soup with kimchi is a game changer. If we knew we were headed to Seoul soon, we treated it as a "foodcation," carefully planning which meals we would eat where. Daegu's non-Korean options, for the most part, weren't on the same level.

With so many nationalities packed in tight, grungy alleys, strolling around Itaewon can feel a bit like some nefarious port of call. I prefer to think of the neighborhood affectionately as Mos Eisley, the spaceport where Luke Skywalker sells his speeder and joins Han Solo in the original *Star Wars*. Not that anyone there is 'alien,' but it's hard to ignore how many kinds of people show up to Itaewon for one reason or another. The entire world is there. Eavesdropping on conversations along the busy sidewalks, you realize that people listen in one language and respond in another. Walk into a bar or restaurant from the narrow maze of streets and sidewalks, and you're never quite sure what, or who, you're going to find. On one occasion I found myself, an American, in South Korea dining in a South African restaurant and striking up a conversation with a group of friendly Swedes. The only difference between that place and the cantina in Mos Eisley is that nobody had the death sentence in twelve systems.

I must mention one more place in Itaewon before we can move on. Maria and I were perusing the overwhelming variety of restaurants when we happened on a café called Tartine. Interested in dessert, we popped in and adored the rows of exquisite, but pricey pies. They all looked delicious, but one drew our attention more than the others by virtue of its name: 'crack pie.' We pointed to the yellowish pie and asked the young Seoulite behind the counter why it was named 'crack pie. She mimed somebody eating nonstop. Aha. The word 'crack,' in this case, was a commentary on the pie's taste and not it's ingredients. We bought one to share and I have to say that the pie lived up to its name. It was merely butterscotch, but the best damn butterscotch pie I've had the pleasure of devouring.

While Itaewon has Yongsan Garrison to thank for its prosperity, it may someday have the same to thank for its ruin. Talk of returning Yongsan to Seoul goes back as far as 1988, when the American and South Korean governments agreed, in principle, that the base should move. The garrison, headquarters of U.S. military forces in South Korea, sits on prime real estate in the center of Seoul. In 2004, the governments of the United States and South Korea agreed to move all American garrisons in the Seoul area south of the Han River, freeing up Yongsan – smack dab in the middle of the city -- for redevelopment. The headquarters are in the process of moving all operations to a beefed-up Camp Humphreys in Pyeongtaek, taking with them the support personnel, military families, and other people that support Itaewon daily. For several years, it appeared that the move would happen slowly, if at all, but construction in Pyeongtaek has picked up. By the end of 2018, such necessary facilities as the commissary and Post Exchange are scheduled to be operational and equipped to handle the influx of new people. In place of the garrison will be much-desired green space, with some of the existing buildings repurposed as museums or gallery spaces. Seoulites will be happy to once again claim Yongsan, which has been a symbol of occupation long before the Americans showed up. It was here that the Japanese built their military headquarters. At the same time, the U.S. military will decrease its footprint in the country and consolidate forces. Everyone's a winner, it seems, except for Itaewon. It remains to be seen what impact the move will have on the neighborhood, but the first and most consistent source of income will be gone. I suspect that the international community that has enmeshed itself into the area's fabric will keep it an interesting place, and enough tourists are told to go there that most things will stay in business. Still, I can't help but feel that Itaewon, my favorite place in all of Seoul and perhaps the country, will look a lot different if I ever lay eyes on it again.

A New School Year

That Time the Principal Was a Dictator

The Korean school year works like this: the first semester starts in March and goes to sometime around late July, when students are off for the roughly five-week summer break. Then sometime in mid to late August, the second semester picks up and runs all the way to winter break in December. Here's where things get kooky. When the students return to school in late January or early February, there's only a couple weeks left of the school year. They finish, and then they go on a 'spring' break until March rolls around and they begin the process over again. How anyone expects students to come back for two weeks after a month and a half of break time and actually learn something is beyond me, especially considering they took their finals already in December.

This system creates two extended periods in which, under normal circumstances, teachers wouldn't be expected to be in school. While nearly every teacher has the freedom to do with their break time what they wish, Native English Teachers are contract teachers and required to fill time at their desks when they are not on their paid vacation. And thus, deskwarming was born.

There isn't a more polarizing aspect of the English teacher gig in Korea than deskwarming. For some, it's a horrific waste of time and proof that the powers that be don't consider Native English Teachers as real educators, or people. For others, it's an opportunity to catch up on "House of Cards" or pursue any number of personal hobbies in what amounts to scheduled and mandatory free time. Personally, I fall in the latter crowd. It's prime movie watching time, an opportunity to plan travel, and a good incentive to write. There's nothing else to do, other than maybe prepare or plan a few classes (textbooks may not even be assigned at this point, so this is not always easy to do). And because these breaks fall on the hottest and coldest parts of the year, it's free air conditioning or heat. That is, if the school lets you turn them on.

Deskwarming also allows teachers to fall down whatever rabbit hole fancies them. For some, that's the YouTube rabbit hole. For me, it's Wikipedia. I remember something mildly interesting that I want to know more about, say, the personal life of Mark Twain. Depending on the quality of the information, I scroll through looking for curious tidbits that I'll likely forget in a minute and a half. I see that Twain was born in the confusingly named Florida, Missouri and wonder what the population of Florida, Florida has gotten up to these days, so I type 'Florida' in the Wikipedia search bar and find that the state has a considerably larger number of old people than when I last looked. But I'm on the Florida page now, which talks about Burmese pythons in the Everglades, so I click on that link. And then I'll think of something else I'm curious about. And another. And another. And another. Before long, it's become extremely important to know the gross domestic product of Equatorial Guinea. I've become acquainted with the teams in the Australian National Basketball League. By the time I remind myself that I'm not actually learning anything important and have better things to do, I've glanced at hundreds of facts and remembered, if I'm lucky, two of them. It's a furious search through the world's compendium of knowledge, but at the end it's not a very useful expenditure of time. To the YouTube rabbit hole enthusiasts, I try to argue that I'm spending my time learning rather than watching junk, but in reality that's not true. I remember practically nothing, and there are some great videos on YouTube. John Green's "Crash Courses through History" series got me through some frigid deskwarming days.

The new school year came with a few welcome and not so welcome changes of pace. Like before, I had no choice but to embrace them and go with the flow.

At the beginning of the new school year in March, Ji Young made the executive decision that she would use her classroom computer as her desk. She didn't get along with Hyun Soo that well, and welcomed the distance between his classroom and hers. Also, she didn't teach in the English wing. The only reason she went over there was because the office was there. So, at the start of the year, I was the office's only tenant.

With Ji Young out, I was left alone to hold down the fort. It made a lonely job even lonelier, especially hearing about other English teachers and the camaraderie they had with their coworkers in their busy offices. The size of the room made it worse. Now, it was the dumping ground of the *waygook*. The fifth-grade teachers continued to meet during 'Happy Time,' which provided a small, limited window of socialization, but otherwise I was alone.

About two weeks into the new school year, Hyun Soo walked in with another school teacher carrying a computer. The teacher dumped the computer onto the desk next to mine and began to set it up.

"You're getting a new officemate," explained Hyun Soo. "A new gym teacher."

"Isn't there an office in the gym?" I asked, clicking out of YouTube.

"Yes."

"And don't we already have a gym teacher?"

"Yes, but he doesn't want to share."

Previously, Ji Young had said she didn't think much of the gym teacher, that he was arrogant and condescending. I didn't always put much stock in Ji Young's appraisals of people, but she had a point about this guy. I knew nothing about him, other than that nearly every day he showed up to school wearing a sweater over a dress shirt, hardly a typical gym teacher outfit. Ji Young explained that he was ambitious and wanted the top jobs available to him, and that was one reason he dressed nicely. I thought it was because he was a pompous turd that couldn't share an office. Then again, I wore dress shirts with sweaters over them and didn't want to share my office with the new gym teacher either.

The following afternoon, while I was organizing plans for an after-school class, I was startled when the door slid open and in came the Principal, followed by Hyun Soo and a man I'd never seen before. I assumed the man was the new gym teacher based on his suit and tie; no one wore suits and ties at my school unless it was their first day or if it was a special occasion. He was middle-aged, short, and looked like he despised nonsense.

I stood up and bowed to the Principal. Hyun Soo gave me the gym teacher's name, which was Lee Jong Young. Because we're getting a bit bogged down with Korean names, especially ones that start with the letter "J," and because this is what Ji Young and I usually called him, from this point on, I will creatively refer to Jong Young as Gym Teacher. The Principal made his exit, as did Hyun Soo, leaving me and Gym Teacher alone.

"Nice to meet you," I said in Korean.

"Nice to meet you too," he replied in English.

We'd both exhausted the useful phrases in each other's language at this junction, so Gym Teacher sat at his desk and fiddled around on the computer. After five minutes, he'd apparently had enough of fiddling and walked around the room, hands behind his back, surveying the contents of the office. There really wasn't much to survey: some old art projects, outdated appliances, and other junk that people had dumped in the room over time. I finished my work and found a live stream of a Blue Jackets game. It was the third period and the game was close. My eyes were glued to the screen, and my headphones blocked any outside noise. It was to my surprise, then, when Gym Teacher's face hovered inches away from mine.

"Ice hockey?" he asked as I slid my headphones off.

"Yeah," I said. "My team. Columbus Blue Jackets."

"Buh-loo jeckets?"

I quickly googled a picture of a Union army soldier and pointed to the color of the jacket.

He pulled up a chair. "Good team?"

"No," I replied, "but getting better." I held my hand parallel to the desk and lifted it.

"Ah," he said. "Rising?"

"Yes."

I unplugged my headphones and we watched the rest of the

game together.

A week into our relationship, I had to admit that it was nice having company in the office again. Most of the conversations between Gym Teacher and I were a mix of broken Korean and English, usually laced with questioning inflections to reflect our inexperience with the opposite language. We taught each other various vocabulary words, and talked sports. He was an inquisitive guy, and a little nosy. The Blue Jackets game wasn't the last time I'd find his face close to mine, looking in wonder at whatever was on my screen. I was often making silly PowerPoints for my classes and looking for fun memes or videos, so it wasn't unusual to see dancing cats or The Avengers on whatever I was making.

It was soon clear that Gym Teacher didn't have much work to do. He taught a few classes, lead an after-school club or two, and then spent the rest of the day looking for things to occupy his time. He had a Bible on his desk; sometimes, when I returned to the office from class, I'd find him sleeping in one of the cushioned seats by the window with his Bible open on his lap. Other times, I'd find him setting up drills for himself in the gym, placing cones across the floor and jogging between them.

My least favorite Gym Teacher activity was when he was learning English. He had found an English-learning website that was probably designed for six-year old's. Even with his headphones in, I could hear the obnoxious voices repeating sentences throughout the afternoon. The worst is when he would start a session and then leave the room. Whatever this website was, it wouldn't shut up. It sang songs too. And here's the weird part: I could never find the damned website on his computer. I'd slide over to his computer to click out of it, and I could never find the ghoulish page.

After class one day, Ji Young asked me, "what do you think of the new gym teacher?"

"He's okay," I replied. "He's nice. We don't really talk much."

"It's probably awkward, right?"

"Yeah, it's pretty awkward."

"No, I mean he's awkward."

"Huh?"

Ji Young explained that my appraisal of the new guy was the same as everybody else's. He was an ajeossi, but unmarried, which was a little unusual. This of course meant that, well into his forties,

Gym Teacher still lived with his mother. We'd only known each other a few days before he asked if I knew any eligible women. I did not. Neither, it seemed, did anybody else. Everyone agreed he was nice, but a bit of an oddball.

Later that week, I walked into the office to Gym Teacher inspecting his gray hairs in a tiny mirror on the wall. When he heard me walk in, he turned around to face me, his fingers still tight around a pinch of hair.

"Metyu, please," he said. He pretended to pluck a hair out and then gestured at me.

"No," I laughed, trying to keep the scene jocular. I waved my hands as if to say, 'no thank you,' even though I really meant 'not now, not ever. Why would you ask this of another human being?"

But he insisted! He kept his eyes locked on mine, waiting for me to give in. "Please."

"No," I repeated. I didn't often refuse people in this country, but there was a line and the gray hairs crossed it.

Gym Teacher returned to the mirror and tried to locate the single gray hair between his fingers. After two or three tries, he pleaded again and shoved the top of his head toward my face.

"Metyu, please."

Sighing, I took the gray hair from his fingers. I'd known this man only a few weeks, yet his gray hair was already pinched between my fingers. I pulled half-heartedly. Nothing happened. I tried one more time, a bit harder. The gray hair was still attached to his head. And then I left the room, squeamish. He never asked me to pull his hair again.

More than anything else, the goal of our orientation seemed to be to tell us that in Korea, you must be ready for change at a moment's notice. 'They'll give you a class at the last minute!' they endlessly admonished us. 'The schedule will change daily!' 'Try to be flexible!' I feel like most jobs I've applied for have cautioned me in a similar fashion, claiming that there is no routine as if to paint themselves as this exciting, Forrest Gump box-of-chocolates place that makes them unlike any other job. "There is no typical day," the ice cream kitchen told me, where they literally do nothing but make ice cream. So I filed all 29 or so cautionary tales of last minute changes and non-emergency emergencies away in the 'we'll just see about that' cabinet.

Well I saw about that.

I was in the middle of a late afternoon slump, too tired from the day's teaching to do anything productive, but motivated enough to do something sort of worthwhile like deleting emails or memorizing the calendar. It's too bad that I didn't have more to do that afternoon, or else I would've really had something to complain about when Hyun Soo walked into my office.

"You need to clean up your desk," he said. "You're going to move to a new office."

"Oh," I said, pretending to be clicking on things and typing something meaningful. "When?"

"In about ten minutes."

I stopped typing. "Oh. So do I need to, like, pack everything?"

"Yes, quickly."

Well, poop. I hadn't exactly kept my area tidy, spreading out projects or stuffing worksheets into cramped files. How was I supposed to pack everything and be ready to go in ten minutes? That question became irrelevant as fellow teachers came to help move stuff.

I didn't have time to evaluate my life and categorize my things into keep or throw away piles. I rushed to make stacks in what few baskets I had at my disposal, tossing in old worksheets and activity materials while teachers pulled desks and other furniture out of the room. Within minutes, nearly the whole faculty had arrived to empty the office and, apparently, turn it into a music room. Yes, it was like a good, old-fashioned Amish barn raising, but instead of raising a barn, we were tearing out what little sense of security I had in a foreign building and moving it somewhere else. How was I expected to perform at my best if at any moment I could be uprooted without any regard to my schedule or workload? What if I was in the middle of some grand project or lesson preparation and the principal decided I needed to move everything? What if I had been in an after-school class?

Ji Ho helped me move my desk into the elevator.

"Where are we going?" I asked in Korean.

"Next to the library," he replied. The elevator slid open and we lifted the desk over to a sliding door next to the library. Inside the door was a room considerably smaller than the one I'd left, and what could accurately be described as a closet. In fact, it was the IT closet.

I told Ji Ho this was stressful.

"What the Principal says, we do," said Ji Ho. With nobody else in the room, he clicked his heels, put a finger underneath his nose, and saluted like a Nazi, laughing. The principal, in this scenario, was Hitler.

He was kind of dictatorial, in a way. I never saw him do any real work, only telling people what to do and overseeing it to ensure it was to his liking. Not two weeks before our eradication from our office, Gym Teacher and I moved some bookshelves into our office and filled them with textbooks by order of the principal. Gym Teacher and I dutifully placed them along the wall behind our desks and stuffed them with the heavy tomes when the principal walked in and decided everything would look a lot better if it was three feet to the left. Heavy with the textbooks, we slid the cases over to where he thought our office would most benefit aesthetically. Then, two weeks later, it all went down to this closet. I'm sure our Principal kept himself busy with real work, but on the surface, he seemed to do little but make knee-jerk decisions.

About an hour later, everything had been moved into my new office, the textbooks had been restacked inside the bookcases, and my desk was put back together. Gym Teacher was elsewhere, probably leading an after-school club. Whether that club was attended by students or just him was another mystery. My computer, while plugged in, was not yet connected to the internet, so I sat in my chair with nothing to do.

Jang Mi walked in with the last stack of textbooks. "Hi Metyu," she smiled.

"Hi Jang Mi," I sighed.

"So small," she sighed in response. "You will miss your old room?"

"Yeah," I responded. "This was not fun."

She found an empty space in a bookcase by the window and shoved the books inside. "I'm sorry. We do what the principal says."

"I know."

I heard the floor creak and saw the Principal standing in the doorway, inspecting the layout of the new office. With him was a new Vice Principal, the third in six months. This one was a tall, crane-like man with glasses. Jang Mi and I bowed. I crossed my fingers that everything was to the Principal's liking and that I wouldn't need to do any more heavy lifting. He pointed to my swivel chair and said something in Korean. Jang Mi responded, and they shared a brief conversation that I did not follow the gist of. The focus then reverted to me.

"The Vice Principal need your chair," said Jang Mi.

"Oh," I responded. I wasn't about to make a big deal out of the chair, but what I really wanted to say was 'this was the chair that I was given when I came here. I don't see what's wrong with the Vice Principal's current chair, but if it's not as nice as this one I suggest you buy a new one because this chair is the best thing I have in this school.' I don't want to sound overly sentimental about a piece of office equipment, but I looked forward to the comfort of that chair every day. No matter what kind of day I was having, I could say to myself 'well at least I still have that really comfortable chair in my office to sit in.' Take my room, but not my chair please. I felt entitled to it. But I gestured to the chair giving my permission, as if I had any to give, for the Principal to wheel my chair back to the Vice Principal's desk. At least he didn't ask me to do it. The Principal took my chair and pushed it out of the room and out of my life. There I stood, once more adrift and wondering what else would be taken from me. My shoes, perhaps. My shirt.

"I need a new chair," I said to Jang Mi, although it was obvious.

Ji Ho walked in, taking in the new room. "Looks good," he said, with a thumb's up.

"The Principal took my chair," I told him.

Ji Ho laughed and did his Hitler salute again. "Follow me."

The three of us walked to the next wing of the school where an old classroom was now a dusty storage closet. Inside among the old tables, desks, musical instruments, and TV's was an assortment of crappy chairs. I test drove a few, leaning back and imagining sitting in them for hours at a time. None came close to Old Reliable. That's the name I'd given my old chair in its' memory. Eventually I dug out an old swivel chair, much smaller and not as stately as Old Reliable. I smacked some of the dust off and sat down. The back support was not as substantial but it would do.

"Good?" asked Ji Ho.

"Yeah," I lied. I sat up and wheeled it back to my room to

further clean it. My friends went back to their classrooms and I was alone once again.

It turned out there was one advantage to this new move, and it was in fact the IT equipment stored behind us. Because said equipment was some of the most valuable and liable to damage from heat in the building, the school was much more lenient about our use of air conditioning. Gym teacher would crank up the air conditioning to a polar level. Whenever a teacher would walk in and protest, he'd calmly point to the IT closet and that was the end of the conversation. I could continue playing the clueless foreigner and pretend that I thought the air was supposed to be on at all times.

In truth, I came to enjoy the coziness of the new office. The bookshelves gave it the feel of a study. The two comfortable chairs from our old office made it down as well and made the perfect reading spot. It's not the way I would have chosen to move, but I soon felt very much at home in my new office.

Right around the same time the Principal unilaterally moved Gym Teacher and I to the IT closet, he decided to repurpose the faculty lunch room as a conference room. Faculty would now eat lunch with the kids in the cafeteria.

By this point in my time at Maecheon Elementary School, I could scarcely walk down a hallway without a horde of kids waving and saying 'hello, Metyu teacher!' They weren't being annoying, most of them, and I'm glad they felt comfortable enough with me to greet me in the hallway. I returned the favor, happy to see them happy. As an introvert, I could manage these short interludes of exuberant attention fine, but these were mostly in hallways with students that I knew. I avoided the hallways with first and second grade classrooms because, by and large, I was still a Martian to them. To put me in a large, loud cafeteria with the entirety of the school's first and second graders was to throw me in with the wolves.

The first days were the worst. To make me eat in the cafeteria, a long, open room with three long rows of tables and stools, was to put me on display while I attempted, fruitlessly, to eat my lunch in peace. Students wouldn't stop staring as I stood in line with them for food. Some of the more cheeky students touched my arm hair as they walked by. Once I had my food, it was imperative to find a seat with other teachers. If I could help it, I tried to sit next to third or fourth graders because they already knew me and would likely leave me alone. The fifth and sixth graders ate in their classrooms, so they were no use to me. I have a feeling other teachers gave me a wide berth, else their lunch be disturbed by children bugging me. I didn't give a choice to Ji Young, or Gym Teacher, or whoever else I went to lunch with. They had to sit with me and help me bear the brunt of attention, especially if there were few seats left and I was forced to sit around kids. The youngest stared at me, forgetting to eat at times. Or, they gabbed on and on until Ji Young would tell them to leave me alone and eat. The level of attention I received ebbed and flowed over time until either students were accustomed to my presence or I got better at ignoring them.

A better change of pace was that two of my English classes were with students in their homerooms and with their homeroom teachers. One of these teachers was Jang Mi. Besides the opportunity to work with someone I knew, I was happy to break up the routine. Hyun Soo's classes were usually dull and I was getting tired of flying by the seat of my pants in Ji Young's classes. With Jang Mi and the other teacher, a kind, soft-spoken woman whose English was passable, I enjoyed structured English lessons in a new environment. Also, because these students were with their homeroom teachers, they were the most behaved.

Jang Mi in particular seemed to plan quiet, individual activities to end her classes, which meant we had time to chat. Ji Young and Hyun Soo were perfectly willing and able resources on most issues, but I found Jang Mi's perspective to be helpful because she was, like Ji Ho, as inquisitive as I was. So, while students colored or practiced writing, Jang Mi and I swapped opinions on movies, of course, but also politics, religion, culture, school, family, and other weighty topics. She was eager to share funny videos, or pictures from vacations, and to see mine. Like me, Jang Mi wasn't from Daegu. While it would be a gross overstatement to say she felt as much an outsider as me, she had difficulty making connections with a lot of people from Daegu. Ji Young, who had spent a year living in Seattle, was better than most Daegu natives at questioning conservative viewpoints, and so the two made for natural companions. Jang Mi, for her part, often called Ji Young crazy in that endearing, 'what are we going to do with her?' kind of way. I felt the same.

The Wedding Factory

That Time People Gabbed During the Processional

In case you've never been married, let's talk for a moment about the list of details that someone, probably the bride, must arrange. Someone must choose where to get married, in the first place, and where the reception will be. Could both be in the same place? Then there's the food. What is everyone going to eat? Drink? Who will be the DJ? Who will be the photographer? What color are the flowers? Is there going to be live music? Where is Aunt Marge going to sit? Should I invite Aunt Marge? Will Aunt Marge bring that guy she's been seeing who eats all the table rolls? What else should go on the tables? Should there be tables? Should there be a wedding at all? What are weddings? Who am I? I've made my point.

Aunt Marge and her tactless boy toy aside, South Korea has developed an industry that renders many of these issues a thing of the past. Wedding halls offer all-encompassing packages so that brides don't have to spend months arranging a big to-do. Rather, they show up like everyone else and what they see is what they get. While a small minority marry in a church, the vast majority of Korean couples get married at a wedding hall for rent.

Here's the sticky thing about wedding halls: they're popular. There may be several rooms to rent in one building, meaning there could be a dozen weddings a day in the same location, some happening at once. They're more like convention centers than sanctuaries. They are, as a fellow waygook so aptly put it, wedding factories, built to churn out as many brides in a day as possible. The result is a highly orchestrated, yet impersonal "best day of your life."

The all-inclusive incentive of wedding halls suits Korea's business-like approach to marriage. I have only anecdotal evidence to support this, but based on the people Maria and I interacted with, I think Koreans (and others, probably) are much happier dating than being married. People in Korea love the idea of getting married, but the honeymoon period seems to come before they even tie the knot. After that, parents start demanding grandchildren and the spare bedroom. Or, even without those pressures, married couples don't seem to maintain the spark. Maria would tell her coworkers that the two of us went on a date and their response would be confusion. "Why go on a date? You're already married." And they wonder why their marriages are unsatisfying.

To be fair, dating in Korea sounds like an exciting time. Couples often meet through a mutual friend who sets them up on a blind date. These blind dates could be exclusive or they could be a more casual hangout with a larger group. Once a couple is together, anniversaries are measured by days rather than months or years. The 100th day anniversary, especially for younger couples, is a milestone that involves gifts and a romantic dinner.

Korean couples love their dates. The 14th of every month is a pseudo-holiday for dating, each with their own particular ritual. There's Valentine's Day, of course, on February 14. March 14 is White Day, when the guys give the gals candy to show their appreciation (guys get their candy on Valentine's Day). June 14 is Kissing Day. August 14 is Green Day, which is a day to go out and enjoy nature.

There is often a counterpart ritual for singles. On Green Day, for example, singles are supposed to drink soju to lament being single. On Yellow Day, May 14, singles eat yellow curry and make plans to find a lover in the next year. April 14, Black Day, is the sole day devoted exclusively to singles, who are instructed to "gather ye singles while ye may" and together eat jjajjangmyeon, which itself has a black sauce, and either console or celebrate one another's loneliness. In case you're convinced Koreans have a screw loose with all these holidays, I'd like to point out they don't actually take these days seriously, but the fact that they exist at all gives the impression that everything is about dating. Everything after that is about duty. There are no days, for instance, devoted to married couples.

Ji Young mentioned one day that she planned to get married within the year, as if getting married was something you could accomplish with an internship and a degree in marketing. I reminded her that she was single, but that didn't deter her. She would find her husband before the age of 30, when most Korean parents begin the "are we getting grandkids or what?" talk. With courtships possibly taking only a few months, it wasn't unreasonable and I silently cheered for a man to come along, if only for her to stop talking about her trouble with men.

Jang Mi was getting married and had invited the entire faculty. I'd never been to a Korean wedding, but I'd heard stories of excessive pageantry, endless photo opportunities, and buffets that stretch for miles. What interested me, other than showing my support for Jang Mi, was the promise of an unadulterated Korean experience, with nobody making exceptions for me. For a few hours, I wouldn't be an employee or a customer or some other sort of person that might change how people behave. I would only be an observer. Maria and I dressed in the nicest clothes we'd brought with us, her a purple dress and myself a pale green oxford shirt and a white tie. We hopped on board a bus into town and Ji Young hopped on at the next stop, outside her apartment complex.

We eventually arrived in front of a massive box of a building. We walked in and, to nobody's surprise, the vast atrium was packed. Wedding guests were coming and going as their respective weddings were just getting started or finishing up. The first order of business was to hand over our gifts. In Korea, the thing to do at such a wedding is to give the couple money in an envelope provided by the wedding hall. In exchange, you receive a ticket for the hall's buffet. Ji Young tracked down the desk where this exchange takes place, and we received our tickets. Some people, according to Ji Young, take their picture with the bride, go eat lunch in the dining room, and then leave without attending the actual ceremony. How nice of them.

Jang Mi's wedding was on the fourth floor. We were early, so the previous wedding was still in the wedding room taking pictures. The room was sanctuary-sized with an elevated marble aisle down the middle, bordered by a water feature, and a thick column of decadent seats on either side. Up front was an altar of sorts, with puffy, white flowers and a large candle on both ends. From the ceiling, just vaulted enough to achieve a vague, nave aesthetic, hung enormous bouquets of flowers and three bright, long chandeliers. There were no doors or walls separating the room from the hallway, so people milled about between the two.

Aside from the 'sanctuary' room, there were two smaller rooms on that floor for photos. In one, family members of the previous wedding had dressed in their finest Hanbok and were taking posed, traditional pictures at a low table. In the other room, sitting on a large, gray couch under a massive chandelier, was Jang Mi in her wedding dress. A line had formed to take pictures with the bride before the wedding, so we stepped in line along with some fifth grade teachers from Maecheon who had just arrived. A professional photographer stood at the ready as group after group sat on the couch with Jang Mi for a picture. I felt sorry for Jang Mi and regretted a little that we'd added to her misery with one more picture to take, one more smile to muster. The wedding hadn't even started yet. She took it all in stride, it seemed, and was happy to see us. From our photo, you wouldn't know she'd likely taken dozens of pictures that day.

Eventually, the previous wedding had all but filtered out and the crowd awaiting Jang Mi's wedding filled the hallway. More teachers from Maecheon arrived, including the Principal and Vice Principal. The Principal was eager to meet my wife, so I introduced Maria. He gave her a very kind reception, saying she was very beautiful. I could never get a read on that man; his decisions at school often felt reactionary and short-sighted, which usually affected me in some negative way, but in person he treated me warmly. Ji Ho arrived soon after with his two daughters and we chatted. Hyun Soo joined the group for a moment, and then disappeared. In the meantime, the older arrivals claimed seats in the wedding room. It was clear that there were far more people than there were seats, and that many of us were expected to stand.

What followed was the least conspicuous start to a wedding I've ever seen. Jang Mi and her fiancé made their way through the throng with the assistance of some photographers and walked up to the front of the wedding room without so much as a 'Canon in D.' I was toward the back of the group, so I had some difficulty seeing what was going on, but the giant bouquets hanging from the ceiling lowered as the couple walked by. Everyone in the room with a camera snapped pictures.

There are three reasons why I wasn't able to discern much from the ceremony. The first I've already mentioned: I was in the back of the standing-room only crowd. The second, the most obvious one, is that the emcee, or pastor, or whatever the man up front was, spoke only in Korean. The third reason, the most bizarre and offensive, was that the standing-room crowd chatted through the entire ceremony. Chatted! Carried full conversations about baseball or TV or whatever came to mind while two people devoted their lives to each other in front of them. I'd never seen anything like it in my life. It's something that would just not fly in America. Someone, either a parent or the bride herself, would start throwing hymnals, but apparently talking during a wedding is not such a big deal in South Korea. To each their own, but I tried my best to stay engaged with what was happening, which didn't really matter because there was no audience participation other than applause. The officiant person would say something, and Jang Mi and her fiancé would move to a different part of the room. The flowers would be lowered again so the photographers could snap some photos. Romantic music, either from the stereo system or the live quartet in the corner, came at different intervals. There were no groomsmen, no bridesmaids. No organ. There were vows of some kind. At the end, a friend of the groom was given a microphone and he began to sing a song. The groom joined in. He was an awful singer. Everyone in the room knew it, including himself, but he leaned into the awfulness and it was actually the most entertaining part of the ceremony. Less than thirty minutes after their unceremonious entrance, Jang Mi and her husband kissed and that was that.

There was no time lost between the ceremony and the typical family pictures in front of the altar. Different groups shuffled up to the front and arranged themselves only to be shooed off a moment later to usher in the next group. There was the next wedding to consider. A new crowd would arrive at any moment and we'd need to scram before their allotted time began. Jang Mi and her husband also wanted pictures with friends and coworker groups. According to Ji Young, if someone was getting married and didn't have many friends, it wasn't unheard of to 'hire' friends for the occasion -- some people to take up space in the picture and make it look like they were popular. She'd done it herself once or twice for extra cash. From the looks of things, Jang Mi and her husband didn't need help in that department, but then again, who would know?

As rushed and impersonal as the wedding was for this Westerner, lunch was stranger still. With our photographic responsibilities finished, Ji Young led us to the basement, where an absurdly long buffet line split a large cafeteria in half. All the weddings shared this one reception area, with guests coming and going at a clip all day long. Rather than find a reserved section for Jang Mi, we had to find whatever seats were available. The buffet itself covered more cuisines than was probably best, and some choices were better than others: meat of all types, dumplings, kimbap, fruit, sushi, octopus, some surprisingly stellar potato wedges, salad, spaghetti, sweet potatoes, kimchi, radish, and too many varieties of bread and desserts to mention. We filled our plates and looked for three seats together, which took some doing in the noisy, crowded cafeteria.

While we nibbled on our pan-Asian, pan-Western lunch, newly married couples meandered through the cafeteria greeting their guests. What a horrifying prospect: searching through 1000 people to find your 200. What if you miss someone? They likely did. Jang Mi and her husband eventually made their appearance. Jang Mi, wearing Hanbok that was bright green on top with a pink skirt, found us as we were finishing our food. She looked tired, as most brides do on their wedding days, but happy. We snapped another picture with her and her husband, whose Hanbok was all pink with a purple sash. Our attention was short-lived as they tried to find as many of their guests as possible. It was perhaps the only part of their day they had any agency over, but that's what they signed up for when they made a reservation at the wedding factory. Custom-made ceremonies are no longer customary.

Despite the relative ease of arranging a wedding, Koreans are waiting longer than ever to get married or perhaps not marrying at all. In 2016, the average age of men getting married was nearly 33 years and about 30 years for women. In 1996, those average ages were 28 and 25 respectively. In 1980, the number of marriages per 1,000 people was 10.6. In 2016, the number was down to 5.5. In part, these numbers can be explained by the increasingly elastic roles for women in Korean society. More are deciding to pursue degrees or careers before they pursue men. Another issue is a declining birth rate, with fewer young Koreans than in previous generations. Other reasons are the same bandied between American Millennials: no money, bad job prospects, too many good shows on.

But it's unlikely people are upset about the lack of ceremonies themselves. Even Koreans tire of the cookie cutter pageantry, the generic buffet food, and the endless photographs. I have to say I find more meaning in the American version, whether it be in a church or not. As Hyun Soo put it, 'once you've been to one Korean wedding, you've been to them all." I'd have to take his word for it.

Seonyudo

That Time I Learned to Stop Worrying and Love the Sea

In South Korea, there aren't a lot of accommodation options in the Best Western range. There are expensive options such as resorts and five star international brands and then there are cheap options, and therein lies the adventure. You could choose to stay at a guesthouse or hostel. You could do as families do and choose to stay in what they call an 'ondol' room, an empty room with a bathroom, kitchen, and a stack of floor mattresses and pillows. Or you could choose a love motel. Love motels are notorious for their ability to accommodate lovers who would prefer to pay for their room by the hour. Prostitutes might bring their clients to love motels, for instance, or businessmen their mistresses. On the surface, they seem like a dodgy choice, but they are typically clean, affordable, and abundant, making them useful when you're stopping in town for a night and just need somewhere to sleep. Such was our lot when, four hours after departing from Daegu, we arrived in Gunsan on the west coast. A friend of Phillip's was visiting and for a long weekend we decided to check out an overlooked island in the Yellow Sea, Seonyudo. It was too late to catch a ferry, so there was no choice but to head for the nearest street with neon and look for the word 'motel' in Hangul.

Immediately there were several options, so we didn't feel pressured to settle. We chose one that looked reasonably well-lit and walked in. A stubbly, old man sat behind the front counter and watched us come in. We asked in Korean how much a room was and if we could see one. He lead us into an empty room on the first floor. There was a dead cockroach on the floor and the rest of the room didn't look especially well-kept. We thanked him and scurried out before we could convince ourselves this was the best we could do.

The second option was much more promising. Rooms were 60,000 won a night, just under $60, and the place looked much newer and cleaner. The adjumma at the counter, however, was a bit dubious about the sleeping arrangements. We were a group of five, see, and apparently this particular love motel was not about that sort of thing. We would have to get two separate rooms. Maria and I showed our wedding rings, so she had no qualms with our room. She was still concerned about the threesome in the other room. They did their best to explain that there would be no lovemaking that night, and the woman finally agreed. She handed us the keys and we took the elevator to the third floor.

As mentioned above, our room was quite nice and would certainly do for one evening. Some love motels go out of their way to create themes for their rooms, but ours was straightforward. The bathroom was tiled and the walls were glass with some elegant frost at toilet level. The room itself had hardwood floors and a big, comfortable bed. The TV came with a standard array of channels and a selection of porn. On the nightstand was an assortment of complimentary lubes and condoms. I couldn't tell you which of these features went used in the rest of the motel, but all went ignored as the five of us spent the evening playing cards. For $60, you could do a whole lot worse.

The next morning, we checked out of the love motel and gathered supplies for Seonyudo, which is off the grid and doesn't offer a lot in the way of groceries or non-seafood restaurants. We purchased breakfast for the next couple days at Dunkin Donuts and popped in a small grocery for some bread, peanut butter, jelly, and snacks. Our bags stuffed with junk food, we hailed a couple cabs and went to the ferry.

Seonyudo is, to put it generously, a smattering of large rocks connected by sandbars, but it is one of my favorite places in Korea. There are very few vehicles on the islands save for the vans that pick up tourists from the passenger ferry and take them to their respective accommodations, all of which likely fit under the 'cheap' option but with no love motels in sight. Most roads are therefore comfortably wide enough for one lane. Our van took us down such a road along the edge of a tidal flat. An inch in either direction would send us into the mud, yet there were plenty of pedestrians and bikers sharing the same cement. By some miracle, everybody remained on the road. Our ondol room was at the foot of one of the 'peaks' of the islands, a large rock a few hundred feet out of the ocean and decorated with some trees. It was on the top floor of a two-story building that couldn't have had more than eight rooms to rent. The room itself was simple, with a sink and stove under a window that looked across the tidal flat to where the ferry was now departing. It was wonderful.

There aren't, strictly speaking, 'things to do' on Seonyudo. To my knowledge there are no tourist attractions or guided tours or anything of that sort. All there is to do is explore. As it was early May and breezy, it was too chilly to swim in the ocean. We rented bikes from the family living below our ondol room and pedaled up the empty roads around the islands, connected by some attractive bridges. Tiny fishing villages appeared around every corner, so we'd stop and take a look around and perhaps buy an ice cream at the corner store before moving on. We spent a good deal of time climbing around the rocky shores and tidal pools, searching for crabs and anemones and little fish. Where there were beaches, we stopped and looked for interesting shells, of which there was an abundance. There was nowhere we had to be and nothing we had to do. If all this doesn't sound charming to you, then I don't know what to say other than maybe your priorities suck, or that you shouldn't go to places like Seonyudo.

Our accommodation was probably the least enchanting part of our stay. The aforementioned ondol room was cozy, and large enough for the five us to spread the provided flimsy mattresses across the floor, but sleeping on an ondol floor is a lot different than sleeping above one on a bed. Ondol style rooms, for the unacquainted, are heated through the floors. The system warms the entire room evenly, much more so than a vent, and is heavenly during the cold winter months. That is, unless you're sleeping on the floor. We played around with the temperature but if it was too low, the room was freezing. If it was too high, our bums started cooking. There wasn't much we could do. Perhaps more knowledgeable people bring their own mattresses in addition to what ondol rooms provide. I don't know, but it was uncomfortable sleeping. My stomach and face would be roasting while my butt was freezing. Every 30 minutes or so, I'd rotate and let one half of me cool down and the other half warm up. This went on all night, for all of us, like a bunch of rotisserie tourists.

The following morning, we were riding our bikes past a few hardy campers on the main beach when we realized there were several people digging in the sand with shovels. Curious, we ditched the bikes and invaded the privacy of a father and daughter duo hard at work in the sand, but they didn't seem to mind. We watched as the father shoveled sand until he came across a small hole no more than an inch wide. The daughter, with a single pink curler in her bangs, poured what I correctly guessed to be saltwater from a bottle into the hole and out popped a razor clam. She grabbed the slender, alien-looking thing and tossed it in a bucket. They repeated this process a couple times before the daughter offered for one of us to grab the clam. Maria volunteered and was successful.

For our second day, we did mostly the same that we did on the first, but in the opposite direction. The sun was warm enough to make the cool weather tolerable. Throughout our exploring, the large rock next to our accommodation beckoned to be climbed. A path led to the base and we surmised that climbing it was possible, so Gail, Maria and I set out to reach the top. It was a steep ascent, one that required coordination, leg muscles, and a comfort with heights. I had two of those things.

Going up was not such a big deal. To reach the top, climbers needed to pull themselves up using two thick, strategically-placed ropes. Since I was only looking up at where I was going, pulling myself up and walking up the mountain with the rope was a lot of fun. The rest of the way was essentially hiking or climbing up some roots and rocks until we reached the treeless top. Our reward was a stunning view. The villages, the sandbars, the mud flats and Phillip and his friend were a couple hundred feet below. The water shimmered in the late afternoon sun, and the rest of Korea sat hazily off in the horizon. What about mountains meeting water that's so pleasing to the eye, I'm not sure, but I had found, at that point, the most beautiful view in South Korea I had seen. We snapped pictures, of course, and enlisted the help of another hiker, a stranger also from

Daegu, to take a picture of the three of us. It was lovely, but when it came time to go back down, I immediately realized I had perhaps bitten off more than I could chew. With every step going down, I was reminded of how high we'd climbed and how steep the rock was. The ropes in particular were dreadful. I was on a mountain side with naught but a rope and, at most, two stray trees between me and the nearest flat land about a hundred feet down. While 'tumbling to death' might be a bit melodramatic, serious injury was not out of the question. I watched Gail and Maria descend the first rope segment not quite expertly but confidently enough. I proceeded to descend the first rope butt first, clinging to the rope for my life. While the going up was assured and quick, the going down was terrifyingly slow. My hands became sweaty as they do in situations with heights. The rope was a bit looser than I wanted so I began to slip, but I pulled it tight and regained my composure. I was afraid to slide my feet down more than a foot at a time, lest gravity shift my weight too far in one direction and I lose my grip. A small line was forming above me at the top of the rope as other hikers waited for me to finish. Maria and Gail greeted me at the end of the first segment of rope and I was, for a minute at least, reunited with multiple points of contact with trees and a relatively horizontal piece of rock. In the interest of eliminating a traffic jam and an embarrassing audience, we agreed to let the hikers behind us, all Koreans, pass us. Each one did what had taken me about three minutes in about ten seconds. They practically walked down the rope face first, as easily as I went up. They might as well have been walking to the mailbox. It's unfair. Koreans really must be more highly evolved beings than the rest of us. They don't sweat, they can squat comfortably for hours, and when it comes to hiking they are sure-footed mountain goats. In a country dominated by mountains, they all seem to have a knack for getting up and down them. We let the last of the Korean hikers pass and then tackled the last rope. The lower of the two ropes, this segment wasn't quite as terrifying as the first. Each step down was a step less likely to result in a grisly death in the event of a fall. At last, all three of us reached the bottom. Back on terra firma, we walked down the rest of the path to the trailhead, where Phillip and his friend waited. We all agreed that we could do with some dinner.

The restaurants on Seonyudo serve seafood and not much else. We found a seaside joint not far from our ondol room that did seafood bibimbap, which sounded easy enough to stomach. It was your standard bibimbap but without the sauce and with some raw fish and additional greens instead, not unlike a bowl of Hawaiian poké. It was staggeringly fresh and delicious, and between the bibimbap and banchon side dishes, we were soon stuffed.

By our last day on the islands, we'd about exhausted our options. We'd ridden bikes, climbed, explored, ambled, and eaten. We were also out of donuts. We walked down a pier to a lighthouse shaped like a giant red hand, as if saying 'stop!' The view was largely the same as everywhere else we'd been, so we didn't linger for long. We found one last beach to look for shells, but ended up finding a good number of starfish, both alive and dead. For our last meal, we chose a restaurant adjacent to the passenger ferry. We ordered a large bowl of kalguksu soup with clams to share. The neighboring table ordered San-nakji, or squirming octopus tentacles. The octopus is good and dead, but the nerves are still active minutes after the octopus is killed and remain wriggling on the plate. If that's not unappetizing enough, the suckers still work and can cling to your throat, making them potential choking hazards. To avoid this fate, diners dip the tentacles in sesame oil to disengage the suckers. While it was interesting to observe from seven feet away, you will not find San-nakji on my plate.

Overall, you will be hard pressed to find a more beguiling place in South Korea than Seonyudo. In a crowded country, it's not often you have a road, or sidewalk, or anything to yourself. Seonyudo is blessedly un-crowded, or at least it was in May. I can't imagine the place is ever swamped; there aren't enough rooms to put people, and camping options are available but limited. Simply put, there aren't a lot of people around and that alone makes it a great place to go. The more people I speak with who have spent time in Korea, the more they confirm that everyone's favorite parts of the country are tied to the shore. This should come as no surprise, given that the peninsula is surrounded by water and that there are over 3,000 islands. There are, of course, glitzy resorts and famous beaches in other parts of the country, but to get a truly unfiltered glimpse of Korea, head to the sea and find a fishing village. Just keep the octopus tentacles to yourself.

The Demilitarized Zone

That Time I saw 'Bob' from North Korea

On August 14, 1945, future Secretary of State Dean Rusk, at that point a colonel, and Army staffer Col. Charles "Tic" Bonesteel spent hours poring over a map of the Korean peninsula. They had been given the thankless task of choosing a line of control that would separate Soviet-occupied Korea with American-occupied Korea. The peninsula had been a Japanese colony throughout WWII, and with the Japanese empire, and the war itself, in its final days, the Americans wanted to make sure that Korea would not fall entirely into the hands of the Soviets. But where to draw the line?

Rusk and Bonesteel knew very little about Korea, about its provincial boundaries or economy. All they had at their disposal was the map. In Rusk's memoir *As I Saw It*, he doesn't mince words about how little they knew about the country they were dividing:

> Neither Tic nor I was a Korea expert, but it seemed to us that Seoul, the capital, should be in the American sector. We also knew that the U.S. Army opposed an extensive area of occupation. Using a National Geographic map, we looked just north of Seoul for a convenient dividing line but could not find a natural geographical line. We saw instead the thirty-eighth parallel and decided to recommend that ... [Our commanders] accepted it without

too much haggling.

So did, mysteriously, the Soviets, who had already begun moving troops into Northern Korea. America's nearest troops, by comparison, were over 600 miles away on Okinawa. Rusk and Bonesteel's expediency paid off, in a way. The next day, Emperor Hirohito ordered the surrender of Imperial Japan to the Allies over a radio address. WWII was over, and the Americans would have a say about what happened to Korea, at least part of it.

What was meant to be a temporary line, within years, became the recognized border between two increasingly hostile nations, each governed by its own brand of dictatorship. On June 25, 1950, the well-equipped and equally well-trained North Korean army flooded over the 38th parallel and rolled over the lightly armed military of their southern neighbors. Within four days, the North Koreans occupied Seoul. The Korean War had begun. By the beginning of August, North Korea had occupied the entire peninsula save for what lay behind the Busan Perimeter, a last stand in the country's extreme southeastern corner. It was here that UN troops, led by the Americans, first joined South Koreans in the fighting and assisted in holding the line. In the meantime, General Douglas MacArthur planned an amphibious attack near Seoul at Incheon (of international airport fame). On September 15, MacArthur and 75,000 of his closest pals came ashore and took the North Koreans completely by surprise. Within weeks, Seoul was recaptured, North Korea was on the retreat, and the war had taken a dramatic turn.

Lest we hope for a minute that the war ended with a swift and happy ending, the fighting would continue for another three years. China sent troops to support the beleaguered North Koreans, and the front line settled with few changes, no matter how many bombs, bullets, or bodies either flung toward the other. This front line settled approximately on the 38th parallel, the original border between the two countries. On July 23, 1953, the two sides signed an armistice to end the fighting, but not the war. The front line would turn into a "military demarcation line," with two kilometers of 'demilitarized zone" extended on either side. This line would serve as the new border between the two countries. The same is true today.

On anyone's 'must see' list when visiting South Korea ought to be the Demilitarized Zone, a misnomer if I ever saw one. The DMZ is the most heavily fortified international border on Earth, separating the Republic of Korea from another misnomer, the Democratic People's Republic of Korea. While many tour companies take you to the border, it's best to go with the guys who help run the place, the U.S. military.

Bright and early on a Saturday, Gail, Phillip, Maria and I took a cab from Haus Guesthouse in Itaewon to the USO office outside Yongsan Garrison. Although it was a humid June day, there were no T-shirts among us. The military requires tourists to dress in a clean cut manner, as not to be portrayed by North Korean propaganda as impoverished. That's the reason our tour guide, a tall, agreeable American man in uniform whose name eludes me, gave us. I wish I remembered his name, because it was something ironically sanguine like 'Sergeant Sunflower.' I'll call him that anyway.

Sergeant Sunflower led us to the tour bus and we made the drive up to the border. The trip is not long, an hour at most, which gives you a new appreciation for how close the 25 million South Koreans in the Seoul area live to one of the most volatile nations in the world, one that is willing to rain artillery on them at a moment's notice. Our first stop, after weaving through cement barriers at a security checkpoint, was Camp Bonifas, a base camp for the United Nations Command Security Group. While it provides security for nearby villages and facilitates diplomatic exchanges at the Joint Security Area less than two miles to the north, on most days it serves as a forward operating base for tours like ours. It has an orientation theater, where we signed a paper stating that we knew violence could erupt at any time and that we promised not to defect. There are also restrooms and a gift shop. I bought a North Korean 100 won note.

The bus then took us to the Joint Security Area, also known as Panmunjom after the village that once stood in its place. This is the only spot on the DMZ where South Korean soldiers routinely stand face to face with their North Korean counterparts, so imagine my surprise when such a tense location featured a lovely roundabout. The bus pulled around and deposited us in front of a large concrete building, where we organized into a single file line. We walked through the building to the other side, where a row of thin, blue buildings straddle the border between the countries. On the North Korean side, a similar concrete building stands in opposition.

Between us and the blue buildings were three South Korean soldiers facing North Korea in a modified Tae Kwan Do pose. There are strict requirements for these soldiers, much like those that patrol the Tomb of the Unknown Soldier in Washington D.C. These men must be of a certain height with a black belt in Tae Kwan Do. They wear shades and stern faces to hide any semblance of fear or remorse. Often, there are North Korean soldiers doing the same on the other side, but there were none that day, for which I'm not sure to be grateful or disappointed. Instead, a North Korean soldier with a round, Soviet-style hat stood on the balcony of the concrete building with his binoculars trained on us.

"That's just Bob," said Sergeant Sunflower.

On either side of the row of blue buildings is a nicely-mown lawn that also straddles the border. I asked Sergeant Sunflower who gets to mow it. He didn't give me an answer. Perhaps concerned about my question, he reminded us not to cross the border, designated with a cement speed bump halfway across the buildings. If we crossed to the other side, he admonished us, he had no authority to retrieve us. As much as I wanted to meet Bob and ask him if he mowed the lawn, I elected to remain on the side that elected their government.

The one place where you can step into North Korea is inside one of the blue buildings. South Korea maintains full authority of at least one of them, which allows tours to enter and walk around the North Korean half of the building. Inside, two more soldiers stand guard: one at the head of a large conference table, and another at the far end with his back to the North Korean door. This latter soldier wins the prize for the last job on earth I'd apply for, but he's there to deter folks from defecting to North Korea, which, while uncommon, happens more often than you'd think. A small number of North Korean defectors, disillusioned with high unemployment and low social status in South Korea, become 'double defectors' and find a way back into North Korea. In 1962, private James Joseph Dresnok chose to deal with his troubled childhood, sham marriage, and disappointing military career by running across the DMZ to North Korea where he lived as a tool of the country's propaganda until his death in 2017. In 2009, a South Korean pig farmer wanted for assault (he'd hit his boss with a hammer) cut through the barbed wire of the eastern part of the DMZ and escaped justice.

There were a lot of stops on the tour, which lasts about 8 hours, so we hopped back on the bus and headed to the first of two observatories on the itinerary. A hazy, hilly North Korea laid before us. In the foreground, a strip of forest likely as riddled with landmines as it was weeds stood as an overgrown fence between the two nations. A small watchtower punched through the trees about halfway through, from which two more North Korean soldiers watched us through binoculars. In the background is the so-called 'peace village' of Kijong-dong, otherwise known as 'propaganda village' by those not of North Korean persuasion. Kijong-dong was constructed in the 1950's to encourage defection from the South. Pyongyang's official stance is that it's a real village with 200 real people living there. Observers from the DMZ have noted that lights turn on reliably at the same time and tend to illuminate entire buildings at once, which likely means the interiors are empty and that there are no floors. The buildings are also betrayed by the fact that the windows don't have glass. A handful of groundskeepers maintain the illusion of activity in the village, but for all intents and purposes, it's not an actual place to live. It does, however, boast one of the highest flagpoles in the world, a result of a flag-pole pissing contest in the 1980's. South Korea had built a flagpole over 300 feet high, so North Korea responded in kind with a flagpole over 500 feet high, at the time the tallest in the world. Rather than continue to build flag poles into the stratosphere, South Korea let the communists have this little victory, so the flagpole remains, flying a gargantuan flag over the empty village. The village is also visible from the Dora Observatory, a larger, more accessible observation deck that provides a panoramic view of the world's most reclusive nation.

If you've ever relished the opportunity to buy a train ticket and not go to the destination, then nearby Dorasan station ought to be on your bucket list. Visitors of the lonely train station, the last before the North Korean border, can purchase a ticket to Pyongyang for about a dollar, walk onto the platform, and see the train that under different circumstances would head north for North Korea's capital. Of course, there are no trains going to North Korea, and the train sits there. It is a bit eerie, though, to look at the north-heading tracks and wonder what waits beyond. How would North Korea react if a train departed from the station? Blow it up, probably. Dorasan does serve a handful of trains a day that depart from Seoul, but is otherwise a ceremonial and useless train station.

The platform is, however, a popular place for photos. Soldiers stand guard and are usually willing to pose for pictures. Tourists stand next to the train as if on their way to the authoritarian nation. Our group decided this was a good idea. We planned our picture out. I would grasp onto the door handle of the train, pretending to defect to the North, while the rest of us would form a line and cartoonishly pull me back to the platform. The problem wasn't the prospect of me defecting; the train wasn't going anywhere and the doors were locked. The problem was finding the opportunity to take the picture. As is often the case in Korea, there were so many people and no conceivable line to determine our turn, so the best practice is to make it your turn by confidently (some might say aggressively) walking forward and ignoring other people. As soon as a group left, we descended on the spot. I took my position next to the train's door, and the rest of our group followed suit, pulling at my shirt, pulling on the person's shirt in front of them, and so on. Our designated photographer snapped the picture, and all seemed successful from our point of view. We moved away from the train to let the next group in, and our photographer shared the image. Three adjummas, either because they liked our idea or thought it was their turn to take a picture, joined in our line and waved at their own photographer. So we have me, allegedly boarding the train to North Korea, a handful of white people pulling at me to save my life, and three old Korean ladies smiling and pretending to do the same. It's one of my favorite pictures.

Back at our EPIK orientation, conversations often sprouted on the subject of what interested us most about Korea. What brought us to the country? What were we excited to see? I had mentioned to one woman that I thought it would be interesting to see the DMZ. She looked at me as if I'd said I might try throwing puppies into lava for fun. Apparently, she boiled down trips to the DMZ as treating military might as a tourist attraction. While I have my own reservations about museums that display missiles, aircraft, and other weapons alongside information on how they are best designed to kill other human beings, I thought her appraisal of the DMZ was reductive and unfair, but I let it go. To her point, some parts of the

DMZ do feel a little too...cheery. This is theoretically one of the most dangerous places in the world, after all. If you throw a frisbee into the woods at the DMZ, that's where it lives now. There are mines and other unexploded ordnance waiting to take somebody's leg off. Back at Camp Bonifas, a nine-hole golf course features the sign "Danger. Do not retrieve balls from the rough. Live minefields." And that's on the good side. A few kilometers north lies the world's most repressive state, where the government not only imprisons the culprit of some trumped up charge, but future generations as well. It's not an amiable situation, yet outside the entrance of the 3rd Infiltration Tunnel, a discovered underground conduit dug by North Koreans in the event of an invasion of the South, stands are selling ice cream and balloons and souvenirs. People take selfies next to a colorful 'DMZ' sculpture. Let's not forget the photo opportunities at Dorasan station. It's just a little weird.

The 3rd Infiltration Tunnel itself feels like a theme park attraction. It doesn't help that the parking lot is full of tour buses and large groups of colorfully-clothed people. An immersive museum at the surface is filled with smiling families and field trips. There are bright, informative signs everywhere. You'd be forgiven for thinking you're at the zoo. We weren't at the zoo, however, so we did what we came to do. We headed to the tunnel entrance, donned yellow hard hats, and descended down the narrow, dimly lit corridor that is, at the best of times, six feet tall by six feet wide. I hit my head a lot.

The South Koreans discovered the tunnel in 1978 after detecting an underground explosion. Hoping to fool any future discoverers that the tunnel was a coal mine, the North Koreans painted some of the rock wall black. Obviously the trick fooled nobody, but it does add to the inauthentic theme park feeling, like you're walking through an elaborate queue line for a dark ride. The precise moment the tunnel becomes a real thing is at the end, where a cement barricade and barbed wire marks the border between the countries and prevents you from going further. Beyond, a spooky distance away, is a cement wall with nothing but a dark doorway and tiny window into God knows what. There were no souvenirs here, only the haunting presence of a dictatorship in the shadows. There is no ride at the end of this queue, it turns out, only the haunting proposition of a thousand soldiers marching from the darkness. That's what the tunnel was designed for -- to invade Seoul. Allegedly, 30,000 troops could march through in an hour. I turned and headed the way we came back to balloons, laughing children, and ice cream. As inappropriate as they may seem, they do serve as an instant shower of sanity after hiking to the gates of hell.

That's precisely what, at every corner, the DMZ seems to offer: a glimpse into hell. You can dance on its doorstep, pay a quarter to get a closer look through binoculars, even dip your toes inside. But here's the thing: the beings that live in this hell aren't demons, they're people unfortunate enough to be born into an authoritarian state. Even the soldiers, the only North Koreans you have the remotest chance of interacting with, are victims of circumstance. When you pay money to tour the DMZ, you're essentially paying money to look at them. Hoping to see North Korean soldiers on the tour, in a way, is almost like saying you hope to see a lion on your safari. Perhaps this is what the woman at orientation was getting at.

I submit, though, that despite the oddities, the DMZ is worth a look because it is history in the making. The Joint Security Area was certainly a more somber experience, and a learning one at that. If you listen to your guide, Sergeant Sunflower or whomever, you stand to learn a lot about the war, the sacrifices made, and the honor it is to live in a safer world. What's more, you learn these things by seeing them unfold before your own eyes. It's live history. The Berlin Wall was a terrible thing to have existed, but my father-in-law was there when they tore it down. He still has a piece of it tucked away in storage. Now that I've traveled to the DMZ, I can say to future generations that "I was there when."

This is assuming that the Korean peninsula will one day reunite. If and when that's the case, a popular idea thrown around is to turn the DMZ into an ecological park to protect the pristine environment that has sustained itself in the absence of development. Endangered animals such as the Asiatic black bear, white-naped crane, and musk deer make their homes in the ribbon of undisturbed ecosystem. It's possible that the critically-endangered Amur leopard lives there too. There are even reports of Siberian tigers. These are creatures long gone from the rest of the peninsula, especially South Korea.

I present one more reason to visit the DMZ. Americans refer to the Korean War as 'The Forgotten War' for the simple fact that it doesn't often cross our minds. In our history classes, we jump from World War II to Vietnam with a passing mention of Korea. This is absurd for two reasons. One, over 100,000 Americans suffered casualties during the war. Two, the war is emblematic of a time when Americans looked at the rest of the world more charitably and fought to make it a better place. Perhaps Americans have become so disillusioned with seemingly endless, fruitless wars in the Middle East that we've given up being our brother's keeper. Let the rest of the world do what it wants, we've decided. Let's focus on ourselves. With the Korean War, though, it's hard to argue that South Korea didn't benefit from the help of the pluralistic efforts of the United Nations, with the Americans leading the charge. Today, 50 million people live in a country that democratically elects their government (or, more impressively, democratically removes people from power, as they did in 2017 with president Park Geun Hye), protects freedom of speech, and generates gigantic sums of wealth as a direct result of American assistance. Their prosperity certainly belongs to their own hard work and perseverance, but America helped clear the brush, so to speak. With our perpetual political dysfunction, angry domestic rhetoric, and a depressing slate of international news throwing the United States into dismal divisiveness, it's important to remember in places like the DMZ that, at least once, America stepped into a mess and measurably made the world a better place. How do we know? Just glance over the DMZ. South Korea has not forgotten, and neither should we.

A Summer of Choices

That Time We Decided to Stay Another Year

The summer heat and humidity came back in June with a vengeance, and I was once again arriving to work covered in sweat. Maria and I had been in South Korea for almost a year and things were beginning to make sense. We knew the bus system well and what took us where. We could navigate through downtown Daegu. Our Korean lessons were coming in handy, in that we could now easily order off a menu and even ask that the restaurant make a change ("no onions on my pizza, please"). Our vocabulary was expanding daily. Remember the militant sounding truck rolling through our neighborhood? The one that sounded as if the North Korean army was on its away? He was selling watermelons. *Subak*, he said. *Watermelons. Come get your watermelons. 5,000 won. 9,000 won for two!*

The new vocabulary range led to some interesting interactions. Maria, excited to use the Korean word for 'verb,' added too much emphasis on the beginning consonant. Rather than 'verb,' she was asking her students if they could identify the 'poop's in the sentence. Actually, a direct translation of the word, pronounced incorrectly, would be 'poop temple.' *Point to the poop temple in the sentence, please!*

I was a victim too. The 2014 World Cup was on, and with it numerous commercials for the tournament's sponsors. I believe it was an SK Telecom commercial that featured several small, cute animals on the bottom of the screen cheering what I thought was, at the time, '*subak, subak, subak*!'

"Why are they cheering 'watermelon?'" I asked Maria.

"I have no idea."

I took my concern to Ji Ho over a spaghetti dinner at his condo. I told him about the commercial and the watermelon. He hadn't seen it, and by the looks of it, thought I was insane. I went through the commercial again, in detail, and portrayed the dancing animals once more. "*Subak, subak, subak*, they say!"

A light in Ji Ho's brain flickered on. "Ah!" he exclaimed. "Not subak. *Baksu*. Applause. Baksu, baksu, baksu!"

We all shared a laugh. I hadn't heard the word 'baksu' before.

Ji Ho and I got along great, but his students were worse than ever. They were never focused, always rude, and beginning to seriously drain Ji Young and I. Whenever their class was scheduled to come in, we steeled ourselves for a hurricane and hoped they'd be receptive to whatever activities we had planned. That didn't happen often. Instead, it was one of those classes where I looked at the clock as much as the students. *Please God, deliver me from this pestilence.*

I will say that the class gave me one of my favorite memories of my time in South Korea. It was one of those days that Ji Ho's class was being particularly terrible. They would not shut up. They were downright hateful, or if they weren't they were the easily distractible and swayed type, complicit in their comrades being hateful toward us. It was clear we would get nothing done that day. Then, for what reason, I couldn't say, one of the ringleaders of the rebellion began singing the "Fast Food Song" by the Fast Food Rockers. Two more joined in, followed by three more. In seconds, the entire class was singing the song. If you've not heard it, the song, if you can call it that, is the type of gratingly infectious one hit wonder that people around the year 2000 seemed to embrace with minimal discernment. It's repetitive, it's fast, and it's awful, so naturally it's a staple of summer camps and kid's programs. The chorus comes with hand motions and goes like this:

A Pizza Hut. A Pizza Hut. Kentucky Fried Chicken and a Pizza Hut.

A Pizza Hut. A Pizza Hut. Kentucky Fried Chicken and a Pizza Hut.

McDonalds! McDonalds! Kentucky Fried Chicken and a Pizza Hut.

McDonalds! McDonalds! Kentucky Fried Chicken and a Pizza Hut.

I have no idea where they heard it. I haven't the foggiest how they learned it, but there I was with Ji Young standing in front of the classroom, with no control over the situation whatsoever, watching our class sing the "Fast Food Song." We shared an unspoken moment of 'let's lean into this' and wrote the lyrics on the white board for the few students who weren't joining along. The class was, after all, singing in English. It wasn't the worst song they could've chosen. We choreographed the hand motions and told them to start over. This carried us to the end of the period, and the students left in a happy mood. I never thought I'd say this, but I'm grateful for the existence of the "Fast Food Song"

I would use the song again for other classes that had too much time on their hands, especially with younger kids. It became the go-to time waster, although it had its uses as a warm-up activity or attention grabber. Much like the puppy song, the Fast Food Song easily got stuck in my head. It was the price I paid to get out of a class or two alive. Summer was approaching, and students were getting antsy.

In May, the big conversation piece among Native English Teachers in the August rotation is whether you are going to renew your contract. EPIK wants to know by May so they can spend the next couple months deciding how many new people to take on and where to put them. Also, it makes sense that teachers should have a pretty good sense of their goals by that time.

It wasn't a hard decision for us. There was nothing pressing us to return to the United States. In fact, it was the opposite. We'd only just paid off our credit card debt and were looking forward to more travel. Teachers who renew their contracts get a resigning bonus. Also, we loved Gail and Phillip and they were staying another year. All arrows were pointing toward a second year in South Korea, so we signed up for one.

Most people went home that summer during break to see their families. Columbus doesn't have a very large airport, so to fly from

South Korea to Columbus is prohibitively expensive. It would be over $2000 a person to fly to Columbus, and we'd only get about a week because of the layovers. Much to the sadness of our parents, and ourselves too, we would not see them or the United States for another year.

We were happy to stay in South Korea, but there came a point where we needed a minute in Western culture again. It was taxing on our brains to spend most of our waking lives in a different world, where we constantly needed to shift our expectations to match those of our surroundings. Every day in a foreign country, you must evaluate how you're speaking, how you're walking, how you're eating. Is what you're doing disrespectful in a way that doesn't exist where you're from? Even though our comfort bubbles had expanded tremendously, that didn't change the fact that the food, the work culture, and the country in general became tedious. For once, just once, it would be nice to walk down the sidewalk without so much as a second glance from a pointing child. "Waygook!" they say. *He doesn't belong!* That's not what they're saying, but that's what it feels like. *You're not at home*!

There's nothing wrong with South Korea that a Chipotle can't fix, but we were in danger of festering an overly critical attitude toward the country. It became all too easy to wish that South Korea would do some things the American way. I know the United States has plenty of problems of its own, but we're not completely useless. For instance, we do a reasonable job of putting trash cans in sensible places. I could not wrap my head around why downtown Daegu had, at best, three trash cans in the streets throughout an area of several square blocks. People still generated trash and had to put it somewhere, and that somewhere tended to be heaping piles on the ground. The United States also does a generally good job of zoning land to ensure that neighborhoods aren't next door to, let's say, a scrap metal dump that makes a lot of noise every morning. These are all pretty minor things, but these and other annoyances continued to accumulate. We needed some healthy time apart, to give our brains a break. You know, a proper vacation. We needed wide open spaces. We needed to get out of the humidity. We needed to eat steak (we weren't willing to pay $30 for average steak at Outback Steakhouse). Above all, we needed people who spoke English. There were cheap flights to Australia, and we agreed that would do just fine.

It was winter in Australia when we went in July, but a winter in Queensland is practically summer in some parts of the United States. We basked not only in the sun but the return to the Western world. Australian culture is approximate to American culture in that they drive everywhere (albeit on the left side of the road), eat large portions of meat, and are much more relaxed about personal appearance compared to places like South Korea. There are some key differences, however. For one, they let famously exotic animals fly and hop about as they please. On our walk to the beach from our bed and breakfast, there were cockatoos and lorikeets looking for food in the grass. Just sitting there, you know? A few feet from my ankles. Australians also indulge in meat pies, which, in one of the world's great mysteries, Americans haven't found a taste for. Seems right up our alley.

The Gold Coast, with its beaches and theme parks and souvenir shops, is more or less the Florida of Australia. With the help of our bed and breakfast hosts, we located an affordable but delicious steak house. At the Currumbin Wildlife Sanctuary, we held a koala while the keeper explained all the ways a koala could mess you up with its sharp claws and teeth. The koala, in my arms, looked at me with those beady little eyes with a sort of cheeky passivity, as if he wanted to say, "I could do those things, but I won't. But, you know, I could." We also found time to take in a whale watching tour, during which we followed not one but two humpback whales breaching together. How precious is it that these enormous creatures, possibly just for fun, will expend huge amounts of energy to jump out of the water? I admit I fought back tears. What can I say? Whales make me weepy. *What a beautiful world this is.* Back on land, we spent some quality hours on the soft, sunny beaches of Surfer's Paradise. We didn't go in the water, mind you – they've got stuff in there that'll kill you just by looking at you. In short, our time in Queensland, and Sydney for a spell, was a much-needed respite in a sunny land of English signage and kookaburras.

Perhaps it was too sunny, or there were too many kookaburras. When we arrived into Incheon, the sky was that same sticky, monochromatic gray when we first flew into the country. Everything, it seemed, was gray. The water was gray, the buildings were gray. It made everything seem dull, especially compared to a country of exceptional vibrancy like Australia. Neither of us were excited to be back. To make matters worse, all the trains to Daegu were sold out or standing room only. We had our suitcases with us, had flown for a long time, and were in no mood to stand for four hours. I still had Ha Young's number from Haus Guesthouse and texted her to see if she had room for us that night. She had exactly two beds left, so we took them. So, rather than take the train home, we took the subway into Itaewon in Seoul.

Maria and I were both in crummy moods. Neither of us were excited about returning to work, or Korea in general at that point in time. Australia had done its job only too well. All I could think about was the sunshine and the wildlife and 'Waltzing Matilda.' Haus Guesthouse turned everything around. A pair of amicable German dudes were passing through the area and were happy to share a conversation. Coincidentally, a young Korean woman who had majored in German was also staying the night. Maria and I watched, ping-ponging between the two sides of the conversation, enjoying the serendipity of the situation. I had to push the pause button and consider that, even a year prior, I'd never expected in my life to be sitting in a tiny guesthouse in Seoul listening to two Germans banter with a young Korean woman, in German! It was a marvelous opportunity to appreciate how wondrous and random life can be, and there's nothing to do but soak it in. Some friends of Ha Young's invited us all to a rooftop pasta dinner above the guesthouse. In one table there were, at the very least, Koreans, Americans, Germans, and a Russian. How dare I, for even a moment, consider that Korea wasn't interesting?

Gail and Phillip had both gone home for their summer breaks, and they had similar initial misgivings about returning to Korea. Within weeks, though, we were all back in the thick of it with classes. We again developed cravings for Korean foods. We sought out cultural experiences again. We let go, for the time being, of the minutiae of life in South Korea. It wouldn't be long before we felt at home once again, appreciative of our lives in a foreign country.

If Ji Young taught me one thing, it was how to complain in

Korean. I suppose this is because Ji Young herself is a bit of a whiner. Every morning, it seemed, her greeting as either she or I walked into the room was "Hi Metyu! (Complaint)." It was always too hot or too cold. She was always tired, hungry, or bored. I'm a bit of a seasoned whiner myself, so I ate these phrases up either because I understood them in context or Ji Young told me what she'd said. I'm not especially good at picking up languages, but I'm proud that I learned how to complain in a different language, with finesse even. She taught me an addition to the phrase in order to say "it's so/I'm so ____, I could die!" We bonded over our shared interest in discontentment.

The best thing to gripe about in July and August is the weather, which takes a sharp turn into monsoon season. For about two months, there's a good chance of rain every day, and I don't mean a drippy rain shower or some atmospheric drizzle. It comes down hard. One morning when walking to school, I was caught in the middle of a torrential downpour. I had an umbrella, but it was useless; the sidewalks were inundated with rain and the wind was blowing in my face. By the time I reached school, my pants were drenched. There was nothing I could do but wait for them to dry. Coming home later that day, the typically tiny creek that flows through the middle of Maecheon was a roaring, muddy river. Gone were the sidewalks along its edges. If one were to stumble into the water (an unlikely prospect, but not impossible) it could mean a swift end.

Griping wasn't the only thing I understood those days. With repetition and a stronger vocabulary, I followed along with most of what Ji Young said in the classroom. When she spoke to the students in Korean, I understood what page she wanted them to flip to, what activity to do, and how to do it. I no longer waited to hear my name as a cue to say my part; I pounced right as Ji Young finished whatever she was saying. We'd also developed good timing with PowerPoint; Ji Young instinctively knew when to change the slide as I was talking, or when we were playing a game. In general, our co-teaching abilities had leveled up.

It was good timing too, because summer camp was just around the corner. Other than deskwarming, winter and summer breaks are synonymous with week-long English camps when students come to school for a couple hours a day rather than sitting at home. Like after school classes, English camps are an opportunity for Native English Teachers to think outside the box -- to invent clever themes and activities to encourage students to practice English, if even just peripherally. For instance, our winter camp was Winter Olympics themed to coincide with the 2014 Winter Olympics in Sochi. I developed a 'finger curling' game where students flicked 1 won coins (pennies, basically) to achieve the best score as configured by the rules of curling. To play, students had to endure a lesson, in English, on the rules of the game. This involved learning some new vocabulary: slide, knock, curling stone. So, you see, they did learn something before they flicked pennies for 15 minutes.

For summer camp, I chose to develop a lesson plan around Vikings to celebrate the release of *How to Train Your Dragon 2*. Students built paper Viking helmets, translated 'runes' into English, and designed Viking shields. We talked about the various types of dragons in the movies and their special abilities. They even generated their own Viking names, dumb names like 'Blast the Dragon Keeper' or 'Burp the Hard Cheese' based on the first letters of their Korean names. These, of course, were complete gibberish and the kids didn't have a clue what they meant. All the more fun for me.

Of course, the main idea of English camps, for me anyway, is that the students have fun and be creative. Their schedules are kept so busy year round. English camps are an opportunity to break the monotony between school and *hagwons*.

There is perhaps no aspect of Korean culture more loathed by children and cherished by adults as hagwons, or 'private academies.' Many of my students, as soon as the last school bell rang, climbed into small yellow buses that whisked them to hagwons to study math, science, Chinese, English, or any other subjects their parents deemed necessary. There are also extracurricular hagwons. Walking to the dry cleaners one day, I passed a music hagwon with the door open. I spotted a fifth-grade girl I knew singing to a piano accompaniment. Soccer hagwons were perhaps the one private academy the students didn't mind.

Between school and hagwons, students spend an average of 13 hours a day studying. It recently became law that hagwons must close by 10pm, but students may continue studying in their bedrooms into the night, and then doze an average of five hours. They wake up the next morning to do it all over again, with dreary but attentive eyes. This was the primary reason I kept English camps silly and included games as often as possible in my lesson plans; they may have been the only games they played all day. It's not just older kids who attend hagwons; in 2017, the Korea Institute of Child Care and Education revealed that 83% of 5-year-olds receive private education, attending extra classes five times a week. These kids are practically leaving the womb with homework.

The existence of hagwons is tied directly to the importance of passing the *Suneung*, or College Scholastic Ability Test. Every fall, the country stops in its tracks for the test. As high school seniors walk to their schools, parents and well-wishers hand out *yut*, a good-luck taffy that will, perhaps, allow the accumulative factoids from years of studying to 'stick' to their brains during the exam. To not disturb test takers, businesses may delay opening times to keep traffic to a minimum. Air traffic routes are rerouted to avoid flying over schools during the listening portion of the exam. Meanwhile, parents and grandparents hike to temples or attend church to pray for their children, and then wait outside the school until the test ends eight hours after it began. The test is, in the greatest meaning of the phrase, a big deal. It determines which, if any, universities students are qualified to attend. In reality, they all covet a spot in one of three universities: Seoul National University, Korea University, or Yonsei University. If one wants to work for Samsung or any of the other massive conglomerates that practically run the Korean economy, it's perceived as necessary to graduate from one of these three. Graduate from anywhere else, and you might as well start making different plans. Students can take the test again after a year, but after at least 12 years of rigorous education, the idea of another year spent cramming for a test doesn't sit well with most.

For an after-school class one day, Maria Skyped with her sister and nieces in Oklahoma so her students could ask questions about school life in the United States. Eventually, the subject came to after school activities.

"What do you do after school?" a student asked Madalyn, in 4th grade at the time.

Madalyn took a moment to consider, grasping for concrete answers. "I go to gymnastics? I do homework. I read. I don't know."

The students didn't know the English translation for hagwon, but Maria deduced that's what they were getting at. She explained that students in the United States don't typically go to private academies. If anything, students struggling in a particular subject may get private tutoring, but that's it.

"Hul!" the class moaned in unison.

"I want to kill myself," said one girl. The class moaned again in agreement.

While it's likely the girl was being flippant, suicide in children is no laughing matter. South Korea has, by a considerable margin, the highest suicide rate in the developed world. In a country as healthy yet stressed as South Korea, the number one cause of death in those aged 10 to 39 is suicide. In 2012, only 60% of students in South Korea agreed that they were content with their school experience. The average among developed countries is 80%.

The obvious solution, it seems, is to cut down on the number of hours spent studying, but it's not that simple. In a country with limited natural resources, the economy progresses only with the ingenuity of the people. Their chief commodity is brain power. It's one way South Korea, in a matter of decades, went from one of the poorest countries in the world to one of the richest. Perhaps one day, they'll figure out a way to balance happiness into the equation.

By the time lunch rolled around, the camp was over for the day and the students went back home. I was still legally contracted to stick around until a normal quitting time hour, so Ji Young stuck around and we ate lunch together. Since the cafeteria was closed for the summer, this was our opportunity to have food delivered. Every day, as the students were wrapping up their last activity, Ji Young would pull up some menus on the computer.

"What do you want for lunch?" she'd ask. We'd eventually arrive at what we wanted for the day and she'd make a call as I kept the kids busy.

It's time I acquainted you with Korean junk food. Delicious, plentiful, and above all cheap, Korean junk food is nearly always available via 24-hour diners and fast-casual restaurants, the kind of haunts that a lower-middle class corner of the city like Maecheon had in multitude. Even better, most of these places deliver. You give them a call, they make the order, and they hand the food to a motorcycle driver who drives primarily on the sidewalk to avoid traffic. Your food arrives as hot as if you'd ordered it in the restaurant, and most places pack banchon side dishes to boot. It's a great system, so long as you aren't between the motorcycle driver and his destination.

But I don't want to smear the good name of Korean delivery drivers; there is dedication there that does not exist in other professions. A peculiar difference between American and Korean delivery is that Korean restaurants still provide their delivered food in permanent dishes; your ramen appears in the same bowl it would appear in had you eaten in the restaurant. This requires the driver to stop by twice: once to drop off the food, and once to pick up the dishes. Ji Young and I would take the food to her classroom, put on some Maroon 5 (her choice, not mine), eat our lunch and set our dishes in a pile outside the door. Later in the day, when no one was looking, the driver would return and take the pile. The tooth fairy is rarely so devoted to her craft, but that's the gig for the Korean delivery driver, the Hermes of fried chicken.

Yes, fried chicken is widely available, but my favorite Korean junk food is kimbap: an easy-to-eat roll of rice, veggies, egg, crab meat, and whatever else you'd like wrapped in thin, flaky seaweed. It appears like an inverted roll of sushi, but with the important distinction that there is no raw fish inside. Popular additions include tuna, kimchi, bulgogi, or even cheese. The best part? If you pay 3,000 won for a roll of kimbap, there'd better be something special about it. On numerous occasions, Maria and I ate dinner, a roll of kimbap each, for less than 5,000 won. That's less than a combo meal at McDonalds, which also delivers, by the way.

But there's so much more to delivery than kimbap. Kimchi fried rice became a quick favorite, made perfect with the addition of salty tuna. Bibimbap, the closest thing to a national dish besides kimchi, literally means 'mixed rice.' It comes in a bowl (a hot one if you order it 'dolsot' style) and combines about the same ingredients found in kimbap with gochujang, a spicy red-pepper paste. If I was feeling especially ballsy about eating spicy food, I'd order kimchi jjigae, which is a kimchi stew.

Occasionally, we'd order pizza instead of Korean food. Ji Young's enthusiasm for Korean pizza was a lot higher than mine. In Daegu, anyway, unless you pony up for Domino's, the options are all Korean and they have their own preferences when it comes to pizza. They come with a side of sweet pickles, for starters. I imagine the first person in Korea to make a pizza rounded up toppings that, on the surface, were American or Italian but didn't altogether belong on a pizza. Mayonnaise comes to mind, and potato wedges. Both are perfectly fine things to eat in the right circumstances -- a Midwestern casserole, perhaps -- but have no place on a pizza. Also, Korean pizza joints have a tendency of including toppings that weren't on the description. A cheese pizza, for example, may come with onions and corn. With such wonky toppings, Korean pizza really is the epitome of junk food: garbage thrown together and thrown into an oven for a couple minutes.

There are more upscale pizzerias available, but they don't deliver. They do, however, still cater to some Korean sensibilities. Some chains will provide honey in which to dip cheese pizza. I tried it; it's not terrible, but it's not right. What's more, when Maria asked her coworkers why Koreans do this, their answer was "because that's the way Italians do it." As an Italian-American, I took umbrage with this statement. I quickly sent a Facebook message to my Italian relatives in Milan, asking if they'd ever in their life dipped their pizza into honey. I was sure the answer was 'no,' but I'd never been to Italy myself and for all I knew I was assuming. I was not. Their answer was a swift and resounding 'never.' It was just as I'd thought: I knew pizza better than Koreans. My cultural supremacy was put in its place, though, when an Italian cousin heard tell of Americans using barbecue sauce in pizza. Surely, Americans wouldn't allow such a travesty to occur. I was guilty as charged. Barbecue chicken pizza is delicious and I won't deny it. There's some in my freezer right now. There's also the fact that I'm only a quarter Italian anyway, which makes me roughly as Italian as barbecue pizza. The moral of the story, I suppose, is to enjoy pizza the way you like it, but maybe know how the original pizza eaters, the Italians, make it. But still, potato wedges?

Do You Know Jeju?

That Time We Climbed a Volcano and Visited a Sex Theme Park

At the beginning of every fifth grade class, two students could ask me any question they liked. The Native English Teacher before me started the tradition and I thought it was a swell idea. The day's students were pre-assigned, presumably giving the students time to think of an interesting question to ask, and they really could ask anything. They didn't even have to ask in English; it was more important to me, for this exercise, that they ask something creative. Over two years, I got some great questions: What is the hardest thing about living in Korea? When are you happiest? Was Maria your first love? But for every thoughtful question like this, I got about 179 dumb questions: Do you run a store? Do you have a watch? Do you like water? One of the most common questions I got, because kids couldn't remember what had been asked, was 'do you know Jeju?'

Jeju Island, a small volcanic island roughly 40 miles south of the Korean peninsula, is to many Korean kids, and probably a large number of adults, the shining star of vacation destinations. It's the first, and in some cases only 'exotic' vacation option open to Koreans who either can't afford to travel internationally or have no intention to, although as Korea's smallest and southernmost province, it's about as exotic to Koreans as New Orleans is to Americans, probably even less so. It's much like asking someone from Ohio if they've travelled overseas and their response being,

"No, but I've been to Florida twice." And Koreans love Jeju at least as much as Ohioans love Florida. In 2017, the air route between Seoul and Jeju was the busiest in the world with, on average, 178 departures every day. By comparison, the next busiest route - Sydney to Melbourne - notched about 149 flights a day.

Jeju is subtropical, despite its nickname being the 'Hawaii of Korea," but is warm enough in the winters for palm trees to survive. The island is dominated by the imposing Mt. Hallasan, a sleeping shield volcano and the highest mountain in South Korea. With so much volcano and so little island, Jeju is listed as a UNESCO World Heritage Site for its extensive lava caves and other geological curiosities. New7Wonders of Nature included the island on its 2011 list, the result of a worldwide popular vote to select seven new natural wonders. Obvious choices such as the Grand Canyon or Great Barrier Reef failed to make the final list, letting you know just what kind of authority this list demands, but that shouldn't diminish Jeju's likeability.

There are a couple routines for a family vacationing in Jeju. First, it's expected that the parents purchase boxes of fruit-flavored chocolates that are bountiful in every Jeju gift shop and report back to work with them. Second, everyone raves about the black pig barbeque that is endemic to the island, so visitors always partake. Third, the family must cover themselves head to toe with clothing at the beach. Koreans value fair skin, yet they travel hundreds of miles to a beach to avoid the sun.

In September, Koreans celebrate the harvest festival Chuseok in much the same way Americans celebrate Thanksgiving: gather with family to eat way too much food, or travel as far away from them as possible because it's a long weekend and 'we just want to keep it small.' Jeju is a popular destination for the latter group. Maria and I joined a guided tour to Jeju to take advantage of the long holiday. We'd been once before on a rainy March weekend, but decided the island warranted a longer, warmer, sunnier try.

The timing of the trip, though, came at a gloomy season of soul-searching for the country. On April 16, 2014, off the southwestern coast of Korea, the junior officer at the helm of the Sewol ferry en route from Incheon to Jeju made an erroneous turn and capsized the ship. The evacuation efforts made by the crew were disastrously uncoordinated, with several employees having little or no training in safety procedures. On board for a field trip to the island were 324 students from Danwon High School, who were told by the crew that their cabins would be the safest place for them to stay. In the end, of the over 300 people that drowned that day, 250 of them were high school students, nearly an entire grade level gone. Ten teachers also lost their lives.

The tragedy only grew darker. Two days after the sinking of the Sewol, the Vice Principal of Danwon High School hung himself with his own belt, overtaken by grief that he had survived while so many students had died. The Principal lost his job by June. For months, the entire country was in a state of mourning. School trips were cancelled, either out of respect or, God forbid, should another accident take place. This decision in turn would hurt the nation's economy, since people weren't attending 'fun' things anymore. The national government mandated that government employees, teachers included, spend their summer holidays in the country to help the economy recover. The knee-jerk proclamation, declared without consideration to existing vacation plans, was rescinded days later.

Of the terrible number of victims, the ship's Captain, Lee Jun Seok, and 14 other senior crew members were not among them. They had left their passengers and crew members to perish in the sea, the most apparent in a long list of ghastly decisions. Captain Lee was sentenced to 36 years in prison for abandoning his ship and the souls still on board. Parents wanted his head. Chief engineer Park Gio Ho was sentenced to 30 years in prison for not saving two cooks he could've helped escape. The other 13 received smaller sentences proportionate to their crimes.

The investigation into the sinking pulled the entire tragedy into some strange waters. The ferry, it turned out, was hauling over three times as much weight as it was designed for. The crew had even drained ballast water -- used to maintain stability -- to make room for more cargo. There was so much cargo, 3,608 tons of it to be precise, there wasn't room to properly fasten it to the boat. Additionally, some cabins had been filled with marble. In short, the Sewol was perilously top heavy. It was incredible the boat sailed as far as it did.

Why was the Sewol so overburdened with cargo? Because someone was getting rich, of course. Korea's Supreme Court charged ferry operator Kim Han Sik, president of the ferry's Chonghaejin Marine Company, to seven years in prison for not preventing the ship from being overloaded. The owner, a son of the enigmatic and wealthy Yoo Byung Eun, was leeching money from the company, forcing Mr. Kim to cram as much cargo as possible in his ferries to make up for the lost cash.

Yoo Byung Eun was a piece of work, a combination of Donald Trump excess and L. Ron Hubbard lunacy. His resume of eccentric interests – environmental activism, martial arts, painting, photography, poetry, entrepreneurism, French village purchasing – make Vladimir Putin look pedestrian by comparison. Yoo became a Christian, of sorts, in 1961 and by 1962 founded the Evangelical Baptist Church of Korea, regarded by other Christian organizations as a cult. His followers, the Salvationists, numbered around 100,000 in 2014 at the time of the Sewol disaster. The Yoo family also indulged in intense business accumulation, owning some 70 companies over three continents. They used these to fraudulently siphon off money and build luxurious compounds. You know, a thing a cult leader would do. The money he'd taken from the Chonghaejin Marine Company left crews with little money for safety training, hence the irresponsible decision by inexperienced crew members to keep high school students in their cabins while the ship sank.

None of this mattered to the Salvationists when word got around that Yoo, on the run shortly after the ferry sank, was wanted by police for possible embezzlement and, tangentially, the overloading of the Sewol. In early June, 9,000 police showed up at the church to arrest Yoo, the largest manhunt in South Korean history, but they were met by hundreds of his loyal devotees protesting the hunt and threatening to die as martyrs. In the meantime, Yoo escaped.

And here's the strangest part. On June 12, police confirmed that a decomposing body they'd found in a countryside ditch belonged to Yoo. He had little with him – some bottles of wine, moisturizer, a copy of the book he'd written, a magnifying glass and extra shirt – and wore an Italian suit. The cause of death is still unknown. It would be months before Captain Lee and the others were sentenced, but for the time being, the Sewol saga ended mysteriously in the grass of a plum orchard.

From a political standpoint, the Sewol incident was the first major blow to President Park Geun Hye's popularity. Although South Korea had suffered tragic accidents before, many of them similarly tied to mismanagement, corruption, and cutting corners, the people wondered why, in the second decade of the 21st century, one of the wealthiest countries in the world still suffered these preventable accidents. Her administration's handling of the crisis was largely criticized as incompetent, not unlike how President Bush bore much of the brunt for FEMA's bumbling response to Hurricane Katrina in 2005. She never recovered politically. By 2017, she was impeached and removed from office for an unrelated but just as interesting charge of corruption. Her approval rating before leaving office was an impressively awful four percent.

With those sunny auspices aside, let's get to Jeju.

Our coach bus was scheduled to leave central Daegu at 2am to make the early morning ferry in Wando. We lived on the outskirts of town, where it would be difficult to catch a taxi at that hour and impossible to take public transportation, so we decided to stay downtown for the evening. After eating a late dinner and getting some drinks we found a DVD bang, where you can rent a movie and a room in which to watch it. As a place with cheap room rentals that frequently feature comfortable beds, DVD bangs have earned a reputation as mini Love Motels. We found one in downtown Daegu that was reasonably clean and didn't make me feel icky within 12 seconds. It had a decent selection of movies, but in this case we only needed a place to doze for a few hours before walking to the bus stop five minutes away. We selected one of the *Lord of the Rings* movies because it was long and would allow us to stay in the room until we needed to. The young man behind the counter took our selection, popped it in the appropriate machine, and told us which room to go to. As rooms go, ours wasn't the worst DVD bang room I'd seen. Some have uncomfortable couches. Others I wouldn't touch with a hazmat suit. The room was just large enough to hold a king-sized bed and a box of tissues. A projector screen covered the entire wall facing the bed. It's actually a great way to watch a movie, given that's what you're there to do. A purple mink blanket covered the bed, so we decided to keep it that way and doze over the covers while Frodo and Sam got lost in the mountains.

A few hours later, with several minutes left in the movie, our alarms jolted us awake. We grabbed our bags and headed to the bus stop, where it was clear there would be two kinds of people on this trip: those that were sleepy, and those that weren't. A large group of Afrikaans friends had clearly spent their evening drinking rather than looking for some way to get some sleep. Most were friendly enough, but they were all very loud and a bit inconsiderate toward the rest of the tour group. While most of us found our seats on the bus and made preparations for a long, sleep-inducing ride, this group of friends stood outside the bus to smoke. When it was clear it was time to go, they couldn't quite put together why, as the last people on the bus, there were no seats left that were together. In happier circumstances, their separation would have ended their conversation, but they were not the kind to let several rows of half-asleep people deter them from continuing. If it hadn't been for our tour guide, a thoughtful Korean-American woman, reminding them that there were other people on board the bus, they might've gabbed all the way to Wando. As it was, their alcohol settled into their systems and they submitted to the wee hours of the morning like the rest of us.

We arrived at Wando's ferry terminal at the crack of dawn. I don't sleep much on moving vehicles, so I was happy to get off the bus and stretch. The next step in the journey, a four-hour ferry to Jeju, carried some trepidation with it. With the Sewol incident still fresh in our minds, the feeling wasn't unlike taking an airplane in the wake of 9/11.

The ferry ride, obviously, was a success. The crew did their best to lighten the mood on board with games and trivia. Most of us on the tour couldn't participate in the trivia for language barrier reasons, but the games were easy enough to catch on to and the crew made an effort to include us. There was a Dunkin Donuts on board as well, and nothing makes people more complacent than donuts. It was actually all a very delightful ride.

There are around 100 museums and theme parks on Jeju, some of them little more than random collections of stuff. There's the Jeju Chocolate Museum, the Teddy Bear Museum, Hello Kitty Island – you name it, they've got it and charge admission to see it. On an island full of interesting geography, our tour's first stop was a cultural curiosity called Love Land. If you go to Jeju without stopping at Love Land, you might as well not go at all.

Being the go-to honeymoon destination for a conservative country such as South Korea puts Jeju in an awkward spot. Many couples arrive having never done the deed. Some barely know each other, having only met months prior. The island, then, has the exciting responsibility of not only encouraging but perhaps educating couples about sex. That's where Love Land comes in. Opened in 2004 with sculptures from students at Seoul's Hongik University, Love Land is billed as South Korea's only erotic 'theme park.' For what it's worth, there are other penis parks in Korea. What makes a park a theme park and not a garden is nebulous and, I would guess, made up on the spot. There are no rides, unfortunately, but the gardens and art are enough to persuade any couple that sex is fun.

The bus dropped us off at the entrance and we ambled into the park, expecting to see throngs of giggling newlyweds posing in front of the suggestive statues. Instead, most of the paying customers that day were old couples, each seemingly a facetious wife and a surly husband with his hands behind his back. Women posed in front of penises, usually pointing and laughing. Whether they were laughing at the statues or their husbands was unclear.

The statues ranged from irreverently sensual to explicitly pornographic. It seemed when the university students who sculpted the park were in doubt, the default was 'make it a penis.' Even the door handles to the bathrooms were phallic. Children under 18 are not permitted inside the park, thank goodness. A statue of Scooby Doo doing the naughty while getting the thumbs up from Shaggy feeling up a female might have scarred some schoolchildren for life. In the center of the gardens was an enormous horizontal penis with a mosaic facade; naturally, we climbed on top of it. In the back of the park is a gift shop with trinkets and souvenirs to match the theme. We selected a stress reliever shaped like a boob. We had roughly an hour to enjoy the gardens, which is all it takes, really. Feeling thoroughly over-educated on adjummas and their sexual fantasies, we hopped back on the bus, the Afrikaans last again, and were taken to our ocean-view hotel before an evening out on the beach.

For me, the education I received on Jeju was what a real beach ought to look like. Before traveling overseas, my only experiences with beaches were those on the Southeastern coast of the United States. I couldn't quite put my finger on what I didn't like about the cold, cloudy water, steep drop offs, and rocky sand, but something told me I wasn't a beach person. That was until I went to Jeju, where many of the beaches slope gradually into the warm, clear ocean and the sand is fine and soft. Hyeopjae Beach was the first we visited. We waded out with some friends into the tropical water, which after walking out for five minutes was still only at my knees. There were no thunderous waves crashing into us every seven seconds, only soothing, gentle ripples. We sat down in the water, the sea tickling our chins. Tiny Biyangdo island sits about a mile out and frames the serene setting. Back on shore, hawkers sell ice cream and fish stands sell grilled mackerel. That's my kind of beach.

Another interesting beach was Jungmun Beach on the southern shore, although it contradicts nearly all my aforementioned preferences. The waves do tend to get pretty powerful at Jungmun, so much so that when late afternoon comes around the riptide becomes too strong and lifeguards patrol the sandbar to make sure no one goes back in. The sand is also volcanic and clingy; my legs were much blacker and rockier than they were before marching down the cliff to the beach. Other than those minor issues, the beach is lovely and perhaps the most tropic on an island that is not in the strictest sense 'tropical.' This alone is probably why Jungmun is Jeju's most popular beach and the center of a large resort complex. A steep, leafy cliff backs the sand; if not for a ritzy hotel on the next cliff, the beach would have a very 'lost world' allure, as if you'd stumbled upon a forgotten corner of Jurassic Park with jet skis and banana boats.

Between the beaches, Maria and I decided to do something stupid and climb a volcano. Most of the tour group slept in before exploring the damp, alien Manjanggul lava cave. We'd seen it on our previous trip – its smooth, wavy walls give the impression that an enormous serpentine monster had tunneled through molten lava to make a nest. Instead, we joined a hardy subgroup to hike the Seongpanak trail up Hallasan. At about 6400 feet high, it's not an especially tall mountain, but it maintains a commanding presence on the island. The tour guide assured us that the Seongpanak trail was the easiest ascent up, albeit the longest at six miles. There are steeper, more scenic hikes to the peak but Maria and I liked the sound of "easiest.' It was not, however, easy.

The first couple hours are simple enough with a gradual incline through a green, monotonous forest. Once the rock steps set in, it didn't matter what there was to see because my attention was on my feet. Each step had to be precise, lest I wanted to reach the summit with a large knot on my forehead. Being the easiest trail, Seongpanak is also the most popular. The entire hike up is spent in line with other hikers. By the time we reached the Jindallaebat Shelter, about three-fourths of the way up, we'd climbed nearly 2500 feet. The shade was sparse on the shelter's wooden benches and the rest was not always a comfortable one. We ate a packed lunch, guzzled some Gatorade, and tried not to sweat to death in the intense sun. We eventually convinced ourselves that as tired as we were, it would be lame not to reach the summit after this much effort so we rejoined the slog up the trail. We'd finished the easy part of the easy trail. Now it was another 1500 feet up to the top.

After over four grueling hours of looking either at a strangely uninteresting forest or our weary feet, the trail broke through the tree line and reached a series of winding, wooden platforms and stairs. The air was cooler, the clouds blocked some of the sun, and the summit was within sight. Although we were still heading up, the view was quite different than anything we'd seen in Korea and we enjoyed the hike. We'd entered a moor that wouldn't have looked out of place in the British Isles, with nothing but rocks and shrubs and little mountain flowers. We took the flights of stairs a few at a time until at last we crested the summit and looked down below at the dormant volcano crater. Hundreds of other hikers had claimed the best spots, picnicking on kimbap or dozing in the mountain air. Their candy-colored hiking clothes dotted the rim like the sugary frost of a cereal bowl. We found a place to sit and marveled at the crater lake hundreds of feet below, which looked little more than a puddle.

From Hallasan's summit, Jeju's unique geology is more apparent. The island is famous for its parasitic cones, baby volcanic hills caused by baby volcanic eruptions along the main volcano's flanks. It's not unusual for volcanoes to have a handful of these cones dotting their periphery. Hallasan has 368 of them, giving the entire island a severe case of acne. We could see many of them at once from the summit.

Because of our slowness, we couldn't dawdle for long. We snapped some pictures, ate a snack, and began our descent. While the going up was certainly harder, the going down wasn't as easy as I would've liked. Again, it was imperative that we look at our feet as we let gravity do much of the work. One false step and we'd stumble down the rocky stairs. It was in the middle of the afternoon and there were fewer people on the trail. It was too late to make the ascent, and most making the descent had a head start on us. My legs were tired, and I feared that each step down would be the one where my knees buckled and I collapsed. By some miracle, both of us made it down the mountain minus any embarrassing stumbles, although my bandana was saturated with sweat. The visitor center at the bottom was still busy when we finished our trip up and down the mountain, a total of almost ten hours on the trail. We found another member of our tour group who was slow like us and split a taxi to our hotel, where the lava tube-goers had long since returned and retired to the pool.

Before our ferry back to the mainland, we had time to take in one last beach on the island's northern coast. Since it was the off-season, the beach wasn't very crowded and most of the service buildings were closed. There was only a disgusting bathroom open in which to change into our swimsuits. The bathroom notwithstanding, Gwakji beach was as bucolic and relaxing as the others, perhaps more so because there were fewer people. The sand was fine, the waves gentle, and the water clear. I was, however, beginning to tire of beaches. I can only stand in the water or lay in the sun doing nothing for so long. I'm a creature of activity. What kept my interest level high was a fish and chips stand just behind the beach. Our tour guide warned us that they sell out often, and if that we wanted to eat lunch there we'd better do it early. We heeded her warning and jumped in line around 11:30, when they still had plenty of food and a fridge full of bottled beverages. We sat in the sand eating our lunch and sipping hard apple cider while much of the rest of the group, including the obnoxious Afrikaans pals, stood in a much longer line and bitched about not getting lunch when the food ran out. I had no sympathy. The group had been tiresome throughout the trip with their inconsideration toward others. The rest of the South Africans avoided them. One or two even apologized on behalf of them. Perhaps it was their lackluster lunch or the copious sun we'd soaked in, but the Afrikaans were silent along with everyone else on the ferry back to the peninsula and the bus to Daegu. It only took five days.

I'd be remiss if I did not give special mention to the island's famed woman divers, otherwise known as Haenyeo. For generations, these women have been the breadwinners of their families. Upwards of 100 times a day, they dive into the often frigid Korea Strait up to 40 feet down and, with nothing more than goggles, a pair of flippers and kickass lungs, collect conches, abalone, and other seafood. Adding to the impressive feat is that 84 percent of them are at least 60 years old, the last of a dying breed. In 2015, the youngest Haenyeo, or 'sea woman,' was 38. Only about 4,000 are left, compared to around 26,000 in the 1960's. It's treacherous work, obviously, but it has determined so much of the island's culture that in 2016, UNESCO inscribed it on their Representative List of the Intangible Cultural Heritage of Humanity, which is a mouthful to say 'this lifestyle matters.' Unless you are a sea urchin, it's not easy to observe them work, but amble along the coast, amongst the lava rock fences and vegetable patches, and eventually you'll spot an orange buoy or two about 50 feet out to sea. A head will pop up with a catch, tread water for a moment, and then duck back down. That is their work. Just off the sea cliffs of 'Sunrise Peak,' one of those volcanic pimples next to the ocean, the Haenyeo have one of many stalls where they sell their catch. After climbing to the top of the peak and looking at the green crater, we wandered over to the stall to see if there was anything to my taste. I don't eat much seafood that isn't fish, so none of it looked appetizing to me. It was also expensive, which is understandable since women are literally dying to grab this food. The women working the stall, all at least 200 years old and as sturdy as the sea cliffs behind me, were a no nonsense bunch, so I didn't even pretend that I was going to buy something. I glanced at the catch and then moved on. For the sake of these women and their way of life, I hope Koreans will do differently.

A Gutenberg Documentary

That Time I Was On Korean TV

I don't mean to brag, but I'm pretty much the world's foremost talent in pointing at things in Korean documentaries about Gutenberg. There are at least two other people that are in the running, but luckily I'm a writer and they are not. To earn this superlative, I had to be a white guy in South Korea and know the right people.

This opportunity came about one afternoon when I stepped into the apartment after work. Maria always beat me home, and we typically talked about our days or what weird, unprofessional conversation she had with her co-teacher, who liked to talk about sex. One day, though, her co-teacher wished to pass on some news.

"Her husband knows a guy who knows a guy that is looking for foreign men to shoot a video this Saturday," Maria said. "You're supposed to find some friends to come too."

"What's it about?" I asked.

"I don't know," she replied. "She doesn't know either. It's up in Seoul and pays 200,000 won."

That changed my tone a bit. 200,000 won, just under $200, isn't a bad haul for a day. "Can you find out more about what it is?"

"I'll try, but you have to decide soon."

When traveling, you have the option every day to do something or nothing. Almost without exception, it's your responsibility to do the 'something.' Maybe it'll be a terrible experience, maybe it'll be an awesome experience, but it will certainly be a memorable experience, which is the best kind of souvenir to be had. So, with that spirit, I said yes to the mystery filming thing. I called Phillip and told him he should do it too, and with a similar spirit, he agreed. What's the worst it could be? Porn, probably. My guess was that it was a promotional video of some kind and they needed foreign people to say how awesome living in Korea was and why we loved everything about Korean culture.

Information trickled down to us throughout the week. The following afternoon, Maria extracted that the filming was a documentary (phew, no porn) about Johannes Gutenberg and his printing press (damn, no porn). I assumed they needed white guys to play the part of Johnny G. and his helpers. I could do that. They'd pick us up at our apartments at 9:00am. They also needed our height, hair color, and a head shot.

The next day, Maria discovered a miscommunication. Filming wouldn't take place in Seoul but north of Seoul in a town called Paju. That's where I hit the pause button. North of Seoul? There's not a lot of South Korea north of Seoul. Pretty soon you start hitting North Korea. Instantly, visions of kidnapping and ransoms and green, moth eaten uniforms flashed before my eyes. How did we know these people again? How were they connected to my wife's co-teacher's husband? Maria pried a bit more, but found few concrete answers. The husband worked for Daegu Health College, that much we knew, but we still weren't sure of the connection between him and this filming crew. Maria asked her co-teacher what the likelihood was of me and Phillip being shipped up to North Korea. The response she got was a giggle. I looked up Paju on the map and noticed that one could practically trip over a flower bed into the DMZ.

Saturday finally rolled around and so did 9:00am. I was ready but my transportation was not. I glanced nervously out the window for my ride, but saw nothing. Did they change their minds? Was I glad? It didn't matter. At 9:30am, a commercial white van pulled up. I went downstairs and was greeted by two young Korean men. We exchanged *annyeonghaseo*s and I got in the van, which was otherwise empty of people but full of video equipment.

Could be a trick, I thought. *To create the illusion that we're filming something. Or maybe we are filming something: a high-quality hostage video. And where's Phillip?*

I asked the two guys up front if we'd be picking up Phillip. They looked at each other like they didn't understand a word I was saying, which was 100% the situation. To recap, I was in a white van with two non-English speaking strangers without Phillip heading to the border with North Korea to film what I was really hoping would not be a hostage video. Gutenberg pornography was starting to sound like a reasonable compromise.

I texted Phillip to see what was up. He was in another van. *Divide and conquer.* My van stopped a few minutes later outside the health college. What I hoped would be another foreigner to glean information from was another pair of ajeossi's carrying a box of sandwiches. *Enough to take us across the border.* I smiled and bowed and they did the same. Luck would have it that one of these gentlemen spoke halfway decent English and explained that we would rendezvous with the other van at a rest stop.

I relaxed a bit. *This is starting to sound like a legitimate plan.*

On the way to the rest stop, I asked as much as I could about the filming. I was correct in assuming that I and the other westerners they rounded up would be portraying Gutenberg and his printing press sidekicks. The documentary would outline how Gutenberg allegedly stole the idea of the printing press from Korea and took credit for the idea. "Is that so?" my euro-centric worldview said, crossing its' arms.

We pulled into the rest stop where the other van, and Phillip, was waiting for us. The Koreans distributed the sandwiches and we snacked before our long drive up to Paju. Rest stops in Korea, the bigger ones, anyway, are one-stop travel shops where motorists can fill up the car, grab some lunch in the cafeteria or other food stalls available, shop for hiking clothes, and take some coffee to go. Korean highways don't have a ton of exits, and the exits don't have rows of fast food joints and gas stations. These rest stops, similar to those found along toll roads in America, are the only option. In celebration of the Pope's imminent arrival in Seoul, this particular rest stop featured a cardboard cut-out of him for people to pose with. When in Rome.

Sandwiches devoured, the crews switched vans and Phillip and I sat together on the drive up the country to Paju. We arrived in the city in the middle of the afternoon in time for a late lunch. We met a third party there, which brought a third waygook with them. Tim, another American, was taller and skinnier than Phillip or I, and I think it was instantly assumed that Tim would have the honor of playing Gutenberg.

Paju is a nice, clean town with a lot of new buildings, and at first glance is unrecognizable from most other mid-sized Korean cities. It's claim to fame, however, is its' gigantic 'Book City' complex. Paju is the publishing center of the entire country, employing thousands of workers in every step of the publishing process. Many of the city's office buildings are large, corporate publishers who sell their books on the ground floor. Used bookstores are popular too, with trendy book cafes, many run by the publishers themselves, dotted in between. It's a bibliophile paradise where books allegedly outnumber people 20-1. Books outnumber people in most cities, I'd guess, but I suppose this is an impressive ratio.

Within the city is a block printing school and activity center with rows upon rows of movable type blocks. While not exactly antiquated, the building would serve as an acceptable filming location for Gutenberg's printing press. The center was still open for business when we arrived, so we waited for the building to empty before the crew could set up their dolly and other equipment. Meanwhile, Phillip, Tim and I changed into our renaissance costumes and went through the makeup and beard-application process, spearheaded by one of the ajeossi's. Our assumptions were correct and Tim was indeed cast as the scissor-bearded Gutenberg while Phillip and I were to play his ink-fingered lackeys. Tim looked downright haggard as Gutenberg. My hat looked more like a winter beanie than anything, but it was brown and nondescript and worked as something someone 500 years ago might wear. Phillip's beard kept falling off.

With each passing hour, I began to wonder how long this day would be. We hadn't been given a definite end time, and it was beginning to get dark. *It's getting late, we're within spitting distance of the Demilitarized Zone, and we look like we're on our way to a Renaissance Faire.*

But the plan was soon apparent. Not only did we need to wait for the center to close for the day, we needed the cover of darkness to disguise its more modern features. The set was carefully lit with candles while black sheets covered as much of the modern equipment as possible. It would be as authentic as we could muster.

Around 7:00pm, we began filming. They handed Tim a large piece of parchment with fancy lettering and told us to point at it and talk about it. We didn't have any lines, so we adlibbed commentary about the quality of the print work. We did so as the camera crew pushed the dolly toward us. The director said 'cut,' or whatever the Korean equivalent is. The ajeossi that met me with the sandwiches had the best English, so he served as the translator between the director and the talent.

"Talk more," he said, his finger scanning the paper, his eyes expressive. "More!"

We tried to be a little more aggressive with our pointing for take two. I tried nodding a bit more without feeling cartoonish, but the director still wasn't feeling it. We did the same thing another three times before our pointing and talking was deemed adequate.

The vast majority of our efforts that evening involved pointing and discussing what we were pointing at. It didn't take long for the three of us to realize that most of the men in the room couldn't understand us and that we could say any old thing and it would work out alright, better even, for the project. The director would say action and we'd begin pointing.

"I'm really good at pointing," I'd say. "And something has to be done about this 'S.'"

"That 'S' is all fucked up," Tim would respond.

"I'm really hungry and tired of pointing at things," Phillip would chime in.

"Cut!" the director would say. Satisfied, he'd motion us over to the camera to see what the shot looked like. Our conversation looked natural, focused, and relevant to the parchment at which we were pointing. Our footage would be B-roll anyway, with some expert talking over our scenes. It looked good. So we did it again, and again, and again.

Eventually we moved on to pointing to other things, namely each other and the moveable type throughout the room. I even had a whole scene to myself, intensely filing through the blocks looking for *the one*. For our last shot, the adjeossi showed us an old painting of three workers appraising a large piece of parchment. We were to recreate the picture so that the documentary could cleverly transition from the painting to our live action scene. The men positioned us into the corresponding positions. I've never felt more like a stop-motion puppet in my life. By this time, the heat of the lighting was melting the glue off our faces, so our beards were almost gone. Phillip's hardly resembled the red, pointy goatee it was when we began. About thirty minutes later, the director was pleased with our position and we called it a night.

We wrapped up filming at around 11:00pm, and besides some snacks they'd provided around dinner time, we hadn't eaten since our mid-afternoon lunch. We were all famished, so after we'd packed the set and taken off our costumes and make up, they took us to a galbi jjim restaurant, the first I'd been to. In general, any Korean food with jjim, or 'steamed' in the title is delicious. Galbi jjim is essentially a pork roast marinated in spices. You can't eat at a restaurant with Koreans without being offered alcohol, so we put away a few beers and soju bottles to celebrate the easiest 200,000 won we'd ever made. I was also really hoping that the vans, when we returned to them, would return south instead of heading further north. The former is, thankfully, the direction the vans turned when we finished our late supper. And here the adventure ended.

Or so I wished.

It being a late night and all after a long day of driving and filming, the guy driving our van was having a time of it keeping his eyes open. There were hardly any cars on the dark, mountainous highway, so the van straddled the lanes. Tim and Phillip had somehow managed to pass out. I couldn't get a wink of sleep, with it being a swerving, exceptionally uncomfortable commercial van, so I took it upon myself to lock my eyes onto the driver's in the rearview mirror. I was prepared to kick the seat, scream, or do anything else necessary if I saw his eyes roll to the back of his head. Occasionally I would feel the van slow and then speed up again as his foot struggled to maintain a consistent push on the gas pedal. I maintained this vigil until the driver finally came to his senses and pulled over at a rest stop to shut his eyes for a quick nap. I was unhappy with getting home even later, and with the plan in general of having somebody drive us in the middle of the night, but I was mostly happy to not be in a car crash in the middle of nowhere in a foreign country.

The van pulled up in front of my apartment at 4:30am. I

mumbled an '*annyeonghigaseo*' to the Koreans and a 'see you later' to the Americans. Maria was asleep when I stumbled in. I crashed, happy to be alive, 200,000 won richer, not in North Korea, and with quite the resume booster to boot.

About a month later, Maria came home from work with a digital copy of the documentary. Phillip and I were anxious to see our contribution, so we organized a little viewing party among our friends and fired up the video.

It opens with a foreboding piano solo and a sneaky camera spying on Germans perusing books in a sidewalk sale. The scene transitions to an older Korean gentleman wandering an empty bookstore as if lamenting a tragedy. Clearly, a grave injustice has befallen the books and the perpetrator, a book-hater, has gotten away.

The music becomes harsher and more percussive, and of all people, the next person we see is Al Gore, who at the 2005 Seoul Digital Forum had this to say about Gutenberg:

> "When Gutenberg invented the printing press, he talked with an emissary from the Pope who had just returned from Korea with drawings and notes on movable metal type, and this emissary was a personal acquaintance and friend of Gutenberg. So in 1453 when he announced to Europe the stunning new invention of the printing press, somehow he neglected to also mention that it had come from Korea."

Cue Tim as the dastardly Gutenberg, plotting how best to destroy Korea's reputation.

The rest of the documentary went about how I pictured it, with talking heads going back and forth between B-roll footage of Tim, Phillip and I pointing at a piece of paper and other things around the room, nodding like idiots. Its appearance was not unlike documentaries you'd expect to see on PBS.

Now, I don't have an issue giving credit for the invention of the printing press to a non-Gutenberg, non-Western individual, but a sense of closure was in order. After all, I was an accomplice in delivering a piece of information that would come as a shock to most

Westerners, and I didn't even know if it was true. Had I sold out my culture for $200? Or was it a small fee for a rude awakening? Given Al Gore's sensitive history with inventions, I did a little sleuthing.

Korea did indeed have movable type before Germany. In 2001, UNESCO's Memory of the World Register recognized the most pronounceable title in the world, "Buljojikjisimcheyojeot," or "Jikji" for short, as the world's first text printed with movable, metal type. The document, whose name means "Anthology of Great Buddhist Priests' Zen Teachings," praises the virtues of Buddha and elaborates on proverbs and meditation. Printed in 1377 by monk Baegun Hwasang, "Jikji" predates Gutenberg's Bible by at least 70 years.

However, to imply that the printing press came from Korea is a trifle misleading. It's possible Gutenberg's inspiration originated in Korea, but the printing press was actually developed first in China.

One of China's greatest gifts to the world, and it has given many, is paper. It's only natural, then, that the industrious country was the first to print things on it. Official reports from the Han Dynasty credit local official and eunuch Cai Lun as the inventor of paper in 105 AD, although recent excavations have yielded fragments of crude paper-like material that push the invention of paper two or three centuries earlier.

By the 8th century, woodblock printing was the dominant method and had spread to Korea, followed soon after by Japan, and branched out into non-religious uses. It was so common in China that people owned personal printed calendars. Alchemist Liu Hong printed thousands of copies of his biography between 847 and 851 (I don't have the name of the biography, so we'll call it *Gold in Liu of Love*). The world's first printed newspaper, *Jing Bao,* began in 713 and didn't fold until 1911 with the fall of the Manchu Dynasty.

Printing was so ubiquitous, in fact, that there was a need for a more efficient printing method. Sometime between 1041 and 1049, another alchemist by the name of Bi Sheng developed a set of earthenware movable type, predating Gutenberg's movable type by four centuries. It was our old friend Baegun Hwasang, the Korean Buddhist monk, who improved on the method with metal type centuries later.

It's clear, then, that Gutenberg was not the first person in the world to invent movable type of any sort. What is less clear is how the idea fell into his lap. Did he innocently design the technology without any knowledge of Baegun Hwasang's movable type, making his 'invention' a happy coincidence? Or did somebody tell him about the idea? This is where circumstantial evidence comes into play.

According to Gore, a papal delegation traveled to Korea and returned to Europe with notes on their printing press, complete with movable type. A 2014 article from the AsiaN news website called "Gutenberg's Invention of Metal Movable Type from Korea?" names Cardinal Nicholas Cusanus as the most likely papal delegate. The author, Park Hyun-Chan, admits that there are no records of Cusanus or any other papal delegate visiting Korea in the early-to-mid 1400's during the rule of the Joseon dynasty. He does, however, believe that Cusanas traveled the Silk Road to Samarkand in modern-day Uzbekistan which was at the time a great center of East-West cultural exchange. From there, Park asserts, Cusanas may have learned about the latest technology coming out of Korea and returned with sketches and a basic understanding of the machinery. According to Park, Cusanas was also a hometown friend of Gutenberg's and would've then passed the information to his friend in the printing business. Their relationship is the key to placing Gutenberg's inspiration in Joseon-era Korea, but I could not find any information verifying that they were from the same hometown or even corresponded with each other. Gutenberg was born in Mainz and Cusanas in Kues, over 100 kilometers apart. I suppose that's what I get for using a news source with a misplaced capital letter.

Conjecture aside, it doesn't appear that Cusanas brought the idea of the printing press to Gutenberg. What's easier to believe is that the Silk Road had existed for over a thousand years before Gutenberg and that information was passing from East to West and vice versa long before he could say the word 'Mainz.' Also, the Latin alphabet is more amenable to movable type than the character-heavy script of Chinese and was therefore a stronger catalyst for the meteoric rise in the printing press. For all we know Gutenberg, either through Cusanas or a prophetic dream, learned about the Joseon movable metal type, slapped his personal stamp on it by making the process more mechanized and therefore more economical, and made movements such as the Reformation possible through his method of accelerated information distribution. Nothing is for sure. History is not known for giving credit to the right people.

Let's give credit to the people of Korea, though, for installing a cardboard cut-out of Pope Francis at a rest stop, a reception so flattering that perhaps that is our answer to the question at hand: if Cusanas had stepped foot on the Korean peninsula, we surely would've known about it.

Two Trips to Busan

That Time a Couple Ignored the Best Fireworks Display in the World

Like Seoul, there was always a reason to go to Busan. A restaurant. A festival. A promisingly-unique temple. Busan was only an hour and a half from Daegu by slow train, about half that by the high-speed version. If ever we needed to get out of Daegu for a minute, to see something different, Busan was the simplest choice.

Busan is South Korea's second city, the Chicago, Melbourne, or Milan of South Korea. It's not quite as cosmopolitan as Seoul (which isn't super cosmopolitan itself), nor does it enjoy as much international attention. What the city lacks in sheer volume it makes up for in aesthetics. Rather than a single dot on the map, the city rests between the sea and the low mountains that rush to meet it, and along the river valleys from the interior. There is no single central business district, making Busan appear as an amorphous blob -- Hong Kong stretched into a web-like tangle of developable land around hills and water. A beach town and port city, with small Chinese and Russian minorities, Busan's 3.5 million people have a greater tolerance for different clothing styles and perhaps thinking styles than those in Daegu. This becomes clear the longer one lingers in the city's districts. There's the glamorous Haeundae Beach area with glittering hotels and condominiums. There's the shopping districts of Seomyeon and Nampo-dong, with the famous and smelly Jagalchi Fish Market. There's Centum City, a business and entertainment district with the country's coolest building -- the ultramodern Busan Cinema Center -- and the world's largest department store that we've already covered. In all these spaces, there just seems to be more variety – in clothing selections, in hair styles, in personalities – than in Daegu.

I've already described our disappointing first trip to Busan with the absurdly crowded Christmas Tree Festival. I'm happy to report that the following trips were much more successful and enjoyable. We'll stick to two of them.

In November 2005, in keeping with the city's desire to become an international convention and conference hub, Busan hosted the annual meeting of Asia-Pacific Economic Cooperation, more commonly known as APEC. To celebrate the prestigious event, the city put on an enormous fireworks display, so well-received that the city decided to do them again. The display was bumped up a month to take advantage of more amenable October temperatures and rebranded the Busan International Fireworks Festival. Since that first display, the festival has established itself as one of the premiere firework displays in Asia, if not the world.

As an American spoiled by patriotic Independence Day fireworks, I require a certain amount of finesse and bombast in my firework shows. If I'm going to travel out of town, pay to stay somewhere, and throw myself into a throng of a million plus people for fireworks, I'd better see some bombs bursting in the freaking air. I was assured that the show would meet my standards, so we went to Busan.

The festival takes place on the less-famous but no less fetching Gwangalli beach. The narrow strip of sand is on a cove in the middle of the city, backed by a busy road of cafes, bars and other diversions with basic names like 'Burger and Pasta' and 'Eat.' There are hotels too, but none of the caliber along Busan's more famous beach, Haeundae. A mile or two out into the ocean, the imposing Gwangandaegyo suspension bridge runs parallel to the beach. It's from this enormous bi-level bridge, the second longest in the country, that the majority of the fireworks are ignited. Maria, myself, and our usual crew of waygooks found a spot on Gwangalli beach by midafternoon and claimed our turf with blankets. Already, the beach was over half full as people swarmed in to find a good spot. The sun was fine and the skies were clear, but the shadows of the buildings behind us crept onto the beach and it wasn't long before we reached for jackets. It would be a perfect night for fireworks. We brought books, games, cards, and enough food to last us the rest of the day. As more people packed the beach, we stationed ourselves on the edges of the blanket, firmly establishing our hold on our territory as sandy real estate disappeared. The skies darkened and thousands of LED lights on the bridge teased us with fun displays. A computer-generated hand on one side of the bridge flicked a light only to be flicked back by a hand on the other. They continued back and forth, faster and faster. What kind of show was I in for if technology was put to such clever use before the show even began?

A spectacular show, that's what kind. Most firework displays run, at the longest, for around 20 minutes. The Busan International Fireworks Festival ran for at least twice that. There were fast songs, there were slow songs. There were whizz bang numbers with Celtic rock accompaniment and gentle ballads with quiet lasers and twinkling fireworks. There were grand orchestral moments with multiple layers of green, red and white flowers in the sky and there were pop songs with strobe lights. The bridge was used well, with fireworks ignited going from left to right, right to left, center to edges or vice versa in time with the music. The fireworks were especially bright and continuous during the "Live is Life" by Opus portion. In another section, fireworks danced to the fiddle of a Spanish song, shooting to the left, shooting to the right, spiraling from the bridge towers. Our ears enjoyed a respite with an "All You Need is Love" section, where the fireworks were fewer and quieter and heart shaped. By far the most astounding part of the show were drones dressed up as birds that flew in front of the beach. They were already lit up looking fabulous when, at a certain cue in the song, each one was engulfed in flaming fireworks. Do you hear what I'm telling you? There were flying fireworks maybe 100 feet above us. I'd never seen anything like it, and haven't since.

Throughout the entire show, through every single riveting moment I've just described, the young Korean couple in front of us faced our way. They'd brought a tripod and a smartphone and were taking smile-less selfies with the fireworks in the background. As the fireworks were their most intense or romantic, the couple would lean in, straight-faced, and snap a picture. One of them would reset the phone's flash and photo timer and, a minute later, lean into their beloved and snap another picture. The fireworks, I assume, rather than their dour expressions were the true representation of their love. I have no idea how their pictures turned out, but I hope they were worth a day spent sitting on the beach. There was a damned good firework show behind them.

The next morning, we showered at our hostel a few blocks from the beach and donned our hiking gear. We had one more sight in mind before we headed back to Daegu. Out in a park on the outskirts of town, there is a temple carved into a mountainside.

Standard logic for going to Buddhist temples in Korea is that they all look the same. Even Koreans will tell you that once you've been to one, you've been to them all. This is generally true. Temples in Korea tend to be small, red buildings with fanciful paintings on the outside and a statue of Buddha surrounded by candles on the inside. Most temples also have a courtyard. It's a tried and true formula, I guess, but they can get predictable very quickly. Eager to find at least one temple in Korea that didn't match the rest, we headed toward Seokbulsa.

It's difficult to find a history of Seokbulsa, but when I told Hyun Soo that I'd hiked to it, he said that it was a new temple. Korea has been around for a long time and things are being rebuilt constantly, so I didn't know if new meant last year, a hundred years ago, or rebuilt after centuries. One blog claims that it was carved into the mountain in the 1930's by a monk, which is good enough for me.

To get to Seokbulsa, we took a cable car to the top of Mt. Geumjeongsan. Before us lay the mixed forests of Geumgang park and behind us lay the sprawl of Busan. It was another comfortable, sunny day and there were plenty of hikers; Octobers in South Korea are reliably gorgeous. The only problem was that not everyone was hiking to the same place. Besides the temple, there is also a mountain fortress somewhere in the hills. There's not a direct path to the temple, so we relied on what little English signage was available along with our wits to take us in the right direction. The path took us through the forest, horizontally at first but with a gradual incline, until we reached a small but busy tourist village of restaurants and badminton courts. Here, the path split and we had to make a choice. Luckily, we chose correctly. Out of the village, a trail followed a mountain stream through a ravine and to a steep, concrete road. Switchbacks led up the mountain as we slowly, with heavy breathing and some water guzzling, hiked this last leg of the journey until at last we saw a red bell tower. Even though the temperature was cool, I was quite sweaty when we reached the breezy temple entrance an hour after we'd exited the cable car.

Right away, to enter Seokbulsa is to enter a secluded, forgotten world. Narrow stairs lead visitors, what few make the arduous journey, between two small, wooden buildings to a rock face carved with depictions of Buddha four times taller than myself. The space isn't huge -- the temple is actually one of the smallest we'd seen – but it was immediately transporting, an easy place to picture yourself in a fantasy land, an ancient kingdom, the gates to an underground civilization. It didn't hurt the magical aesthetic that the few trees in this small mountain crevice draped the entire temple in an autumnal red. Looking back from the bell tower, a distant corner of the city was visible behind a ridge of verdant, pine-filled mountains. What a quietly epic temple this monk had built eighty years ago, though none could tell; it might as well have been 500 years old. This was easily my favorite temple in all of South Korea. We couldn't stay long—cable cars and trains to catch back to Daegu and all that—so we hiked back the way we came down the concrete road and to the path along a ravine. Some of the fun ups before were now somewhat treacherous downs, but it was an enjoyable hike. We found some boulders good for sitting along the stream and we ate our lunch of peanut butter and jelly sandwiches, fruit, and nuts. There are worse ways to spend a Sunday afternoon, let me tell you.

For our 5th wedding anniversary, Maria and I decided to book a hotel on Haeundae beach and spend a romantic weekend in Busan. It was June, but rates at the Novotel Ambassador hotel were oddly affordable. It's right on the beach too. We arrived expecting to find a catch – a twin bed, a leaky bathroom, a dead body behind the couch – but never found one. The indoor pool was luxurious, the king size bed comfortable, and the room spotless. By all appearances, the hotel was a legitimate four star establishment. I'm not sure what they're playing at over there with their prices, but good on them. The hotel's restaurant, however, looked more the part: expensive and unexciting. Instead, Jang Mi had recommended an Indian restaurant within walking distance of the hotel for dinner. We celebrated five years of awesomeness with mango lassis and curry.

Other than our anniversary, there was one more thing bringing us to Busan. We'd heard stories about a colorful hillside neighborhood called the Gamcheon Culture Village, that it was full of quaint coffee shops and art galleries and a good place for a stroll. The next day, eager to find corners of Korea that looked unique, we took the subway to the complete other end of town and hailed a taxi outside the station. We gave the driver the address, but this rarely helps. Neither do maps. Phillip and I once hopped in a cab to take us to a disc golf course on the edge of Daegu. We handed him an address, and he rejected it. We handed him a map, and he rejected that too. He couldn't read it, on account of his poor eyesight. What a terrific career, I thought, for a man who can't see. We did end up leading him, through some poor Korean and by shoving a smartphone with a map in his face, to our intended destination. By the looks of the driver Maria and I had found, we would likely need to do the same.

"Gamcheon Culture Village," we said slowly in Korean. We showed him an address, and repeated the words again. He seemed to have some idea of where to go. I knew Daegu's layout enough to know if we were headed in the right direction. I did not have such an intimate knowledge of Busan. Our driver whisked us away from the station in the direction of the mountains, which seemed a pretty good start.

Luckily, he took us to the right place. On top of a hill, the high rises disappeared and we were in a world of colorful houses and large murals. We hadn't the foggiest where we should get out, and neither did the driver. The cab climbed up the mountain, passed an intersection that might've looked like an entry to a culture village, and went right back down it on the other side, back to gray buildings way past what was now the apparent start of the cultural trail. Through the magic of solitary Korean words and a shared understanding of a group mistake, the driver turned around and headed back up the mountain, back to color. We paid what we owed him and left.

Gamcheon came to being soon after the Korean War. At the time, Busan was a messy place. Refugees, homeless and starving after much of the country had been destroyed, flooded into the city since it had never fallen under attack. The hillside that is now the culture village was mostly empty at this point, but families built make-shift shacks out of what they could find: scrap iron, wood, even rocks. Eventually, these dwellings were swapped out for brick and concrete buildings, but the folks that lived on the steep hill remained some of the poorest in Busan.

By order of the city, the first 800 or so families that moved into Gamcheon belonged to a semi-religion called Taegukdo. Founded by a man named Chol-je Cho in the beginning of the 20th century, Taegukdo asserts that the *taeguk*, the yin-yang symbol on the Korean national flag (the official name of the flag is *Taegukgi*), is a representation of the universe's order. Life, Cho told his followers, could be summed up in this symbol. No longer persecuted by the Japanese colonial government for his beliefs, Cho practiced openly again after the war, setting up shop in Gamcheon where most of the inhabitants were either already followers or converted. The headquarters for the religion is still there today.

As Busan built upwards and outwards over the next several decades, Gamcheon remained mostly the same, and its families remained poor. The first decade of the 21st century brought two major art projects that would permanently transform the fabric of the neighborhood. The first, the Dreaming of Machu Picchu project in 2009, provided money for artists to paint murals or build art installations in the streets with the assistance of locals. In 2010, the Miro project brought an additional 12 art installations and murals, as well as a designated path through the neighborhood. The Ministry of Culture, Sports and Tourism hoped that the art would entice tourists to step away from the beach and spend time and money in Gamcheon. Thus, the Gamcheon Culture Village was born.

Their methods must have paid off. It was a gray, sticky afternoon but the culture trail was brimming with people, not exactly a horde like at the Christmas Tree festival, but enough to generate excitement. The main drag, if you can call it that, rounds the top of the hill through a maze of tightly-woven alleys and houses. Cafes and art galleries intermingle with private residences. The dense assortment of houses, blue-roofed with walls of faded reds, greens, yellows, oranges, and so on, cling precariously to the steep hill, facing each other in the secluded valley shaped like a cove in the sea. Indeed, the village is billed the 'Santorini of Korea' even though the ocean is down the road a piece.

Maria and I took our time, wandering into galleries that piqued our interest and stopping to take pictures of funky art along the way. Above the doorway to one of the galleries were porcelain pigeons with Buddha faces. Elsewhere, potted plants sat in dismembered pairs of pants appearing to walk away. Around every corner, quirky installations entice pedestrians to continue into the neighborhood. This bibliophile couldn't resist snapping photos of an alley painted as a library.

We'd already eaten lunch elsewhere, but we felt compelled to spend money and support the village. About halfway through the trail, we stopped at a café and I bought an iced coffee. Next door was a tiny shop that sold customized bracelets at a reasonable price. To commemorate our 5th wedding anniversary, we told the guy doing the customizing that we wanted bracelets that said 'Matthew and Maria, five years.' He painted our wish in Hangul on two tiny plastic rectangles, attached them to our bracelets of choice, and slid the bracelets onto our wrists.

The main drag ends unceremoniously into a jumble of terraced vegetable patches. Visitors can either stroll around the gardens and turn back the way they came or explore the lower haunts of the neighborhood down a series of narrow and steep flights of stairs. Not thinking ahead, we elected to do the latter. There were fewer people down these corners, probably because most people are smarter than us, but it was fun to imagine living away from busy streets and intimidating high rises. The streets were much too narrow for cars to get through, so I imagine the residents have no choice but to walk past their neighbors and, God help them, build relationships. They all practically live on top of each other anyway. I could see that being a charming existence. We made it to the bottom of the hill where a museum and art center stood as a sort of community hub. We walked inside, convincing ourselves that the reason we'd chosen to hike down a large hill was to explore this building. In actuality, we'd spent a couple hours already immersed in art and color and decided we'd reached our saturation point. With that in mind, we had nothing left to do but head back up the hill. The way we came looked much too imposing so we tried to find an alternate, more staggered climb. After some false starts and dead ends through empty alleys and stairs, we eventually found ourselves more or less where we'd started, but all the more sweaty and tired for it.

While the art installations and promotion of Gamcheon as a 'culture village' has infused cash and spunk into the neighborhood, some residents are less than happy with the attention. Around 10,000 people still live there, about half the population of its peak decades ago. With houses emptying out, entrepreneurs move in to fill the space with new art houses and cafes, drawing in more visitors and convincing more shy residents to move away. In some regards, I don't blame them. The entire trail is basically one gigantic photo opportunity; I wouldn't want my home, or my person, to be the constant subject of selfies and well-meaning, but perhaps intrusive photographers. The powers that be stress that residents don't wish to be in pictures, but I suppose even an obtrusive 1% of thousands of people a year can be tiresome. Still, Gamcheon isn't quite a major tourist draw yet. It's not front and center on most Busan itineraries. It doesn't pack in the masses the way department stores or beaches do. At the time of our visit, the village seemed to enjoy a thriving bustle rather than a debilitating flood, but how the village will balance success with preservation in the future remains to be seen. There are worse challenges.

A Second Round of Holidays

That Time I Resisted 'Air Refresh'

On July 8, 1973, a 20-year old man was found dead in his bedroom. The room's windows and doors were shut, you see, and the man had turned on two electric, oscillating fans before breathing his last. Never minding the curious jars of chemicals in the room, the consensus from many newspaper readers was that the fans were somehow to blame. The man's undoing, they said, was the fans.

Much to the bewilderment of the rest of the world, Koreans take the theory of fan death, or death by fans in an enclosed space, extremely seriously. Well into the 21st century, evening news bulletins across South Korea report on fan death every summer. Electric fans in Korea are designed with timers on them so they don't run into the night. In 2006, the Korea Consumer Protection Board named fan death as one of the five reoccurring hazards in the summer months, warning readers that sleeping in a room with closed windows, bad ventilation, and a running electric fan could cause bodies to lose water or catch hypothermia. Worse, the board warns, direct contact with an electric fan could lead to "death from increase of carbon dioxide saturation concentration and decrease of oxygen concentration." And that's not all. Some believe fans suck oxygen from the air and cause victims to suffocate, or that fans convert oxygen into carbon dioxide, or that fans chop oxygen molecules (but no other kinds) in half. Ask five Koreans how fan death works, and you're likely to get five answers. Most of them will agree, though, that fan death is a thing and not to be taken lightly.

It's unclear when the idea of fan death first came about. A 1927 article published in *Jungoe Ilbo* ("Domestic and International Daily") claimed this new-fangled technology, the fan, could cause nausea, facial paralysis, and asphyxiation. One conspiracy theory asserts that the authoritarian government in the 1970's told citizens rumors about electric fans to keep them from using too much electricity. The dictatorship withered away, but the rumors persisted, and rumors they are. There is little, if any scientific evidence that any of the aforementioned explanations of fan death are remotely true.

To prove this, a professor at the Korea Advanced Institute of Science and Technology set up a little experiment. In 2008, Professor Chun Rim put his 11-year old daughter (there were no other willing participants) in a closed room with an electric fan and checked her temperature and blood pressure every five minutes. Her vitals remained steady and she bravely survived the experiment.

I don't bring fan death up to make fun of Koreans. Goodness knows Americans believe some weird shit. 5% of Americans, or around 15 million of them, believe that the government controls our minds and possibly the climate with 'chemtrails,' the exhaust from airplanes in the sky. An unsettling number of Americans, and others around the world, believe that the earth is flat and surrounded by an impenetrable wall of ice. In September 2017, rapper B.o.B even began a crowdfunding campaign to send a satellite to space, take a picture, and prove that there is no curvature of the Earth. I believed, until an age I'm not willing to disclose, that buffet was pronounced to rhyme with 'toupee.' A good comparison is the common myth that you shouldn't go swimming within thirty minutes of eating, that digestion takes too much blood away from your limbs and that you could drown from severe cramping. While digestion does divert a percentage of blood, it's not enough to debilitate your entire body. You may get a cramp, one just annoying enough to whine about, but you're not going to die. No, I bring this up because it was December and one of the season's first snows was blowing outside. I was enjoying the warmth of my office when Gym Teacher walked in and opened the window. The snow that was swirling outside was now swirling inside, with the heater straining to maintain a comfortable temperature. I put my coat back on.

"Air refresh," said Gym Teacher.

I said nothing. Fan death, or any other issue with open windows, is a lost cause to discuss. You are starting on the offensive from the get go, and if you don't want feelings hurt, there's really not much to say. I couldn't tell Gym Teacher that he was wasting heat, or fuel for the heater, or that most people around the world don't open the window when it's snowing outside, so I sat huddled at my desk until it was time to leave for class.

Gym Teacher began to make it a habit of opening the windows in the dead of winter, and sometimes leaving them open. When he wasn't around, of course, I took the opportunity to shut them. After the eighth or ninth time, I decided that this was my office too and that my sensibilities counted for something. Rather than get into an open argument about windows and air and molecules, whenever he opened the window I let my protest known by saying "why?"

"Air refresh," he'd say again. I'd point to the heater's fuel gauge. The limited fuel was a genuine concern. Supposedly, what we had been given at the beginning of winter was supposed to last us the entire season. There was no chance that was happening with the windows open all the time, and I wasn't willing to freeze for two months because of 'air refresh.' Nevertheless, I'd return from class and the window would be open.

The last thing a teacher wants stepping into the classroom is uncertainty. Planning ahead is a good way to avoid it, but since Ji Young didn't really do the whole planning thing, there was always a degree of 'what are we doing again?' whenever I walked through the door. There was also, about 2 out of 5 times, a degree of 'where the hell is Ji Young and why are students wrestling on the ground?' Usually the answer was that she was brushing her teeth. I knew this because the bathroom was on the opposite end of the corridor from her classroom, and I would watch her casually saunter back with a toothbrush in her mouth.

One day, I walked into the classroom a few minutes before class started and, as described above, Ji Young was nowhere to be found. Mercifully, this class was a fourth grade class and one of the best behaved in the school. I waited as long as I could before quieting the students and displaying the vocabulary words on the projector for them to copy. But damn that good behavior, the students finished writing in three minutes. Their feverish desire to please the teacher and learn was, for once, a nuisance. They were ready for the next activity. Still, there was no Ji Young. We recited the vocabulary words they'd written in their notebooks, eating up another minute and a half. I had no idea what Ji Young planned for the day, so I pulled up a song on YouTube they'd been singing.

At last, Ji Young arrived with a stiff walk and closed eyes.

"Metyu," she whispered. "I'm really sick."

She told the students to put their hands on their heads and close their eyes. They obliged.

I'd known Ji Young long enough to know when she was being whiny and when she was feeling ill, and this was certainly the latter. She delicately lowered herself into the computer chair.

In my experience, whenever I told a Korean that I was sick, their first question was 'why?' This stuck me as almost offensive the first time I was asked, as if I did something wrong and my carelessness was the cause for my ailment. My first instinct was to reply with something cheeky like 'I checked the calendar and today was available' or 'because there's a sale on Robitussin this weekend,' but I always went with the simple 'allergies' answer, which was not untrue. But the tables had turned and it was my turn to ask the questions.

"Why are you sick?" I asked her, smirking inside at the chance to ask.

"I don't know," she said. "I think food poisoning. I went to the nurse's office."

"What did she say?"

"Your skirt is too high."

"Pardon?"

"She said 'your skirt is too high.'"

I laughed then asked if the nurse had anything to say about her feeling sick.

'No," she moaned. "Any time she sees me, even if it's just in the hallway, it's always 'your skirt is too high. And now that I'm sick, she's like 'see? Your skirt is too high.' A girl student walked in after me saying she had a cold and the nurse said 'your skirt is too high.'"'

I knew from a handful of interactions with the nurse that she was a very conservative Christian. On one of our teacher trips, we toured an old Confucian academy. While the tour guide explained the particular and not exactly egalitarian rules of the academy, the nurse occasionally leaned over to Ji Young and whispered 'never mind what he says.' This is overall a good thing, I suppose, that she found happiness and equality from the church, but perhaps the rigidity of her beliefs didn't make her the most empathetic school nurse.

Ji Young flipped to a page in the textbook and pointed to where the class had last finished. I took the class by myself that day while she returned to the nurse's office to rest. It probably wasn't the most fascinating English class for the students, with little Korean translation from myself to aid comprehension, but we got through it, and I played some sing along videos that they liked at the end.

The next day, Ji Young came to school feeling better. She brought me a bag of tiny, individually-wrapped chocolate squares as a thank you for taking all the day's classes. It wasn't the first time she'd brought me candy to smooth things over; every once in a great while she'd show up late and completely unprepared. I would then have to figure out on my own what to do for about 15 minutes during the first period. On those occasions, the chocolate was more appreciated. This time, it wasn't her fault.

Hyun Soo was giving me more autonomy in class too, although not because he was sick. Whether because he was busier than usual or because he thought maybe I'd like to do something more substantial, I was leading half the classes by design. It was a good arrangement, much closer to what EPIK probably had in mind when they implemented a co-teaching system. Hyun Soo would introduce new units and I'd come in to reinforce retention with PowerPoints, activities, and games.

The increase in actual teaching time was great, but with new responsibilities came new exhaustion and I was ready for the holidays. For Thanksgiving, we again ordered the turkey dinner out of Camp Walker and gathered a large number of friends – not just Americans but South Africans and Kiwis too – to fill in the rest with a potluck. That afternoon, crammed into a small living room with our plates full of food, we did the cheesy thing where, one at a time, we shared what we were thankful for.

"I'm thankful to speak a language that gets me a job," said the first of us. That about said it all. The rest of our answers were moot, or at least it felt that way. None of us would be there if we didn't speak English as a first language. We were blessed with a mother tongue that is in high demand.

For Christmas, we dismissed any grand travel plans and decided to, as a large group again, treat ourselves to a buffet dinner at the Hotel Ariana. The food was average—a combination of Western and Korean food like most buffets we'd been to—but there was lots of it. Additionally, part of the package was unlimited beer and wine. A trio of women were the evening's entertainment, singing Christmas songs and selections from the *Frozen* soundtrack on a stage up front to appease the younger eaters in attendance. In all, it was a much more festive, roundly successful Christmas than the disaster in Busan a year before.

I had zero interest in the weeks of school between Christmas and winter break. My head was somewhere else completely. If you remember, a trip to New Zealand was promised me as an incentive to teach English in South Korea. While I'd long felt rewarded for making the decision, the fact remained that we hadn't made the trip. We simply didn't have the funds to make it happen after one year. By staying a second year, we would have the money and the added bonus of going in January, which is the beginning of summer down there. We booked our flights to Auckland and made preparations for what was to be a trip of a lifetime. I was beyond excited. Between classes, I'd iron out itineraries, make reservations, and do any research that was required (and not required) of me. I wrestled over routes to take, this hotel over that one, whether we should rent a car or just take planes and buses everywhere (not a good idea). Most people go on vacations to relax; this was to be a 'see everything you can because you'll likely never be here again' type of vacation. All that stood in my way were a couple days of school, two layovers in Japan and Hong Kong, and a long flight over the Pacific Ocean.

That Far, Marvelous Country on the Bottom of the World

That Time We Went to New Zealand

My first surprise in New Zealand was a Wendy's. We were on the bus from the Auckland airport to downtown and I noticed one as we whizzed by. I had no idea there were Wendy's in New Zealand, but there were no Wendy's in South Korea. I immediately drew up a map on my phone to find all Wendy's locations along our travel route. It was a non-negotiable stop.

We finally got our fix in Hamilton, a couple hours south of Auckland, where a fellow Native English Teacher lived now that her and her boyfriend had finished their contracts. While they were off at work, Maria and I took their car (with their permission) and drove to the nearest Wendy's a few miles away. Inside, Maria and I stared at the menu as if we'd never seen the color red before. We didn't eat fast food often in South Korea, mostly because we don't care much for McDonald's, Burger King or KFC. We had to make our choices count; we wouldn't get another shot at Wendy's for a long time. But how to choose? Each variation of hamburger seemed more pleasing than the last. *That sandwich doesn't include lettuce and tomato. Do I care? Do I want bacon on my sandwich and how much of it do I want? Should I splurge and get a combo meal? Or order a ton of crap off the value menu?*

"Can I help you find something?" asked the bewildered girl

behind the counter. I can't imagine what she thought of us: two Americans drooling over very average fast food in a country with much better options at every corner.

"You don't understand," Maria tried to clear up. "We don't live in America. This is a big occasion."

The girl said nothing but smiled. There were few other people in the restaurant. She probably would've preferred a few more, in case the Americans did anything untoward for the sake of hamburgers and a chocolate Frosty. What she didn't understand was that Wendy's was about the last thing we expected to find in New Zealand. Our expectations for the country were already sky high. Apparently they weren't high enough.

On October 11, 1999, film director Peter Jackson and a crew of over 2,000 people began the most ambitious filming project in history. *The Lord of the Rings* trilogy was to be shot simultaneously, out of sequence, and across over 100 locations throughout the North and South islands of New Zealand. While *Rings* author J.R.R. Tolkien envisioned his trilogy as a sort of mythology for England, the modern day British Isles are much too developed and peopled to represent an extremely old, geographically-diverse continent. Therefore, the crew needed a much emptier, vaguely European-looking locale to bring Tolkien's Middle Earth to life, and Jackson's New Zealand fit the bill. He and his location scouts took advantage of the country's wild and contrasting landscape to transport viewers to Tolkien's imagination, to mountains, deserts, marshes, plains, and pristine farmland. New Zealand has them all.

The movies went on to become fabulously popular and well-received, so the local Kiwis did what only makes sense: they marketed their country as Middle Earth. They established tours of the filming locations, some of which are in very far-flung places. They plastered the characters on their airplanes. By the time we arrived in 2015, Air New Zealand's safety video starred the cast of Tolkien's *Hobbit* trilogy, also filmed in New Zealand, as well as Jackson himself. The Kiwis clearly knew their audience. By 2012, the country had seen a 50% increase in international visitors since the first of the films, *The Fellowship of the Ring*, was released in 2001. By 2015, 13% of visitors said that the *Rings* movies, and the subsequent *Hobbit* trilogy, were a primary reason for visiting the country. These days, tourism is the number two industry in New Zealand after dairy. That's saying something, considering New Zealand is close to nowhere. Australia, the nearest continent, is over 1,000 miles away. South America, going in the other direction, is well over 5,000 miles away to the east. There's nothing north of New Zealand for over 6,000 miles, save for tiny Polynesian islands, all the way to Russia's Kamchatka peninsula. To the south? Antarctica. You've really come to the end of the world when you've made it down here.

But first things first. Even if you've never heard of a hobbit, New Zealand is a fascinating place to visit. If you like the outdoors, there's no finer country. If you like the indoors, there's plenty going on there too. If you consider yourself someone who breathes oxygen, someone who eats food, or something similar to a person, then you'll find something to love about New Zealand. It is a country of devastatingly stupendous (and sometimes stupendously devastating) countryside with the kindest people I've ever met and more peculiarities and things to do than any country of 4.5 million people and 29 million sheep has any right to. Even without *Lord of the Rings*, it's a wonder.

For one thing, the landscape is not only stunning, it can change by the minute. On our drive to Waitomo, famous for its caves with thousands of celestially blue glowworms, I had a hard time placing what biome I was in. Before, on the bus ride from Auckland to Hamilton, we passed through hours of cornfields that wouldn't have been out of place in Ohio. Now, driving to Waitomo through neatly trimmed pastures, I thought the land had a faint Mediterranean shine, with tall, thin pines along the hedges and ceaseless rolling hills like a mildly disheveled beach towel. We pulled into the parking lot for the caves but first took in a small walking path down the hill. The path meandered through a primitive, temperate rainforest of ferns and moss. This, I believe, is what covered most of the island before the Maori arrived around 1300 and the Europeans in 1769, when British explorer James Cook mapped most of the two islands' coastline.

The day we went to Waitomo, I was having one of those

dilemmas that only come about when your life is, for the moment, entirely too blessed. Later that day, my beloved Ohio State Buckeyes would play Oregon for the college football national championship. I was considering finding some way to watch the game: streaming on someone's laptop, begging a pub to find the correct channel, buying 50 binoculars and laying them end to end. Maria patiently reminded me that I was in the country of my dreams, and that I should spend every waking moment breathing it in. As it turned out, as we walked up to the window to buy our tickets for the cave, a group of four older folks walked in behind us with Ohio State hoodies and hats on. They were taking a month to see the country, a retirement gift to themselves, and planned on watching the game at their hotel. What a universe this is. Even in Waitomo, on the complete other end of the earth, there were Ohio State fans, and they were on the same cave tour as us. Ohio State went on to beat Oregon and I would watch the game later on YouTube. I have no regrets.

The retirees had it right; New Zealand is for groups of close friends. Luckily for us, Maria's sister Jennifer and her husband Ricky were coming to join us. They met us in Hamilton the next day. Jennifer and Ricky liked *The Lord of the Rings* movies well enough, but neither was an avid fan like Maria and I. Therefore, I took special care to sell the scenic or cultural significance of our destinations outside the specter of visiting Middle Earth locales.

The first of such places, and there was no getting around it, was the Hobbiton Movie Set Tour. Deep in the center of the Alexander sheep farm outside Matamata, Hobbiton was the principle filming location for the idyllic, pastoral Shire. For *The Lord of the Rings* movies, the set's hobbit holes were built with temporary materials and were mostly torn apart after filming commenced. That didn't stop the Alexanders from arranging private tours for desperate film fans. Pictures of Hobbiton from these years are a bit eerie, like an abandoned Cold War bunker inside an otherwise green and pleasant knoll. When Jackson decided to film the *Hobbit* trilogy, the Alexanders gave him permission to film on their farm again with the stipulation that he rebuild Hobbiton with permanent materials; that way, they could make something of a real attraction out of it and charge a lot of money. That's precisely what they've done. They knew that people like me would pay about anything to step inside the Shire for a couple hours. It costs about $60 a pop, and it is worth every cent.

You don't just drive up to Hobbiton, snap a few pictures, and then drive off. Visitors park in a lot about a mile or two off, then get whisked away on a bus through the grassy and expansive farm to a gravel lot. We got out, wondering how far we'd have to walk to see the set. I hadn't noticed anything on the drive in. A path leads down a hill, through tall grass and scrub, and then the Shire appears in front of you as it does in the movie.

I can't begin to describe the happiness that overcame me. The best estimation I can give is the scene in *Willy Wonka and the Chocolate Factory* when Mr. Wonka opens a small door and reveals the main factory floor, where 'you can eat almost everything.' Apparently, the child actors had yet to see that particular set; their faces in that scene are genuine reactions of awe and joy. That's the closest I can describe how I, a grown-ass man, felt walking into Hobbiton.

Every inch of the set is as it appears in the movies. There are flowers everywhere, and vegetable patches. Round, welcoming doors with the knob in the middle greet you at every corner, with some woody and warm underground home presumably on the other side. With dishes in the windows and smoke coming from the chimney, you might suppose someone is cooking supper inside. Our tour guide walked us through the village, explaining some of the behind-the-scenes effects to achieve the correct scale for the hobbits, who are very short people. I won't spoil the mystery for those who want to hear it for themselves, but I will share one fact about the filming. Months ahead of when filming was scheduled to begin, the production crew busied themselves making Hobbiton look like a real, lived-in place. They planted crops to look like the hobbits were actively growing things. Additionally, it was somebody's job for weeks on end to walk between the hobbit holes and do 'laundry.' In doing so, that person's feet would wear paths in the grass, like people had been walking those shortcuts for years to hang the laundry to dry. Astounding, isn't it? I dare you to find a movie more lovingly and considerately made.

Tongariro Park was a four-hour drive from Matamata, and we arrived late at our motel. I felt bad that we'd made the owner, a balding guy in his 50's, stay up past midnight to let us in, but he showed us our room without a harsh word. The next morning, we awoke early to hike what we could of the Tongariro Alpine Crossing. The trail would lead us past the foreboding cone of Mt. Ngauruhoe, otherwise known to *Rings* enthusiasts as Mt. Doom. Mt. Ngauruhoe, which I haven't a clue how to pronounce, is actually a parasitic cone of the smaller, less-active Mt. Tongariro (it's the same concept as the cones around Hallasan on Jeju Island. See? Don't tell me I don't teach you anything). A third and very active volcano, Mt. Ruapehu, is taller than both and sits just to the south. When not spewing primordial debris, Mt. Ruapehu is a ski resort.

Unlike Waitomo or Matamata, the alpine crossing through Tongariro National Park is desolate. There are no trees -- only tough, windblown tussocks that give way to dark and sinister rock and lichen. It is an empty, jagged land of unworldly reds, oranges, and browns. It's no wonder Jackson chose the park to film scenes in Mordor, the evil land of the story's main antagonist, Sauron.

From the Mangatepopo parking lot to Soda Springs, the trail stays horizontal but then begins an upward trajectory to the base of Mt. Ngauruhoe. The higher we hiked, the more the ratio shifted from plant to rock. The temperature dropped too. Until 2007, the trail had been known just as Tongariro Crossing. Folks were coming to do some or all of the 19 kilometer hike in tank tops and flip flops. Concerned that the relatively straightforward hike lured too many unprepared people out for a morning stroll, the park added the word 'alpine' to better describe the elements that hikers may experience. The park is, after all, in a volcanic zone a few thousand feet above sea level. The closer we got to the cone, the more 'alpine' it became.

At last, we reached a plateau. The cone was to our right, Mt. Tongariro to our left, and the trail shot straight in between. Perhaps 50 or so people were ahead of us, tiny dots with legs either coming up or down the slope straight ahead. Tinier dots still were slowly making their way up the cone, most of which is at a 45-degree angle with loose volcanic pebbles. The sun was hot, the air was getting colder with the altitude, and Jennifer and Ricky were doing all this without their luggage, which was still on its way from Los Angeles. We wouldn't be hiking up a serious mountain that day. Instead, we settled for the slope ahead to the red crater of Mt. Tongariro, not quite the top but almost. It was still difficult, with the same loose stuff impeding our upward progress. It was always one step forward, six inches back. A tumble down either side would likely result in a bumpy, but probably not mortal slide down hundreds of feet of rock. When we finally reached the chilly, breezy top, the view was pristine in every direction. Ahead were the undrinkable Emerald Lakes. To our right was the red crater, a deep chasm which lives up to its name. Behind us, the cone stood in plain view, no longer hiding behind smaller ridges. We found some mildly comfortable rocks to sit on and ate our lunch in the harshest environment I've ever seen, made beautiful by its treachery and otherworldliness. We couldn't linger long, though. We were due in Wellington that evening, and already by midday there seemed fewer people on the trail (and there weren't droves of them to begin with). We returned the way we came and, seven hours after we'd left the car to better acquaint ourselves with the word 'inhospitable,' drove down to the bottom of the North Island to Wellington.

We were all due for a good night's sleep. In two days, Jennifer and Ricky had covered Matamata, Rotorua, Tongariro National Park, and driven in between all of them. They did all this with nothing but what they put in their carry-ons, and on the kind of sleep you get on a flight from Los Angeles to Auckland. Maria and I were exhausted ourselves, and we'd had the fortune of spending a couple leisurely days around Hamilton. It was with this exhaustion we rolled into our hotel in downtown Wellington, where Jennifer and Ricky's bags were faithfully waiting for them after the airline dropped them off.

Wellington is a fun-sized Seattle with a windy waterfront, a plethora of coffee shops, the kind of people that frequent coffee shops, and a backdrop of green, residential hills. The central business district is compact and good for walking, a great place to slow our pace for a minute. The next day, Maria and I had a few filming locations in mind to look for, so Ricky handed us his GPS device and we went our separate ways. I had ordered *The Lord of the Rings Location Guidebook* by Ian Brodie, which points the way to the trilogy's filming locations. Some tours charge a premium to point at rocks, stumps, and empty fields only to say, 'the thing you like was filmed here once.' The book, which went so far as to include GPS coordinates for each location, would save us a lot of money. Still footsore from the alpine crossing, Maria and I took a bus to the top of Mt. Victoria, a forested hill overlooking

Wellington's central business district.

Not all of the filming locations are in remote locations. There are a handful along the paths of Mt. Victoria, smack in the middle of a major city. Unfortunately, some of the directions in *The Lord of the Rings Location Guidebook* are less than precise. Maria and I had several false starts before we found a path that seemed to match what the book said and take us in the general direction of the coordinates. The paths from the summit skirt the side of the ridge through tall pine trees to the bottom of the hill, where the city starts once again. It was down one of these paths that actor Elijah Wood famously tells his friends to "get off the road!" in the first film, *The Fellowship of the Ring.* The four hobbits hide beneath an oversized root just as the hooded and creepy ringwraith arrives on his black horse. The root and tree were fabricated for the movie and are no longer there, but the coordinates place you in the exact spot, where there is a ditch. When we arrived, a group of friends were taking turns sitting in the ditch, as the hobbits did, and taking pictures as part of a guided tour. We asked the guide, a guy about our age, if this was indeed the spot, but he was unwilling to answer our question since we hadn't paid him to point at it. I understood his reluctance to share information that gave him a livelihood, but he remains the only person I met in New Zealand I didn't like. As soon as they buzzed off, we took the same picture.

Later, we met up with Jennifer and Ricky on Cuba Street for dinner. Why it's called Cuba Street, I couldn't say, but it's a pedestrian road with some turn-of-the-century buildings and an endless supply of ethnic food. It's the kind of place where you make a food decision and instantly regret it not because it's bad, but because the next option looks that much better. Most prices are very reasonable as well. There ought to be more Cuba Streets in the world.

The last thing we did in Wellington, after taking in the waterfront and the free and excellent Te Papa museum, was tour the Weta Workshop. Founded in 1987, Weta Workshop has made a name for itself as the go-to producer of film props and special effects, whether they be practical or digital. Besides *The Lord of the Rings* and *Hobbit* movies, Weta has been deeply involved with films such as *Avatar*, *The Chronicles of Narnia* series, and Jackson's version of *King Kong*. They offer tours of their workshop, with hundreds of swords, guns, masks, miniature sets, and other props on display from these and other films (they've had their hands in far too many to mention). Like most New Zealanders we'd met, our guide, a woman about my age, was very personable and easy to talk to, the kind of guide that you're genuinely sad to leave after the tour. During her 45-minute presentation, she bestowed upon us wonderful nuggets about the filmmaking world and the highlights of working behind the scenes on such memorable films. I am by no means handy with machinery or tools, but I instantly wished I was. That way I could work at Weta, live in Wellington, and be the happiest human being for the rest of my life.

⸺⸺⸺◈⸺⸺⸺

The North Island is wonderful, don't get me wrong, but there's a sense that you've not really been to New Zealand unless you venture down to the South Island. I'd reckon even North Islanders would tell you that. It's here that the scenery really takes on an untamed persona, unlike the relatively populated North Island. With such emptiness, you're reminded that you're not in Seattle but at the bottom of the world, as far as you can be from practically everyone. There is no city further away from London than Dunedin on the South Island, which tells you that if you're trying to put some distance between you and your parents, and I mean some serious distance, there's no better place to go than here.

We flew from Wellington to Christchurch and spent the night at the Jailhouse hostel, formerly the Addington Prison from 1874 to 1999. It was a four-hour journey by tour van, including stops, from the Jailhouse hostel in Christchurch to Mt. Sunday. We were, of course, on this tour to see a *Rings* location. Although we'd found locations on our own easily enough, we thought such a remote destination in the bush, through empty lands and down gravel roads, was best left to the professionals. Our tour guide and driver for this excursion was a retired chaplain in the New Zealand army. He had a scruffy white beard and a belly and, with his calm sense of humor, it took no imagination at all to place him as Santa Claus. He dutifully drove us through the flat farmland of the Canterbury plains, framed by the approaching foothills of the Southern Alps, to Mt. Sunday in the middle of the island.

Because we were paying a large sum of money to drive all day for one thing, I had to really sell this one to Jennifer and Ricky. Mt. Sunday, I explained, is a solitary ridge in the middle of a massive, yellow-grassed valley enclosed on all ends by snow-capped mountains. As far as epic scenery goes, it's a humdinger. That's why Jackson and company chose the ridge as the location for Edoras, home of the horse-lords in Tolkien's kingdom of Rohan. Tolkien, and the film crew by extension, envisioned these people as Norsemen of the plains, with the horse rather than the ship as their center of gravity. Construction crews built a town center of thatched roofs and wooden huts on the summit of Mt. Sunday, with a horse motif prominently featured in each building. It's a stunning location in the movies. Nothing remains of the set, but it hardly matters. If I'd come all this way to the end of the world, I was going to stand on top of Mt. Sunday.

After the tiny town of Methven, where we stopped for a toilet and a flat white (New Zealand's coffee drink of choice), the fields of crops gave way to sheep pasture and then, as we drove into the mountains rather than along them, empty, brown land surrounded by peaks. A small holiday community tucked between Lake Camp and Lake Clearwater is the last settlement of any kind before Mt. Sunday, a half an hour away. At last, the van turned a corner and I knew the sight immediately. There, below us in a vast, wide valley, was Rohan.

Mt. Sunday is little more than a giant, obstinate rock rising out of the tough grass like an iceberg. The climb through tussocks up the hill isn't difficult, but more so than it would appear. It's steeper than it looks, for one, but it's also unbelievably windy. Our tour guide warned us not to get too close to the edge, and I was inclined to listen to him; it's difficult to stand straight up. The view, though, is immaculate. The valley meets the floodplain of the Rangitata River, and behind that is the main range of the Southern Alps. The nearby sheep station, the last before the road dead ends into the mountains, is called "Erehwon," which is "nowhere" spelled backwards. It really is nowhere out there.

While on the summit, we had the privilege of handling replicas of the movie's swords and flags. Scoff if you'd like at my propensity for being an incurable nerd, but I ask you the following: what could be more captivating than holding a sword in your hands, with the heart-wrenching lilt of a Hardanger fiddle from the film soundtrack playing from your iPod, the wind blowing through your hair, all while surrounded by majestic mountains? Nothing, that's what.

Our tour guide had one more activity up his sleeve. In fact, it was a sleeve of bread. At the second to last station on the road, Mt. Potts Station, he pulled the van over, away from lingering sheep, and walked up to the skimpiest of wire fences. Holding a slice of bread in the air, he hollered for a good minute. From the other side of the vast field trotted a herd of very orange and fuzzy Scottish Highland cattle. We each held out our own slices of bread and let the cattle come to us, taking the bread out of our hands with their lips and tongues. It wasn't something I expected to do in Rohan, but it was fun all the same. The station's hedges and trees are visible, if you know what to look for, in a handful of shots in the movies.

We'd been to the end of the road, yes, but not quite the end of the world. We didn't have time or interest to make it to Invercargill, the southernmost city in the country, but that's not the end either. Stewart Island, with a permanent population of 381 as of 2013, floats 19 miles south of the South Island. South of that is nothing but Antarctica. Instead, we drove 12 hours down the spine of the island and through it to see what Rudyard Kipling pegged the 'eighth wonder of the world.'

As the crow flies, Milford Sound (which is a fjord actually, or 'fiord' if you're in New Zealand) is only 43 miles from the nearest city, Queenstown, yet because of those beautiful but pesky Southern Alps, there's no direct route. Instead, drivers must go down and around 178 miles of sparsely populated bush to get there. It took us about eight hours to drive to Queenstown from Christchurch, with stops at Lake Tekapo and Twizel, so another four sounded doable. There's something oddly macabre about the mountain range across Lake Wakatipu opposite Queenstown, which is perhaps why Weta Digital superimposed them with computer generated images to establish the mountain range of Mordor. The range is called the Remarkables, shooting about 6,000 feet up from the lake. After Queenstown, much like before Queenstown, is a lot of yellow, grassy fields, tall-ish mountains with a dusting of snow on the top at most, and sheep. When we grabbed dinner at a no-frills seafood joint in Te Anau, the last town and gas station before Milford Sound, we asked the 50's something woman behind the counter how she managed to live in such a remote location.

"You've got to be organized," is all she offered.

After Te Anau, it's nothing but remote farms and mountains as far as the eye can see. The pass narrows and the road winds through valleys and short, tangled forests rather than farms. It was getting late and low clouds were moving in. Surrounded by mountains, the road became dark just as the rain moved in. The dim clouds and rain eliminated all visibility past 100 feet, so to our surprise the road curved past rushing waterfalls, from what heights I couldn't say. After the long and skinny Homer Tunnel through the mountains, it was another 20 minutes to the rustic Milford Sound Lodge, where we found our rooms in the pouring rain. It was completely dark outside by then, and our rooms were chilly, save for the thick covers on the bed. I hoped for the best for the next day, when we intended to actually see something after driving for 12 hours. It rains 252 inches a year in Milford Sound, so it's a bit of a gamble as to what you're going to see once you're there, and 'there' is so utterly far away: two hours from Te Anau, which is itself two hours from a city of any size. More so than in Tongariro National Park or on Mt. Sunday, on this empty, rainy, dark road hours away from civilization, it truly felt like we were at the end of the world.

The next morning, we arose from our rooms early to catch a sea kayaking tour. Our surroundings had changed dramatically. The last wisps of cloud from the night's rain were evaporating with the morning sun. We were encircled by shimmery, snow-capped mountains, from the tops of which hundreds of waterfalls, swelled from the night's rain, dropped thousands of feet down the steep, gray rock faces like tears into the rainforests that filled the valley floor. We drove down the road to the end of the sound, where our sea kayaking journey would begin.

I find I'm out of words to describe Milford Sound; this country really does put a thesaurus to shame. How do I convey something so obviously and stunningly beautiful when I've already labeled the rest of the country as such? I can't go back and tell you Mt. Sunday is actually a bit ugly, that Hobbiton was 'meh,' or that Tongariro was just a bunch of rocks. They were all uniquely gorgeous, but you're going to have to take my word for it that Milford Sound is, by a spectacular degree, more beautiful than all those places, indeed any place I'd ever been. Heaven, it turns out, is not reached by stairs or wings but by boat. Or kayaks, if you were the four of us and a third pair on their honeymoon.

You're never going to believe this, but our tour guide -- a 20-something named Tim out of Dunedin, I believe-- was a wonderful human being to spend a few hours with. Seriously, New Zealand's tour guides are on point. Maria and I wanted to be friends with every single one of them. Tim had only been a guide for a month or so, but he was personable, knowledgeable, and brought us back alive. The water, protected in the sound, was calm enough for this writer with an aversion to deep water. The seven of us paddled in our tandem kayaks, save for Tim, past Bowen Falls, one of the few permanent waterfalls tumbling straight into the seawater. While in the sound, we kept a sharp eye for marine life. Dolphins, seals, and penguins frequent the waters in some numbers; as we slid our kayaks into the water earlier, a pod of dolphins was heading back to sea. Other than a solitary, lazy fur seal sunning itself on a rock, we didn't see much as we skirted the north shore.

I couldn't put my finger on it as we made our way into the sound, but there was something eerily prehistoric about our whereabouts. Something about the way the wet, verdant forests clung to the cliffs told me that we'd discovered some lost world of dinosaurs and ill-advised theme parks. I had the urge to climb aboard a helicopter and find some velociraptors. Indeed, location scouts considered the area for the second *Jurassic Park* film, the flora is so similar to what dinosaurs would've trampled back in the day, but chose to return to Hawaii for budget concerns. Milford Sound is, as I've already explained, a long haul from anything.

This doesn't keep tourists from coming. 585,000 people came in 2016, most making a day trip of it from Te Anau or Queenstown. They arrive in tour buses, cruise the sound for a couple hours in boats that hold a few hundred folks, and then go back to their hotels. I can't imagine a worse way to see Milford Sound for the simple reason that the scenery demands your undivided attention, away from crowds or cameras. Once you're there, you realize there isn't enough time in the world to look at it. We would have to settle for one rainy night and a sea kayaking excursion. The bonus of the rainy night was that we were already in the sound first thing in the morning and most people wouldn't be around for another few hours.

This meant that, save for a half-dozen early cruises and a smattering of other kayakers, we had one of the world's most astounding views to ourselves.

The water widened and we reached a fork in the fiord. Here, on a rocky beach, we took a break and ate lunch. Tim, wonderful Tim, brought a portable kettle to warm ourselves in the exhilarating, but chilly midday with tea and coffee. There in front of us, across the fiord to our left, was Mitre Peak, a gigantic incisor of a mountain named after the pointy hat worn by Catholic bishops. It's more than a mile straight up from the water to the top. Apparently, people climb these things. I was happy to wonder at its height from sea level.

The wind was set to change in the afternoon, into the sound rather than out, so Tim had a plan. We rowed to the opposite shore and he presented a sail. My job, as well as Maria's, was to cling tight to one kayak on our left and the other on our right and therefore become a sort of 'super' kayak. On the other two kayaks, the back person tied the sail to their oars and held them high above their heads. The front two held the bottom of the sail. We would let the wind take us back to where we started. While this seems the lazier option, and it probably was, it still wasn't easy. The sail holders had to position the sail just right or else it would flap in our faces. Meanwhile, the cold water splashed Maria and I's fingers, grasping with less and less iron will, as we held the kayaks together as one unit. Tim, his plan working only too well, paddled hard to keep up with us while attempting to explain Maori beliefs about the area. I'm sorry to say my attention was more on my surroundings and my fingers, but it was fun to watch him breathlessly attempt to relate a story and paddle at the same time.

We made it back in good time. After we changed into dry clothes, we began the drive back to Queenstown, where we would spend our last couple of days in New Zealand. Already, the traffic coming the opposite way was thickening. With the clear skies, we enjoyed the views that had been robbed of us the previous night: more mountains, more waterfalls from the rain, more superlative majesty.

Yes, more, more, more. Gorgeous. Beautiful. Breathtaking. These words don't help you learn anything about New Zealand, but I'm telling you that no words do this place justice. Few countries on earth offer such a variety of absorbing features in such a relatively small space. I haven't even touched half the things we did while there: the beach in Raglan, a Maori 'hangi' feast and haka performance in Rotorua, a winery in Wanaka, extreme sports (some more extreme than others) in Queenstown. I'd love to share about all of them, but this book is about South Korea after all; I've only included the trip because it was the impetus to get me to teach English overseas in the first place. What's more, my journey home was at a crossroads. For the first time in my life, I found another place I would seriously consider uprooting myself for. I fell in love with New Zealand and could see myself living there. It sucks that it's on the absolute other side of the world from Ohio.

My lasting impression of New Zealand – that far, marvelous country at the bottom of the world – is that Middle Earth exists. I was deathly afraid that, having been to many of the film's locations, the magic would be lost and the movies would never be the same. Nothing is farther from the truth. The trip spoiled nothing, except for perhaps myself. It was the most indulgent thing I'd ever done, traveling to New Zealand, and I'm not sorry about it at all. Not one bit.

Badminton in the Gym

That Time With the Noodle Smell

The new school year, my last semester as a Native English Teacher in South Korea, brought its usual round of changes, both welcome and unwelcome. Once again, we had a new Vice Principal. This one was a bit younger, early 40's by the looks of him, and athletic. He wandered the hallways often, either because he was surveying his dominion or bored.

When the pompous gym teacher accepted a job at another school, the Principal decided to hire another contract teacher, like Gym Teacher, to replace him for the upcoming semester. He also made the decision to put him in our office. News circulated that the guy he hired was, as Jang Mi put it, a 'troublemaker.' I didn't know if this meant he was dastardly or just didn't play by the rules, but I wasn't thrilled with sharing my office with another outcast. I was already outcast enough. But Jang Mi brought me another piece of news.

"I will be the new music teacher," she said. "And I will move into the office with you."

I was beyond excited to have somebody to talk to in my office other than Gym Teacher. During the Winter break, we moved in some more tables and computers and she set up her desk next to mine. Gym Teacher sat facing me, and the new guy would sit facing Jang Mi.

On the first day of the new semester, I walked into the office to find none of my officemates present. However, on the new gym teacher's chair was draped a winter coat. My nostrils were inundated with the salty stench of cheap ramen; there, on the new guy's desk, was an empty bowl. I signed in on my computer when Jang Mi walked in and made a face about the smell.

"He's already a problem," she said, sitting at her desk. We didn't have time to discuss the new guy any further. I had to run to my first period class and so did she. I was in and out of the office throughout the day, but still he was absent. When I came in to drop off my books before lunch, Gym Teacher was sitting at his desk with his headphones in.

"Happy lunch time?" he asked.

"Yes," I replied in Korean, although I was hoping to stall until Jang Mi came back. I was tired of going to lunch by myself, trying to time my arrival with Ji Young's or Hyun Soo's. It would be nice to arrive at lunch with somebody, as a group. Somebody who wasn't Gym Teacher. Someone who wasn't an outcast. Jang Mi was that person. She was elsewhere, though, and Gym Teacher was looking at me expectantly, so we walked down to the cafeteria together.

I knew nothing about the new teacher other than he wore a winter coat and ate food, so I expected to at least see him at lunch. However, he was absent from the noisy cafeteria as well. I sat with Gym Teacher with my lunch, which other than the daily portions of rice and kimchi consisted of roasted potatoes and the kitchen's variation on pizza toast. Not quite pizza and not quite toast, the junky invention combined what are normally American ingredients to create a food that is nothing at all American. The bread, the whitest you've ever seen, appeared to be baked with a type of tomato sauce that could only come out of a nuclear lab smeared on top and sprinkled with corn, onions, and other marginally-acceptable pizza toppings. The melted white stuff to top it all was, I assume, the cheese part of the equation but it was tasteless and made the whole thing less appealing, which is the opposite role of cheese. I was halfway into my first slice of pizza toast when Jang Mi and Ji Young joined us. Ji Young, ever the lover of junk food, devoured the pizza toast. Jang Mi nibbled at hers. I was glad at least one other person in the room was suspicious about the fake-tasting food.

It wasn't until about an hour before quitting time that I finally saw the new guy. I was typing out a new PowerPoint when a tall, lanky adjeossi slid the door open and bowed. He had short hair, like Gym Teacher, wore glasses, and looked exactly like the kind of kid that hates gym. We introduced ourselves and then he sat at his desk. He knew less English than Gym Teacher, so our opportunities for conversation were severely limited. Still, you don't need to speak the same language to be annoying.

Gym Teacher took a shine to the new guy and within about three minutes it was clear that they were going to be best friends. They began a conversation that didn't end until it was time to go home. During that time, Jang Mi shifted uncomfortably in her chair and finally put on headphones. I pulled up the messenger app on my desktop and sent her a message.

"WHAT ARE THEY TALKING ABOUT?" I typed. I waited for a response. The program said she was typing.

"YOU DON'T WANT TO KNOW," she responded.

"YES, I DO."

A moment later, she typed back. "THEY ARE TALKING ABOUT NOTHING. I'M JEALOUS. YOU DON'T KNOW KOREAN."

Later, presumably after a conversation with Jang Mi, Ji Young explained that the two gym teachers talked about anything and everything and that none of it made sense. I could easily tune it out, but Jang Mi had difficulty concentrating on her work and began spending more time in the music room than the office. So much for an office friend.

The new guy quickly gained a reputation for being awkward, which I'm sure came as a relief to Gym Teacher who was up to that point the most awkward person in the school, except for possibly myself. The pair were inseparable, never wasting an opportunity to shoot the breeze and laugh. And they laughed all the time. It would've been kind of cute, if it wasn't so pathetic. The new guy laughed more than Gym Teacher. Sometimes, when Gym Teacher wasn't around, the new guy would sit at his desk and watch funny videos on his computer and laugh loudly at them even though he was in an office where Jang Mi and I were trying to work. He did this more often than not with a bowl of ramen on his desk. I've quite forgotten his real name, so let's refer to him as Ramen.

Gym Teacher and Ramen's antics became a big enough issue

that Jang Mi requested we install some dividers to maintain some sense of privacy and separation. After classes one afternoon, we slid the dividers between the desks, making the room much less personal. They had an immediate effect; Gym Teacher and Ramen silently entertained themselves while Jang Mi and I worked. That lasted for about 30 minutes, when Gym Teacher decided to lean back from his desk, in sight of Ramen, and incite a conversation again.

In truth, the dividers did eventually lessen the noise. Gym Teacher and Ramen either got the message and took their tomfoolery elsewhere, or were running out of things to discuss. There was some normalcy in the office again.

Unfortunately, the dividers did nothing about the ramen smell. Every day, Ramen brought in a plastic bowl of the soup, ate some percentage of it for breakfast, and then left the remnants to fill the room with odor. Some offices light scented candles. We had a cooling bowl of spicy MSG.

One morning I walked into the office with everybody already present. When I logged in, Jang Mi opened a conversation immediately.

"MATTHEW....TELL HYUN SOO....YOU ARE DISTRESSED," she said. And then nothing.

I'm distressed? Why am I distressed? I knew she was formulating the answer, so I waited to hear what was distressing me. "BECAUSE NOODLE SMELL."

I saw her plan immediately. Nobody was going to listen to a young, female teacher's gripes about co-workers older than herself. However if the foreigner, who is oblivious to the cultural nuances that prohibit this kind of complaint, made a comment to somebody with authority, something just might be done. I assured her that I would say something to Hyun Soo.

That afternoon, I made a comment to Hyun Soo that our office was a little crowded, and that perhaps everybody would be best served if the gym teachers spent more time in the gym office. It sounded logical to me. It probably sounded logical to Hyun Soo as well, but he didn't quite have that much authority to make that big a change. He probably mentioned it lightly to the principal and waited, like the rest of us, to see if something would change.

Of course, very little changed. Gym Teacher and Ramen, while spending perhaps a little less time in the office, didn't move to the gym. The ramen smell didn't stop either. It was settled then: if the gym teachers wouldn't leave, then we'd spend less time in the office. After lunch, Jang Mi and I began taking walks around the school grounds, sometimes bringing Ji Young or other teachers with us. The official excuse for wandering outside for a walk was for 'digestion,' but really we were just lazy. I'd taken walks with Gym Teacher many times, stopping to observe the trees and flowers growing in the garden. Our conversation topics had been limited, as always, so I enjoyed my walks with Jang Mi more.

We also took to playing badminton in the gym in the afternoons. After we'd gotten our work done, and sometimes before then, we grabbed some badminton rackets in the gym closet and hit the shuttlecock back and forth. I'd never played badminton before, and so we spent most of our time just keeping the thing in the air. Students, or Gym Teacher, might wander in and ask if they could play a game with us. Jang Mi told them all we were only practicing.

There was one afternoon that a local badminton coach was with a handful of my students in the gym. Jang Mi assured the coach that we were there to practice and only needed one side of the gym, but we got roped into a doubles game: Jang Mi and I versus the coach and one of his best players, a fourth grade girl in one of my classes. Jang Mi and I took our positions and the coach served. I swung my racket and hit the shuttlecock. It was a great shot, landing between the two of them. The swiftness of my hit had caught the girl unawares, and she received an admonishing glare from her coach. The score was 1-0. That was the last time we'd be in the lead for the entire game. The student got her game face on, and the coach was naturally the best of all of us. I don't remember the exact score, but I didn't repeat it to anybody the following day. I'm sure the student did: she'd just beaten the music and English teacher at badminton.

So ended my brief stint playing real badminton. After our embarrassing defeat, Jang Mi and I returned to our 'practicing.' It turned into an opportunity to discuss politics, our families, and our countries. This is what I appreciated most about Jang Mi, that she was as curious as me about other cultures. She was always perceptive about how I might be viewing events or information that transpired within in the school or in Korea. For instance, one day in the office, the Principal said I'd put on weight. As soon as he left she explained that he meant that as a compliment, that I was looking healthy. In this way, Jang Mi became the natural person to share my frustrations and concerns. These were often shared in the gym, hitting the shuttlecock back and forth.

Jang Mi also picked up Ji Young's slack in informing the waygook about last minute changes. Ji Young was good about informing me of schedule changes or administrative needs, but she wasn't there every day and some things fell through the cracks. Jang Mi filled that void. I'd often walk into the office in the mornings with two messages waiting for me: one Korean message shared to all the teachers with information pertinent to the day and then Jang Mi's English translation. She had an inkling when I might be in the dark, and did her best to bring me back to the light.

And thank goodness. Google Translate was zero help with the Korean messages, vomiting sentences like 'Sorry for the boring table,' 'Map does not rain in the playground,' and 'Contact threesome teacher jobs hump, I'd greatly appreciate it right now.' My absolute favorite was, at the end of a long message, the helpful 'If you are interested, please contact Doris Nuggets.' I think it goes without saying that there was no Doris Nuggets in my school, but on the plus side, we now have the incredible name Doris Nuggets.

Some more winners:

Elementary tyranny 14:00.

School-related staff development slapping: 15:00.

Today the spaghetti is somewhat inadequate.

The youth group meetings colon (Girl Scouts, Syrians, Sea Cadets).

Do not forget to drink before work today, thank you.

Sexual submission - by tomorrow.

So you see why I was at the mercy of a friend's translation. I would've been standing on the roof with my shoes on my hands otherwise.

Unfortunately, Jang Mi and our walks and badminton days were short lived. One too many times, the Vice Principal had walked into the gym, doing what I'm not sure, and seen us not working. We decided that it probably didn't look good on our parts to be seen in the gym every day, so our badminton practices became few and far between. Jang Mi went back to avoiding the office, to get work done away from the chatter of two strange, older men. I missed having her around, but I'd still arrive in the mornings with two messages blinking at me on my computer.

Gyeongju Marathon

That Time "Big Wall" Built a Temple

About once every three years, I remember that, as a college student, I ran a half marathon. I didn't finish with an especially good time, something in the two and a half hour zone, but the fact that I ran it surfaces from time to time as the misguided notion that I am a runner. This is false. I hate running. It's boring, it's exhausting, and I don't enjoy it at all. Plus, I seem to weigh more every time I put on the tennis shoes. But every three years or so, I forget and convince myself it's time to jump start a running routine.

One such season occurred while in Korea. Some friends of ours, including Gail, ran a local 10K during our first April. Maria, Phillip and I woke early on a Sunday and watched from the sidelines and I was at once transplanted back to my own half marathon. In truth, I really enjoyed my experience running through Cincinnati. The energy is positive throughout a marathon morning, with crowds cheering and offering genuine encouragement along the entire route. It's encouraging as well to see how many types of people sign up to run: young people, old people, families, military, first responders, people with disabilities. I had prepared for the run and I made it through without any major stops, for which I am immensely proud. In the last half mile, I'd expected to be crawling across the finish line feeling defeated and deflated. Instead, I felt hungry and nearly sprinted the rest of the way. If you've never had the pleasure of bounding through a horde of tired joggers to the finish line as hundreds of people cheer, you really must sign up for one of these runs. It was exhilarating, and so were the complimentary post-run snacks.

The marathon in Daegu looked no-less exhilarating, and on a much more horizontal axis than the one in Cincinnati. Again, it was inspiring to see who showed up to run; everyone from troops (both American and Korean), taekwondo classes, mothers and their children, fathers and their children, and so on made the early morning starting time. This marathon had the added bonus of culturally-themed support along the route. Not far down from where we stood, a company of elderly citizens played janggu drums and sang. So, with such sunny memories coloring my mood that morning, I vowed to join Gail and others on a future run. But not too soon. Summer was approaching, and I wasn't keen on starting a jogging routine in Daegu's humidity. So I was possibly interested in starting in the autumn, but it really is the best season in Korea and I didn't want to get tied down to plans. Next Spring sounded lovely, provided the weather cooperated.

I did end up going out for a few jogs in the autumn time. Gail and I met once a week for about a month and jogged along the river in town. Jogging is not a big activity in Korea, or Daegu anyway, so occasionally we'd receive glares from Koreans walking along the path, particularly older pairs ambling with their arms behind their backs. To my delight, I was still able to run about 30 minutes, albeit at a deliberate and embarrassing pace, without stopping. That's all I would need for a 5K, so we looked for an interesting one to run. We selected the Gyeongju Cherry Blossom Marathon in the upcoming April.

Gyeongju is the perfect day trip from Daegu. About an hour and a half away by bus or train, the city was the ancient capital of the Silla dynasty for a millennium. At its peak in the 9th century, it boasted a population of one million and its rulers and aristocracy wielded enough power and money to govern the entire peninsula from its remote position in the southeast. Centuries later, it's still rather off the main grid -- a medium-sized city flung indiscriminately, by the looks of it on a map, between the much more expansive metro areas of Daegu, Busan, and Ulsan. It's near the coast, but not quite on it, removed from the main high-speed rail line, and not all that big -- not quite touching 300,000 residents. Despite its geographical oddities, the city and its surrounding national park are among Korea's top tourist attractions. Gyeongju National Park preserves what remains of the area's archaeological treasures, which is to say not much. Baekje, a rival kingdom, sacked the city in 926 A.D., the Mongols followed suit in the 13th century, and the Japanese did their part in the 16th century. Luckily, Gyeongju was tucked just inside the Busan Perimeter during the Korean War, or else there might be nothing left to see. Such as it is, what remains of the capital city makes for a splendid stroll or, even better, a bike ride. You can hire a bike steps outside of the train station for, last I was there, 10000 won for the day, or roughly $10. Then, the city is yours to explore.

We'd come once before to explore the city's historical offerings. The most unusual of them are the tumuli, or royal tombs. The interior of these conical, earthen mounds is a wooden chamber filled with, alongside the body, riches suitable for royalty. The Gyeongju National Museum, which itself sits inside the national park, is a wonderful museum that displays many of these excavated treasures. There's also Cheomseongdae, the oldest surviving observatory in East Asia. Dating back to the 7th century, the building is small and shaped like an upside down goblet, but is fully intact and worthy of a look. All these sites and more are linked together by paths through yellow rapeseed and wildflowers. And, if you play your cards right and arrive in April, there are scores of cherry blossom trees throughout the entire place. If there's a lovelier place for a bike ride in Korea, I haven't found it.

Not to miss an opportunity to make a few more bucks, Gyeongju has developed a resort area to the east of the city surrounding Bomunho Lake. Resorts, 5-star hotels, spas, water parks, and other tourist traps dot the shores. The area is exceedingly expensive, and poor and stingy as I am, I never had the pleasure of going to, say, California Beach, a water park whose every billboard sported smiling girls in bikinis, or the Love Castle, a museum/theme park every bit as naughty as Love Land in Jeju. I am being selective; there are plenty of establishments in the resort area that are wholesome, ritzy, or any other adjective that suits your fancy. All I'm saying is that the city planners had the good graces to put the Orlando side of town 10 kilometers away from the rest and plant cherry blossom trees along the roads connecting the two parts. And that is why, at 7:30 on a chilly, cloudy April morning, Gail and I stood several thousand people behind the starting line of the Gyeongju Cherry Blossom Marathon which started and terminated in the heart of the resort area. We'd trained up as best we could; that is to say we ran two or three times in the weeks leading up to the race. Mostly, my goal was to run the 5K within a half-way respectable 30 minutes, but I had one slight problem: I woke up that morning with a really sore throat. One can run with a sore throat of course, but it would not be fun. Also, my nose was becoming stuffy. They were the beginning symptoms of a nasty sinus infection, but I would need to run through it. Maria and Phillip, ever the supportive kind ("do you really need me to come out?"), stood somewhere along the track waiting to watch us run past them for 10 seconds.

Some small fireworks and an explosion of confetti signaled the beginning of the race, and the more serious marathon runners at the front bolted past the starting line. It took a few minutes for the rest of the horde to get rolling, and by the time us lazy 5K runners got to move forward, at least 10 minutes had passed. I was raring to get it over with, with my sore throat and all. Also, it was not a warm morning and I wanted to move. We passed the starting line and began to jog only to nearly run over a group of girls who were posing for a picture. What a wonderful place to stop moving. We maneuvered around them only to do the same to a family who had stopped in the middle of the road to take a picture. With the few serious runners long gone, it quickly became apparent that most participants in the race were going to treat it as a nice stroll along the lake to take pictures of cherry blossoms. And why not, I suppose. Cherry blossom festivals around Korea are notoriously crowded and far flung; a family could spend a day driving to the festival location, waiting hours for a parking spot, spending a terrible time shoulder to shoulder with other cranky families, and then driving back home. A marathon is a clever subterfuge to see the trees in a much more relaxed environment, minus the flustered foreigners taking their run times too seriously. Thus, our first two kilometers or so of the run were very slow going.

Some way into the run, another thing occurred to me: there were no spectators. There were cheering people at the start/finish line, but people didn't show up in droves to watch the runners like they did in Daegu or Cincinnati. Half the fun of a marathon is the positive environment emanating from onlookers, but we were forced to create our own positivity. With a sore throat and what was looking to be a terrible finish time, this was easier said than done. I didn't envy the folks running anything longer than us; what could be worse than running along a deserted marathon course?

I did, at one point, decide to do as the Koreans do and snap a picture, only I took mine mid-run. To this day, I am extremely proud of how horizontal and focused the photo is. It shows the line of runners, the cherry blossoms standing sentinel beside us, and the lake behind. Ansel Adams couldn't have asked for better.

Maria and Phillip planted themselves near the end of the course where they did their due diligence and cheered Gail and I toward the finish line. My time ended up being just over 30 minutes, which wasn't so bad all things considered. Gail and I agreed that we'd have run the thing in under a half hour if it weren't for them meddling photographers. The skies were getting grayer, and I was looking forward to a hot shower, some hotter tea, and a change of clothes, so we grabbed a cab back to the hostel.

The hostel we stayed at, a few blocks from the train station, is worthy of note in that it had the strangest rules of any hostel I've stayed in. Take the co-ed rule: they didn't allow opposite sexes to stay in the same room. Since we were traveling with a group of four evenly divided between males and females, this worked out fine, but it's just a little weird to be told that I can't sleep in the same room as my wife. I could let this go, if it weren't for the odd inverse curfew hours in the afternoon. We weren't allowed on premises between something like 12:00pm and 5:00pm. What if I wasn't feeling well and wanted to lie down with the lights off, which was very much my situation? Didn't matter. We needed to be out. To appease our hostel managers, we decided to check out the famous Bulguksa temple on the outskirts of town. We took a cab, navigated through some residual marathon traffic, and drove past the rest of Gyeongju's sights to a far suburb, where the driver dropped us off at a busy parking lot.

As I said before, Korean temples can become tedious once you've seen a few, so when a temple is supposed to be particularly good, it means you're looking for three things. You're looking for a beautiful natural setting that separates it from the hundreds, if not thousands of temples scattered across the country. You're also looking for size. Lastly, you're hoping that the temple is actually from antiquity, that it wasn't destroyed and then rebuilt forty years ago. Bulguksa delivers on two and a half of these fronts. The temple is tucked in the bottom folds of Tohamsan, a modest mountain but one tall enough from which to see the ocean from the peak, with cherry blossoms and other flowering trees scattered throughout. While not large by historical standards -- many temples surpassed it in size in its heyday -- it is an expansive complex by today's standards. The half points it receives is in the authenticity. The wooden buildings were burned to the ground when the Japanese invaded in 1592 and have been rebuilt or restored several times since then. However, the stone terraces on which the buildings sit and the rest of the masonry structures are original, dating back to the 8th century.

I must mention here the description provided by the website Asian Historical Architecture of Kim Daeseong, Bulguksa's architect. It explains that the man "overcame extreme poverty and ugliness to become a great believer in Buddhism." What on earth does being ugly, or good looking for that matter, have to do with joining a religion? Kudos to Kim, I suppose, for making the commitment to set aside his notoriously flat forehead, earning him the moniker 'Big Wall,' in order to adhere to a stoic set of rules. At any rate, legend tells that he dedicated the construction of the temple to his parents, the very folks who endowed him with that forehead, so to speak.

I knew none of this as we purchased our admission tickets and walked through the gate to the complex. I knew exactly three things at that moment: it was crowded, the rain was picking up a bit, and I was getting a massive headache. I pushed on anyway. The front of Bulguksa is impressive, with a grand staircase leading up to the main building. Visitors aren't allowed on the steps, being part of the original construction of the temple, so to go up to the central courtyard you must go around a long outer wall with an intricate green and red roof and up a less impressive set of stairs. A large, stone pagoda stands in the center of the courtyard and features more steps that you're not allowed on. If it weren't for the crowds, the temple courtyard would be a seriously tranquil and inviting place. As it was, and with my head and the weather, I was ready to go back to the hostel, rules be damned. We wandered for a while longer, but the details are mostly the same: wooden structures, intricate, colorful roofs, and stone. Even within the same temple, the design can become tiresome, and most temples follow the same pattern. Paintings on the outer walls can be fun, however. Often they depict dragons, but this is not always the case. My personal favorite is of a tree growing out of a weeping whale like a spout. I have yet to discover the meaning of this.

Another notch for Bulguksa is its gift shop. Most temples have them, but they are usually small and don't carry anything exciting. Bulguksa's shop occupied a large side building of the complex and sold the typical knick-knacks, but also paintings, ceramics, and other artistic endeavors. I put up with my headache while we perused the wonderful store. We ended up buying a painting of musicians parading across the paper. Once we made our purchase, I made it known that I wasn't likely to last much longer on my feet so we walked back to the parking lot and hailed a cab. At this point, the headache was probably the worst of my life. The cab took an hour to get back to the hostel, thanks to the marathon crowd which refused to go away. Once we finally did exit the car, the rain was steady and the temperature not above 50 degrees Fahrenheit, which is excruciating weather for a headache. Each step felt like a punch to the brain. My strides were much longer and faster than those of my companions as I hastened back to the hostel, eager for some acetaminophen and a lie down. Luckily, we'd made it back just within the bounds of legal hours so there would be no arguing over access to our rooms. I bid my wife and Gail adieu and laid in the dark, hoping the pain would recede quickly or that I'd fall asleep. Neither happened.

The Korean Bucket List

That Time Dinosaurs and a Penis Park Were a Priority

During our first year in Korea, the decision to stay another year was easy. We were young, we had traveling to do, and we liked making money. When the opportunity came around a second time, the choice was not so easy. Two years was a long time to spend overseas, but three? You're in danger of planting roots. As luck would have it, the decision was largely made for us. Budget cuts swept through EPIK and they would not be offering as many positions the following semester. If we stayed, it was likely we wouldn't be in the same school, and it was possible we'd need to teach in multiple schools. None of that sounded appealing, so when EPIK needed a yes or no, we gave them a no. We were going home.

There came a point, roughly four months before leaving Korea, that I had a bit of an identity crisis. It had taken over a year to settle into life in a different hemisphere, and I don't just mean getting used to the job or learning Korean, although that's true as well. It took my brain that long to adjust and comfortably look around and think "this is not America." The United States was the only place I'd spent extended periods of time, so that was where, according to my brain, I was most likely to be. Up to that point, according to my brain, I might've been in some unexplored corner of the United States that speaks Korean and has less stringent road laws; an alternative West Virginia, perhaps. Now, after a year living in Daegu, I could firmly say I was not in West Virginia. For most of my life, if I looked at a map I'd mentally view the world from Ohio and look at places like South Korea and think, "gee, that's really far." It had become the other way around. Ohio was the place that was far now. What a weird feeling that was, coming to the realization that you've planted yourself somewhere else, that your perspective has shifted. I began to prefer the world maps where Asia was in the middle rather than Europe and Africa. Suddenly, the prospect of leaving South Korea made me very sad, much sadder than I thought would've been possible. I'd forgotten the whole point of this adventure was to go home to Ohio.

The most alarming realization was that there was still so much to see and we were running out of time. Weekends were filling up with plans; there were only so many left. Maria and I made a Korea bucket list of things we wanted to do or places we wanted to see before we went back to the United States. We wanted to make sure we ate all our favorite Korean foods before we left: kimchi jjim, jjim dak, dak galbi, the bulgogi tents, and so on. We wanted to learn how to roll kimbap. There were places to go, people to go there with, and things to do that wouldn't be available to us again. We took in a 4-D movie, with moving chairs and everything, for the first and only time. This bucket list included a couple places on Korea's southern and eastern coasts. I've said it already and I'll say it again: a trip to South Korea must include the sea.

The top item on my list was Goseong. Almost due south from Daegu, Goseong is a bit off the beaten path but is famous for its well-preserved fossils of dinosaur footprints. To add to the drama, these fossilized prints are on the coast itself, only visible at low tides. It just so happened that the movie *Jurassic World* was opening in Korea soon, so we coordinated a dinosaur-themed weekend. Gail and Phillip were game, so the four of us took a direct bus to Goseong and caught a local bus from the center of town to the Goseong Dinosaur Museum.

The first thing that greeted us outside the museum was a rather convincing life-size replica of a Tyrannosaurus Rex. Walking past it toward the museum, there was another replica of a pack of velociraptors killing a mama iguanodon while its young stands and watches in horror. I liked this museum already; there would be no Barney's here.

As far as dinosaur fossils go, you can't do much better than the

Goseong Dinosaur Museum, standing sentinel atop a coastal cliff over the fossilized footprints below. For a mere 3,000 won (less than $3), not only are visitors granted access to one of the world's largest concentrations of dinosaur footprints, they're treated to a small but memorable collection of actual fossils. There are replicas, too, but not every natural history museum boasts an actual dinosaur fossil, let alone an entire Protoceratops skeleton. Because Koreans never miss a chance to install a trick eye photo opportunity, visitors can pretend they're steering a raft through the Cretaceous period with a Pterodactyl flying above their heads. Phillip and I couldn't say no.

The museum was perhaps my favorite place to practice my Hangul reading. An entire wall labeled 'Dino World' listed dinosaur names in Korean. We could've spent all afternoon competing to see who could read the names fastest ("Ti-Ra-No-Sa-U-Ru-Suh!"), but we had to factor in the tides. The footprints would not be visible all day.

A path from the museum leads down to the shore, past recreations of dinosaurs both friendly and hungry. A flight of wooden stairs later, we descended into the Cretaceous period. There are several sets of dinosaur tracks ambling through this world of rock and tide. The first we saw were plate-sized tracks headed toward the ocean, inching closer with the tide. Most tracks at Goseong are round imprints on the rock, both because they were made by large, plant-eating creatures with flat feet and because of millions and millions of years of erosion. I placed my foot on top of a track, in awe of the notion that a dinosaur once stood where I did.

It was a sticky, hazy day, so there weren't many people out, making the time warp seem all the more real. The trail lead us past sea caves and cliffs to another briny outcropping of rock. Here, below a boardwalk, were more sets of tracks. These were smaller and deeper, made perhaps by a bipedal fellow in no particular hurry. Curiously, they appear in a single line rather than set off from one another, as if the dinosaur had been pulled over for drinking. We saw several other sets of footprints, but the novelty wears off a bit quicker than expected without live, fire-breathing dinosaurs to track, so we headed back toward the museum. Don't get me wrong, though. I was happy we'd made the trek to see them. I'd never been to a fossil site of any consequence and it was completely off my radar until sometime into our second year in Korea. The tracks and the museum are well worth the effort.

The path had taken us farther from the museum than we'd anticipated. We took a shortcut through a parking lot with, by way of some shoddy translation work, an encouraging bright yellow sign saying, "The Way to go Parking Lot." This led us to a trail, a dinosaur-themed pedestrian bridge, and finally the bus stop at the top of the hill. The aforementioned Tyrannosaurus stood about a hundred feet away watching us as we waited for the bus. If lightning struck and it came to life, we would be the first to know.

———⋙⋘———

If Goseong is off the beaten path, Samcheok is into the weeds and down a mudslide. Even from Daegu, with buses and trains going every which way, it takes three buses and four and a half hours to get to this remote town two-thirds of the way up the eastern coast. It's a beautiful three bus rides, though, the second leg out of Pohang hugging a highway with the ocean on the right and mountains on the left. In reality, it only takes two buses to get to Samcheok, but we wanted to check out a curiosity a ways out of town, for which we needed to get off early and catch a local bus. By 'we' I mostly mean Gail. It was her birthday weekend and we let her call the shots on this trip. Also her mother was visiting for the week, all the way from South Africa, and she wanted to give her mom some one-of-a-kind Korean experiences. Thus, we found ourselves at the entrance to Haesindang Park.

Technically, Haesindang Park isn't one-of-a-kind; there are other penis parks in South Korea. We'd been to one already in Jeju, but Haesindang is regarded as the best. It's certainly the largest, taking over a forest along the coast, and the most scenic. If ever you decided that you needed some ocean in your life, but you also needed to see dozens of penis statues and you only had one day to see both, well you're in luck.

Unlike other penis parks in South Korea, which are typically tourist traps, this one comes with a story. Legend tells of a young couple, engaged to be married in some versions, sitting on the shore when a strong tide comes in and carries the woman into the sea, drowning her before they could consummate their relationship.

214

Soon after, the fishermen return to the docks empty-handed; the fish were gone. An evil spirit, they said, was keeping them at bay. Then, desperate to revive the village's fishing industry, a man waded out into the sea and masturbated. Sure enough, the fish returned. In order to forever appease the evil spirit, the villagers built a shrine on the shore to the lost woman, and built penises over the hill leading to the shore.

From the parking lot, it's a general downward walk through woods and handsome flower gardens until you reach the shore. Like Jeju's Love Land, most of the visitors that day were older folks having a laugh. Everything in Haesindang Park, after all, is a penis. The statues, totem poles the majority of them, take on different interpretations of male genitalia. Some have faces. Some have additional penises pointing out. There's a penis seesaw, a penis cannon, a courtyard of the zodiac characters (all sitting in penises). A small lighthouse at the end of a seawall below is a penis. Even the benches are penises. Some are metal, others are stone. Most are wood. Gail's mom, like the rest of the older people at the park that day, seemed to get a bigger kick out of the park than we did. While I wouldn't say it's worth four and a half hours and three buses to be aggressively inundated with phallic symbols, there are worse excuses, I suppose, to get outside and enjoy a beautiful, sunny day.

In truth, the scenery at Haesindang Park is wonderful. The hills come right up to the ocean and form a rocky shoreline begging to be climbed on. Between the rocky outcroppings are tidal pools with crabs, sea urchins, and small fish. We couldn't linger long, though. We still needed to get to Samcheok and find a hotel somewhere. We climbed back up the path and stairs, passing all the same phallic symbols we'd seen before but at a much slower pace with the climb. On the penis seesaw, three adjummas, all with short, curly hair, sat on one side while a single adjeossi sat on the other. Eventually we made it out of the park and to the bus stop.

We were a large, odd-numbered group, so finding a hotel would take some doing. Our original plan was to find a hotel on the beach near Samcheok. The bus let us off and we looked for a hotel that looked cheap enough for our budget. There were fewer choices than we'd anticipated and all were booked. We were running out of options as the sun was beginning to set. While the families and couples that had long since booked their rooms enjoyed the sand and ice cream stands, we were in danger of not having a place to sleep for the night, at least a place close to the beach. There was no choice but to head into Samcheok instead and find a regular love motel. Once we found two cabs together that would take us into town, a task that again took some doing, we arrived in the central part of the city and, with some luck, found a clean love motel near the bus station with enough vacancy for all of us. At 70,000 a night, it was slightly more expensive than the average love motel, but we didn't have a choice. After we'd settled in, we needed to figure out dinner. Maria and I were in a season of wanting only American food, so we walked back to a Domino's we'd passed in the cab. I'm not at liberty to disclose how much we paid for Domino's Pizza, but I will tell you that it's exactly what we wanted and that's all you need to know.

The next morning, the plan was to buy tickets to Samcheok's rail bike along the coast. Samcheok is one of several places in the country with these rail bike systems where groups of two to four pedal open air cars along a fixed-rail path. Daegu doesn't have one nearby, so we thought we would take this opportunity to check it off the list. We arrived at a tiny tourist office across the street from our love motel to purchase the tickets, but evidently rail bikes are a popular thing to do and tickets were sold out days in advance. I had come to Samcheok more interested in the bike rail than the penis park, so I was unhappier about this news than everyone else. The woman working the office kindly suggested that we check out one of Samcheok's caves instead. We'd come a long way to get to Samcheok, so we decided that a cave would be a worthwhile alternative to a breezy bike ride by the sea. It'd be cool inside, at least. The woman directed us toward the correct bus stop and we hopped on when the appropriate bus came by.

Hwaseon cave is in the middle of a karst mountain range just outside of Samcheok. The dark, foreboding entrance lies about halfway up one of the mountains, not unlike the Grinch's lair in Dr. Seuss' *How the Grinch Stole Christmas*. It's a 45-minute hike up from the parking lot, but an incline is also available. We were in no mood to hike up in the humidity, so we were all too thankful for the incline. We didn't know this at the time, but Hwaseon is the largest limestone cave in South Korea and one of the largest in all of Asia. Over six kilometers of the cave have been mapped, but visitors only see about 1600 meters. Walking in, the interior is vast and deep, like walking into a stark and empty cathedral with an aversion to windows. The cave is relatively well-lit, at times with colorful greens and reds, further proving the hypothesis that the Grinch lurked nearby. Metal, grated steps and pathways looped us through the cave, not so much filled with stalactites and stalagmites but with interesting rock formations and water features. In fact, much of the path was wet and I'd only worn my sandals. I wasn't prepared for a precarious jaunt through a cave, but I managed without tumbling into the various shadowy pits of uncertain depths.

Back in town, we had time to spare before our bus took us back to Daegu so we ordered too much food at a Chinese restaurant. South Korea, like the United States, enjoys Chinese food but has developed its own dishes to the point that it's no longer actual Chinese food. Again, like the United States, this hybrid cuisine is delicious. My favorite, *jjajjangmyeon*, is a noodle dish with a black bean sauce and bits of pork. Imagine slurping a savory beef noodle soup when you were sick as a child and you've about got the gist of what makes jjajjangmyeon appealing. Even better is to put the jjajjang sauce on fried rice. There is some overlap with American Chinese food too. *Tong su yook* is basically sweet and sour pork. At any rate, it's common to find Korean Chinese restaurants next to bus terminals so it became a tradition of sorts to eat Korean Chinese on trips. We ordered tong su yook this go around, and ate maybe half of it between all five of us. The other good thing about Korean Chinese food is that it's typically very cheap, so we didn't feel terrible about not finishing our food.

And that was all we got to see of Samcheok. There are varying ways to measure the success of a trip, and I suppose many of them would've deemed this one a general failure. We didn't get to spend time on the beach or ride the railbikes, but the fun quotient never went down. We got a cave out of it, and some scenery, and we still got to see the penises. By God, did we see the penises. By some measures, it was a roaring success. Complications arose and were overcome with everyone still in high spirits at the end. The railbikes never did get crossed off the Korea Bucket List; someone else will have to tell me if they're worth it. That's how it goes with travel. Sometimes, you have to read somebody else's travel book.

It doesn't take long to tire of Korean architecture from this or any other century, I'm sorry to say. Palaces look much the same. Temples are all but indistinguishable aside from their size or what surrounds them. Don't get me started on modern, shoebox developments. I don't mean to dump on Korean architectural history, but you could find more historical variety in one block in Rome than you could find anywhere in South Korea, and Korea has just as long a history to refer to. I don't think this is because Koreans were or are incapable of designing unique buildings. I think it's because Koreans have a history of finding what works for them and sticking to it for a really long time. Like a temple? Build it again.

My interest was piqued, then, when I learned of an attractive fortress in Suwon. While there's no shortage of temples and palaces, intact fortresses are a bit in short supply. It's not unusual to pass some ruins of an ancient fort's walls on a mountain trail, but nothing to the magnitude of a fully-formed fortress. Suwon was officially on the bucket list.

Originally, we were going to pair Suwon with a stop near Osan Air Force Base, the largest American airfield in South Korea. I say near because we can't just waltz into a base as civilians. To accommodate the needs of the American military and their families, a large shopping and dining area grew outside the base's gates much like Itaewon in Seoul. It was here, according to Maria's father who was stationed there in the 2000's, that you can get anything from $5 mink blankets to customizable jerseys. The latter interested me greatly. Daegu's much smaller Camp Walker has a similar street devoted to things Americans might be interested in, so one day we walked into the jersey store to look for anything Ohio State. There was one XXL Eddie George jersey. We went ahead and bought it and Maria took it to a seamstress to adjust. We wear roughly but not exactly the same size of clothes, so she used herself as an example for the seamstress to adjust to, adding the word 'bigger' in hopes that she would leave a little extra room. She did not. The jersey came back fitting Maria perfectly. I would have to find my own. In the end, we decided that it wasn't necessary to go to Osan and that we'd just go to Suwon. That was a useless story. I apologize. Anyway, now you know why Maria has an Eddie George jersey and I, the much bigger football fan, do not.

Our train pulled into the Suwon train station, bright and sterile like many large train stations in Korea, and very clean. We took a cab to a nearby Hyundai apartment complex where our Air BnB host lived. It can be a chore in the large apartment complexes to find the correct building out of thirty, but they were numbered on the sides and we eventually found where our host lived. She was a kind, young mom who spoke passable English. Her daughter was shy, her husband somewhere else. We didn't dawdle long before we took our day trip bag and set off for the fortress. We hailed another taxi, and a few thousand won and a couple minutes later, we were at the main gate of Hwaseong Fortress.

Hwaseong Fortress was initially built by King Jeongjo to house and honor the remains of his father, the late Crown Prince Sado. The Crown Prince Sado was the mentally unstable son of King Yeongjo of the Joseon Dynasty. In 1762, as punishment for an altercation with an official at court, King Yeongjo ordered his son to commit suicide. The prince refused, naturally. Therefore, by command of the king, the Crown Prince Sado was tied up and locked into a rice chest where he died eight days later from dehydration and starvation at the ripe old age of 27. Jeongjo eventually assumed the throne and years later, adamant about restoring his father's good name, moved his father's remains to Suwon where he built a tomb.

The tomb was only one part of King Jeongjo's master plan to move the capital from Seoul to Suwon. In 1794, he began building a grand fortress around the tomb that could also serve as city walls. Common practice during this time was to protect a city with serviceable but unfortified walls and then evacuate to a nearby mountain fort if the need arose. Jeongjo's fortress, Hwaseong, would be strong enough to forgo the hike to the mountains. The walls, three and a half miles around and piled high with stone, would take quite an army, one larger and more powerful than the Japanese brought with them in the 1500's, to penetrate. Additionally, the fortress was designed with a host of features in case of a siege. Periodically along the walls, Jeongjo built watch towers, artillery towers, floodgates, bunkers, arrow-launching platforms, and beacon towers. Secret gates in the walls allowed for covert operations and offensive maneuvers. King Jeongjo also built Hwaseong to be beautiful. Most city walls or fortresses were utilitarian in nature, but Hwaseong incorporated what was fashionable in Joseon Dynasty architecture into the roofs of the towers, namely the colors green and red. All told, Hwaseong fortress was a big deal and an honorable bid to move the capital from Seoul. It never happened, but he did successfully move the court to Hwaesong, and the city grew and prospered.

Today, much of central Suwon still lies inside the walls, which are still intact and mostly original. Modern multi-lane roads either weave under the gates or, in some cases, bulldoze through. The entire structure is maintained, and a trail snakes along the top of the wall. Our cab dropped us off right outside the archery demonstration area, which had sounded fun on paper. Of course I wanted to shoot arrows in an old fort. A closer look at the participants rendered them all under the age of 10, though, and we realized that no real arrows would be shot. We moved on.

The outer walls are a breezy, pleasant stroll. Costumed characters interpret the various features of the fortress and how they were used. One gentleman in colorful traditional garb explained to us how his cannon worked. As the fortress sits on high ground, the view encompasses nearly the entire city of Suwon, with its sports complexes and high rises and other indistinguishable landmarks from any other city, save for Suwon Jeil Church, a 10-story gothic building. Rather than invaders, the walls keep out a neatly manicured row of pink flowers. A pile of shoes outside a pagoda indicated that the inside was open for resting, so we slipped off our shoes and joined a handful of people already inside enjoying the shade and a sit away from the city noise. I don't recall how much admission was to the fortress, but it wasn't more than $3. I've paid more for much, much less.

While the area of the fortress near the main gate is parklike, it doesn't take too long to reach the section of the city still inside the walls. There are no high-rises here, but most of the buildings are still modern and drab. A creek meanders through the middle, so we went down some stairs to join a path that meandered with it. Stepping stones allow pedestrians to cross the creek intermittently through the neighborhood. Herons and little fish still thrive in the watery grasses despite living smack dab in the middle of a large city. Ahead, a traditional-looking floodgate marked the boundary of the fortress walls. We walked underneath it to exit the fortress and look for something to eat. Not far from the walls, a fried dumpling restaurant beckoned at the head of a narrow but busy street. We ordered too many and then sat in the cramped second floor, watching motorcycles and pedestrians navigate the bustle below.

I'd be lying to you if I said the Hwaseong Fortress was the only thing bringing us to Suwon. Word gets around, amongst foreigners, of unusual museums and parks around the country. Millennials are especially fond of finding tacky, one of a kind attractions, as if on a mission to collect the strangest, most unique experiences if only to say "look where I am, ironically enjoying this weird thing." Thus, we hopped in a cab and told the driver to take us to the Mr. Toilet House.

Sim Jae-Duck, Mr. Toilet himself, is perhaps most famous for his campaign to modernize Suwon's restroom facilities before hosting the 2002 World Cup. Before the campaign, the city's restrooms were typically disgusting affairs. As mayor of Suwon, he oversaw the removal of these facilities, often squat toilets, and their replacement with clean western-style toilets. Although the upgrade was surely appreciated by western butts, the campaign was mostly used as a means to shine a light on hygiene, or the lack thereof, in many of the world's bathrooms. According to the Center for Disease Control, "88% of diarrhea cases worldwide are linked to unsafe water, inadequate sanitation or insufficient hygiene." The resulting dehydration leads to 1.5 million deaths a year, and those are mostly children. Hardly a sunny statistic surrounding a man named Mr. Toilet.

To that end, Mr. Sim accumulated an impressive resume of achievements and titles surrounding his work in sanitation. He was a chair of the organizing committee to establish the World Toilet Association, president of the Korea Toilet Association, and established the world's first Public Toilet Act. Also, in 1939, he was reportedly born in a toilet. To celebrate the inauguration of the World Toilet Association, he had his house bulldozed and replaced with a new house shaped like a toilet bowl. I suppose with a moniker like Mr. Toilet, you might as well lean into it. After his death a few years later, his family donated the house to the city of Suwon, which now houses the Mr. Toilet House museum and gardens. Its' official name is Haewoojae, roughly translated to "a place to solve one's worries," which is certainly what I do when dropping the kids off at the pool.

From the front driveway, Mr. Toilet House looks less like a toilet bowl and more like an Epcot attraction: white, with a stripe of space-age tinted windows and a crown of flags over the top. A sculpture of an orange pile of poop with big eyes, an inquisitive little mouth, cherubim wings, and, distressingly, a branch sticking out of its head adorns the front lawn. This mascot, whose name I can only begin to dream, showed up throughout the museum inside, this Epcot's Mickey Mouse. Never has an orange, coiled turd been so overutilized in the name of edutainment. An entire wall was devoted to children's artistic renderings of the character, as well as other interpretations of poo, in a prominent hallway of the museum.

The building does try to hold up its 'museum' end of the bargain with exhibits on toilets from around the world. Another exhibit chronicles Mr. Sim's sanitation and hygiene efforts in Suwon and elsewhere. It doesn't stay serious for long. A visiting exhibition portrayed send-ups of famous artwork with new toilet-themed contexts. My personal favorite was Rodin's The Thinker, or perhaps 'The Tinkler,' sitting on the john. I was sorry to see that I would not be in the area when the special exhibits 'Poop! Save our Earth!' and 'Poop Painting Contest' would arrive. A staircase to the roof allows visitors to stand in the 'bowl' of the building. There isn't a view, or anything remotely interesting up there, so we allowed ourselves a moment to think 'yep, looks like a bowl' and went back inside.

Strangely enough, there are no public bathrooms in the Mr. Toilet House. Instead, they direct people to a building across the gardens that belongs to the city's park department. The facilities are, I'm delighted to say, satisfactorily clean and well-equipped. This is not always the case in South Korea – bathrooms famously are short on soap, toilet paper, or both -- so I'm glad the museum made a point to demonstrate how a tidy, hygienic bathroom ought to look. Relieved, we took a turn about the gardens, which were verdant, sunny, and full of toilet and poop-related sculptures. Some were educational depictions of historical outhouses and hygienic practices. Others, like toilet bowls filled with flowers, people squatting to take care of their business, and more piles of dung, bordered on overkill. The inside of the museum straddles the line between education and tacky kitsch. The garden leaps over that line, does a summersault in the grass, and then takes a dump. In fact, there's an entire wall devoted to this very illustration. Naked butts squat and release some smiley-looking feces in colors that would suggest a severe health disorder. This was all beginning to get tiresome and repetitive. We were a good walk from a main road, so we had the lady at the front desk call us a cab to take us to more civilized haunts. One can only ironically appreciate poop for so long.

Leaving Korea

That Time We Were Sad

It's amazing how many things you can accumulate over two years. When we moved to South Korea, we each brought a suitcase, a duffel bag, and a backpack stuffed to the brim with what belongings seemed necessary at the time, including our not insignificant DVD collection. There wasn't a prayer of fitting all our stuff in the same space now, so we shipped four boxes of belongings ahead of time. Since it was August, we departed with our winter clothes first, and some souvenirs we'd purchased throughout our travels. We'd also collected a lot of clothes and other things that had amusing or incorrect English phrases, honest mementos that would be impossible to find in the States. Many of these featured characters from popular culture that in places like the United States would be subject to stringent copyright laws. For instance, for Maria's birthday I bought her a hoodie with a surly cat and the words 'hakuna matata.' How, might I ask, am I supposed to pass that up? I also got a giggle out of a children's pencil case with a cute kitty and pastel lettering that said 'I like pussy.' Maria found some winners too. At Homeplus, she picked up a green sweater with a bunny-thing with a bow walking a turtle on a leash. The wording on the sweater goes as such: "He is Akira. Akira has a turtle." Who Akira is, why he is dressed like a girl, why he walks his turtle and what he has done to deserve a sweater are all mysteries to us, but clearly the sweater needed to be bought, and so it was. These were all dandy purchases at the time, but after a while we'd gotten a little ahead of ourselves. Into the box they went, as we would not need them on our trip to Europe.

Yes, we were headed to Europe. It was about the same price to fly over either ocean back to the east coast of the United States. In addition, the euro was down and we were soon to be unemployed with an unlimited amount of time, so the time was right. My grandfather came to America from Italy as a boy, and we still keep in correspondence with the distant relatives that remain in Milan. I'd met them a few times when they visited the United States and they were eager for us to see them in Italy, so it was the perfect time to oblige them. It didn't hurt that I'd always wanted to go to Italy and see the 'homeland,' so we made plans to tour Italy and then head up through Austria and into Germany, where the rest of me is from.

While we packed up our belongings, we also packed up our life. We canceled our phone plans, filed some paperwork for our severance packages and tax reimbursements, and sold off what we could. We said our last goodbyes to our students. I took my selfie stick with me every day one week. In each class I held it over my head and let the children fill the space around me with sweet, silly faces. I bought rice cakes for the faculty. Ji Young helped me write a message in Hangul saying "thank you for two wonderful years." My desk was easy to clean, since I'd brought very few belongings. I nabbed my nice headphones before anyone could incorrectly claim they belonged to the school.

On my last day of school, I went to my last meeting in the Vice Principal's office. I'd long since given up trying to look engaged with the meeting and was playing a word puzzle on my phone under the table. About five minutes before the start of the meeting, Hyun Soo had hinted that I might prepare a farewell speech. Even though Maria and I had taken private lessons in addition to lessons through EPIK, my Korean was not good enough to string together meaningful sentences for a farewell speech. I suppose I'm dense like that. Hyun Soo waved it off, claiming that the faculty knew English well enough that they'd understand. The Principal said my name. Hyun Soo, standing with the Principal, ushered me to the front of the office where everyone's eyes were on me. He handed me a glass plaque, much like the one handed to the first Vice Principal I'd met two years earlier. It read, "We hereby express our sincere appreciation to Matthew Caracciolo for your dedicated efforts and outstanding performance as an English Teacher at Maecheon Elementary School. You are an inspiration to others." I chuckled a little on the inside as I read the last part. Hyun Soo asked if there was anything I'd like to say.

Whatever I did end up saying, it's not what I wanted to say. What I wanted to say was that I was entirely grateful to be made part of the group, so to speak, for two years. I'd been humbled by the faculty's kindness, patience and hard work. I wish I had known more of them better, spoke better Korean, and could repay their generosity in some way, but I knew that unless they came to Ohio, there was nothing I could give.

"Do you have a favorite memory you'd like to share?" asked Hyun Soo, sensing my failure at speechifying.

"Field Day," I lied. I had too many memories to process. The school had hosted a Field Day a few months prior, and it was a much grander community affair than any field day in my elementary school experience. Entire families came and participated and shared picnics outside. It was a wonderful day, but it wasn't even close to my favorite memory. What to choose? The uninitiated rendition of the Fast Food Song? I wasn't telling everyone in the school about that. At any rate, the teachers applauded and I was allowed to sit down again.

Some of the hardest goodbyes were to our fellow waygooks. These people hailed from Ireland, Australia, New Zealand, and other places I wasn't likely to reach anytime soon. Some of these friends were perennial wanderers, always on to the next thing so long as it wasn't home. These people would be even harder to reconnect with. For our fellow American expatriates, I suppose the opposite was true. Places like Boston or Kansas seemed next door in comparison. We would practically be able see each other from our living rooms.

Gail and Phillip were especially hard to say goodbye to. South Africa is an awful long way away, and not exactly a cheap flight. We all loved each other too much not to see each other again, but there was no telling when. We decided, for our last day together, to do all the things we'd loved doing in Daegu. In one Saturday, we went to our board game cafe to play Ticket to Ride, took a group picture in a tacky photo booth, played arcade games, went bowling, ate kimchi jjim, enjoyed dessert and coffee at a cafe, and got some drinks at a sidewalk bar. Unwilling to admit that our day was over, we sang karaoke into the night at a multibang.

On the day before our flight to Rome, we packed up our life. We ended up having to throw away a lot of stuff: t-shirts, furniture, dishes nobody wanted. Our stuff just, and I mean just, fit into our bags. There wasn't room for a single other thing. A pencil eraser would've sent my suitcase into 57 directions.

I wasn't the only one leaving Maecheon Elementary School. For once, the Vice Principal was staying and it was the Principal who was leaving, or in this case, retiring. His retirement party was on the evening before our flight to Rome the next day. Somehow, I ended up sitting with Gym Teacher and Ramen. After the food and the speeches, people wandered between tables like at weddings, and I not-too surreptitiously moved to a different table and found a seat next to Ji Ho. I told him he was welcome in my house at any time, should he find himself in the United States. Then we said our goodbyes. I said my goodbyes to Hyun Soo too. I thanked him for everything and wished him well; he and his wife had another baby on the way. Despite it all, I did end up saying goodbye to Gym Teacher and Ramen. Despite their peculiarities, they were very nice people.

After the dinner, I returned to the apartment to retrieve Maria and we went to a cafe to say our goodbyes to Jang Mi and Ji Young. These were hard goodbyes to make. Jang Mi had been an indispensable friend. I would miss our badminton, our walks, and our conversations. I wished her well, and that she might move back to Busan with her family. Perhaps her husband would get a job there. They were big travelers too, so like Ji Ho, I told her (pleaded, perhaps) that they visit us in America. The four of us talked into the night, but the following day would be a big one and we still had a few things to pack. We crossed the street and hailed a taxi. Jang Mi lived nearby, so after we all gave our hugs, Ji Young, Maria and I climbed into the cab. That was the last I saw of Jang Mi.

And then I looked at Ji Young. Other than Maria, there wasn't a person I spent more time with in the last two years than her. As frustratingly unstructured as our classes could be, as illogical as her decisions were, I'd grown rather accustomed to having her around. I came to rely on her in the way I relied on a Chicago weather report: she was available every day, often wrong, but consistently unreliable enough that I could adjust to and even come to enjoy the mystery. As often as she made things hard, she also made things right. She'd taken me to the doctor's, helped me make travel reservations, showed me how to use the bus system, and argued with phone companies. Behind the scenes, she did a considerable amount of paperwork to make my life in Korea sun smoothly. In all, she'd done far more than I gave her credit for, and by the looks of it, she wasn't ready to stop. As the cab stopped at our intersection, she teared up.

"We'll see each other again, right?" she said.

"Yes, it'll happen," I replied. And I meant it. Maria and I got out of the car and the driver took off immediately. Ji Young turned and waved from the back seat.

The next morning, we had one more goodbye to make. We stuffed a cab with our belongings and headed to the bus station, where our last bus trip would take us to Incheon International airport. The bus pulled in on time and we loaded our heavy bags into the storage below.

We took our seats and I pulled out my neck pillow and iPod for the journey. I queued up *Angels and Demons* on my Kindle. We were heading to Rome, after all, and I wanted Dan Brown to take me to as many famous landmarks as possible and color them with conspiracy before walking the streets myself. But before I dove into the novel, I looked out the window one last time. The bus was already on the highway. To our right was our neighborhood. To our left was Daegu. The road turned a corner around a mountain and the city was gone.

Two years before, we drove out of Chicago and I didn't look back. On that bus to Incheon, I buried my face in my neck pillow and cried. I didn't cry during any of our individual goodbyes. I didn't cry leaving the school. No, the feels snuck in and slapped me in the face all at once, in public. In some ways Daegu felt more like home than Chicago ever did. Talk about unexpected. So there we were on the bus sad to leave our life, but happy to go home, but sad to have no job, but happy to go to Europe. I don't think I've been more emotionally confused in my life. I just sat in the bus thinking "God, what do you want me to do with this day?" There was nothing to do but hope that the emotions ended somewhere positive, tell Maria that I loved her, and feel small against an incredibly blessed life. That, and find the Illuminati.

We would have one more adventure in South Korea, although I use the word adventure here loosely. Our bus arrived at the airport a comfortable three hours ahead of our flight. We were among the first in line to check our bags and print out our tickets. With all of our bags, we were well beyond the one free checked bag policy enforced by the airline and were mentally prepared to pay a few hundred bucks for the rest. We walked up to the counter and the gentleman gave our luggage an appraising look.

"How many bags?" he asked.

"Four," I replied. Two extra bags. "What's the extra bag fee?"

"Please put your bags on the scale."

I heaved our bags onto the scale one at a time. The man spent a moment typing and, without a change in tenor, said "$1600."

I might have laughed in his face.

"For two extra bags, it's going to cost us $1600?" I asked. He might as well have said $1.6 million. The idea that we would pay that much for two bags was laughable. Surely he didn't expect us to pay that much. We'd sooner throw our bags in the ocean.

"Some routes into Europe base the rate on kilograms and not per bag," he explained calmly. "Also, the length of the flight is a factor."

We were going to fly from Seoul to Rome, easily 5,500 miles away.

"What are our options?" asked Maria.

"Can you consolidate bags?" he suggested.

We explained that wasn't an option. He looked at his watch. "The post office downstairs closes in 45 minutes."

We told him we'd be back. He told us to skip the line once we did. For a man who had to say absurd things to people like "Your bags will be $1600," he was very accommodating. We rushed to the escalator, and by rushed I mean trudged under the unrelenting weight of two bags and a backpack apiece, and down to the floor below and found the post office thankfully free of long lines. We bought four of the largest boxes they were selling and unfolded them. Maria began the paperwork while, out in the hallway along the railing, I sprawled all our bags and began stuffing the boxes with anything I didn't think we'd need in Europe. As it was August, I packed most of what remained of our cold weather clothing, saving only a pair or two of jeans each. Thankfully, I had the foresight to remember we would be heading through the Alps and that a jacket might be useful. That foresight, however, did not reach past Europe and we would go well into October in Ohio with a minimal amount of warm clothes. Superfluous knickknacks, t-shirts, and underwear were thrown into the boxes, which quickly filled up. Mind you, I did this in full view of any passerby's who, I presume, found great sport in watching the foreigner take up half a hallway with his stuff. It was one more chance to be the strange waygook.

Meanwhile, Maria was hard at work with the paperwork. Her Korean handwriting was capable but slow, so after the first of four forms she asked the bewildered lady at the desk to help her with the other three, using the first as a reference.

With a sufficient amount of our stuff in boxes, my next task was to consolidate and then pack the extra bags themselves. I moved what remained in our duffel bags to the larger suitcases and then folded the bags themselves into what space was left in the boxes. With 10 minutes until the post office closed for the day, we closed the boxes and presented them to the counter where the lady taped them up, added the address form, and set them on the scale. Our total to ship four boxes to Ohio was $300, about what I expected to pay in extra baggage fees to begin with. The added bonus was that we wouldn't have to haul the stuff around Europe, which in retrospect would've been about the worst idea in the world. For one last kind gesture, the women working the post office took pity on us and gave us juice boxes and snacks. Grateful for their help, their patience, and their snacks, we headed back up to the ticketing level where the gentleman awaited our return. True to his word, he let us skip the now formidable line and took our suitcases without question.

Our two and a half weeks in Europe were wonderful, so wonderful that they would hardly make a good story, so I'll paraphrase. We arrived in Rome at 7:00am local time, much too early to take a nap, so there was nothing to do but stay awake and see the sights. Jetlagged and sun drunk in the Roman August heat, we walked from north of the Castel Sant'Angelo where our hotel was all the way down to the Vittorio Emanuele II monument, stopping at nearly everything interesting in between. If we kept moving, we were fine, but the moment we stopped to eat or drink or rest, our exhaustion became apparent. I was in very real danger of making a new hotel out of the cafe in the Vittorio Emanuele II monument.

Our Europe trip took us in a generally northward direction. From Rome and its ancient ruins we took a train to Florence, where we were whisked away to the Renaissance. On a gorgeous evening we hiked up to the Piazzale Michelangelo to take in the Florence skyline under a red sunset. The railing facing the city was crowded with people, like us, trying to take the perfect picture. We took the opportunity to startle some Korean tourists when we asked if they wanted us to take their picture. From Florence we headed to Milan, decidedly more transformed by the Industrial Revolution than Florence or Rome, where we met up with my distant Italian relatives. They took us in warmly and wheeled us around the Milan area. My cousin is something of a smooth talker, and I mean that in the best way possible. He's entirely capable of making a friend within seconds and convincing that friend to let us do things that are off limits for others. On that end we found ourselves, for 30 seconds tops, next to the starting line of the Monza Autodromo where, hours before, the Formula 1 Italian Grand Prix had just wrapped up for the day. My Italian is a bit better than my Korean but I still don't know what my cousin said to persuade the security guard other than we were Americans in town only a short while. Perhaps we looked pathetic.

We bid our Italian family farewell and took a bus through the Swiss Alps, where we played Ticket to Ride Switzerland on our Kindle en route. If you fly over the Alps, you completely miss the experience of transitioning between cultures. In Switzerland, anyway, you go up a mountain surrounded by places with names like Bellinzona and Lostalo and go back down to places with names like Nufenen and Splügen, with an appropriate architectural costume change. Seven hours after we departed Milan, the bus dropped us off in Munich, a completely different world. This is a foreign concept for most of us Americans. You drive seven hours out of Chicago and you're just getting out of Gary, Indiana. To drive seven hours through a mountain range and come out the other side to a different language and culture doesn't happen for us. We'd sooner expect to find Narnia in our wardrobes.

Munich, on this day, was only a stop and we took a second bus to Salzburg. The next morning, we saw the town with Fraulein Maria's Bicycle Tour, which is somewhere on my unwritten list of the five best things I've done in my life. Fraulein Maria, for the unfortunate souls who don't know, is the main character in the musical *The Sound of Music*, which takes place in Salzburg. The movie was also filmed there, thus the bicycle tour that took us to the movie's filming locations and, by extension, around the city itself. It's marvelous.

We returned to Munich, which was to be our last stop and a home base for day trips throughout Bavaria. This was September 2015, the very beginning of the refugee crisis that would dominate Europe, and the Munich Hauptbahnhof was the center of operations. Already, people were arriving in droves and authorities were doing what they could to help. It's a bit awkward, I have to admit, to stand in line at the train station for your tour to Neuschwanstein Castle within view of haggard-looking families who have slept little and gone through God only knows what to find safety. We had our bag for the day. They had their bags for their lives. At the time, the Germans looked relatively well-prepared, with shopping carts upon shopping carts of clothing, bottles of water, and other necessities. I have no idea if it was enough. On one of the three trains it took us to get to Rothenburg ob der Tauber the following day, a family en route to a new home was passed out. I quietly hoped that they were near their destination.

On our last day in Europe, we were beat. We'd had enough of trains, of figuring things out, of full itineraries. We were anxious to go home. I'm sorry to say that Germany did not receive our full admiration for these reasons. What we saw and ate was wonderful, but mentally we were already looking forward to the United States. On our last day before flying to Washington D.C., we made a change of plans. Rather than look at another priceless piece of art or impossibly ornate palace, we sauntered about the Englischer Gardens in Munich with no set agenda. We stopped at beer gardens, rented a swan paddle boat, walked past nude sunbathers, and generally soaked in German culture in a way I think most Germans would appreciate: drinking beer, walking in a leafy park in the sunshine, and averting the eyes of old, naked men.

Epilogue

The first thing we did in the United States, after two years of being away, was eat a burrito at a Chipotle 10 minutes outside Dulles airport. We sat inside the near-empty restaurant—it was well past dinnertime—and savored the faux-Mexican goodness before any reverse culture shock set in. Two years is a long time to be away, and I'd since pivoted toward a new normal. I looked at the restaurant, and later out the window of the CR-V, like a foreigner looking at the United States for the first time. I'd never been able to do that before. What did the menus look like? What was the interaction like with the guy behind the cash register? How did the road signs differ? How well did people adhere to the road rules? I was tired, so the easiest way to keep a conversation going in the car was to compare everything we saw with the Korean way or European way of doing things. We probably did that all the way to College Park, taking advantage of the fact that we'd just returned and making comparisons would later become annoying. The moment we stepped foot in my parents' home, Maria and I had officially circumnavigated the globe, having visited their house before leaving for Korea and, since then, gradually made our way west back to College Park. I don't know what to tell you, flat earthers. Try it for yourself.

Within hours of activating our new phones in America, Maria began receiving mysterious calls explaining that her student loans were in default. The woman on the other end claimed that Maria owed $12,000 more than we thought she did. I told Maria to hang up the first couple times, that it was likely a scam. It was not. They had been trying to get a hold of us for two years about the loan. They started with snail mail, sending notices to our address in Chicago beginning one month after we left. Wonderful timing, loan providers.

Our trips to the Department of Motor Vehicles were no more welcoming. My driver's license had expired while we were out, and I needed to get a new one without a permanent address. On our first trip, we waited for three hours in a frigid air-conditioned lobby only for the woman to tell us we didn't have the right paperwork. I needed one more piece of mail with my parents' address to make it, for a couple weeks at least, my permanent address.

Before we left for South Korea, we'd deposited our stuff in three separate houses. The owners of all three promised they had no intentions of moving within the year. To their credit, that was true. They didn't move within the one year we originally planned to stay. Two of them, however, did move the following year. By the time we returned to Ohio, our things were distributed across six locations. One of those was a storage unit in which a family of industrious mice had happily chewed into half our boxes and pooped on our dishes, linens, and clothes.

Our belongings in the storage unit weren't the only casualty to furry rascals. Our 2000 Honda Civic had admirably served us in Chicago and in our subsequent travels before we left the country. By the time we deposited the car in Oklahoma to live with Maria's parents' while we were away, the cruise control no longer worked, it needed a new muffler, the auxiliary port wasn't working properly, and the air conditioning was shot. We should have sold our good and faithful servant then, but the proposition of returning without a car didn't sound appealing, so we hoped it would stay alive until we returned. A family of mysterious creatures (mice again, probably) had other plans. They made a house out of the engine. We got $300 off of Craigslist.

"Have you hit the ground running?" friends and family would ask as we reunited over the next few months. Hit the ground, yes. All told, our first couple months back in the United States were a painful reminder that, sometimes, longing for home can be a lot more romantic than coming home. I was under the delusion that everything would work out once we returned for the simple reason that it was home. I'm afraid, if you're under such delusions yourself, that this is not the case. I'd been prepared to go home for a long time, but I hadn't considered that home may not have been preparing for me. I was back to square one, it seemed, on the job front, and would-be employers weren't nearly as excited about my two years as a Native English Teacher as I hoped they would be. Also, it's easy to imagine that when you leave a place, everything pauses until you come back. People you know aren't moving houses, having babies, or switching jobs; they're sitting on their couches doing a crossword patiently waiting for your return. In that regard, returning to Columbus was something of a disappointment. At family gatherings, there were babies I'd never met, and kids that were two years older and taller. Among friends, there were new friendships made, new lovers. There were too many people to meet, too many new names to learn, and they'd all made memories without me.

Before Korea, I'd avoided moving back to Columbus because I wanted a proud return, with a full treasure chest and banners caught high in the breeze. I didn't want to return empty handed, with the flag drooping over my shoulders. It certainly felt that way at holiday parties when people politely asked how the transition was going. For the first Christmas, I had to navigate how to tell people about our low job prospects. The following Christmas, it was the frustration and pain of back-to-back miscarriages. This wasn't the home I'd been missing, or at least it didn't feel like it.

Home itself changed while we were away, and I can't say most of the changes have been for the better. We returned to the United States in the midst of the 2016 presidential campaign, if that tells you anything. I needn't say more about it other than it was an atrocious and embarrassing marathon of people, either on my Facebook wall or on my TV, making reductive assumptions about people that weren't their people and then responding accordingly. On the evening of the election, as results filtered in, my Facebook wall exploded with angry, knee-jerk comments like 'Fuck white people!' Conversely, in my two years abroad, I didn't see anything half so startling as a house waving the Confederate battle flag on the road to my grandma's house. I never felt more like a waygook in my own country. I had half a mind to knock on the door and point out the irony that he lived in Union County, Ohio, and that thirty miles away in Columbus the NHL's Blue Jackets are named as such because Ohio supplied more Union troops in the Civil War than any other state, but what would've been the point? People believe what they want to believe. That isn't a new development, but it's made it all the more difficult to adjust to my country after two years of, by necessity, questioning everything I was ever taught about how the world works. Mark Twain famously said it best 150 years ago: "Travel is fatal to prejudice, bigotry, and narrow-mindedness, and many of our people need it sorely on these accounts. Broad, wholesome, charitable views of men and things cannot be acquired by vegetating in one little corner of the earth all one's lifetime." Watching America divide itself from afar and then coming home to see it up close has been the hardest dose of reverse culture shock to swallow. Again, the home I'd envisioned for years, in a way, no longer existed.

I'm reminded, though, by the very nature of Central Ohio's boring geography, that home is what you make of it. The flat farmland and indistinguishable geographical features are a blank canvas. We don't have the luxury of famous monuments or mountain ranges. Everything Columbus has is the result of hard work, of somebody looking at a piece of land, framing it in their fingers and saying "I can make that a coffee shop. I can make that a park. I can make that a university. I can make that a home." Columbus is worth living in because people made it that way. Goodness knows nobody lives here for the weather or the view.

So I've had to reinvent myself. I've had to start over from scratch, to fall in love with my home all over again. Granted, it wasn't as hard the second time around. We have Chipotle back in our lives, after all, and football at normal hours. We have a membership at our beloved zoo, which never seems to be short on adorable baby animals. Columbus itself continues to surprise with new places to explore and new things to eat. As an added bonus, when I speak to people around here in English, they respond in kind, which generally makes things easier. I have a bike again, and metro parks to ride it in. Finally, it goes without saying that we're tickled to be on the same continent as most of our family and friends, many of which dutifully make Columbus a better place every day. I admire their pursuits to make things, start businesses, and serve the community. It inspires me to give more of myself to my city, rather than expect it to give something to me. If this is my home, after all, then I have an equal stake in making it a better place. I've helped write for startups and volunteered with my church. I've patronized local businesses. It can become too easy, as a traveler, to show up and say 'what do you have for me?' That's not how you make a home. That's how you make a scrapbook. That's looking for the next high, demanding that every place impress you a little more than the last. Traveling is reduced to an addiction.

Every day, little by little, I feel more at home. I get excited about traveling again, but I also get excited about the prospects of a new sandwich place, a favorite trail, or next year's football season. We make plans with friends and take advantage of events happening around town. Our conversations with the people we love have become less about our time apart and more about our recent time together. We're growing roots, as they say, and they are not a bad thing.

Still, not a day goes by that I don't think about South Korea. I still get emails from my Korean bank, for one thing. I don't know how to turn them off. I still talk to Ji Young, and Jang Mi and Hyun Soo on occasion. Sometimes, when I'm feeling a bit like a waygook again, I remember that it's not just my home that's changed, but that I've changed too, that part of me is still in South Korea. I still find it weird to wear shoes in someone's house. I have a craving for kimchi fried rice that never seems to go away. I miss the movie theater popcorn in multiple flavors, the comprehensive train and bus system, the clothing that completely disregards copyright laws. In some sense, it feels like I'll never be in one place again. Too often my mind strays to memories, becoming ever more distant, and to friends a million miles away. To Ji Young, to Jang Mi, to Ji Ho, to Hyun Soo, to Gail, to Phillip. To Daegu.

Bilbo Baggins faces this dilemma too, upon returning from the Lonely Mountain in *The Hobbit*. "Something is the matter with you," says Gandalf as he and Bilbo step into the Shire. "You are not the hobbit that you were." Indeed, after reestablishing himself at his house in Bag End, Bilbo takes to writing poetry and visiting with elves and dwarves and other outsiders. This diminishes his once considerable reputation as an upstanding hobbit, that is, a neighbor who doesn't do anything unexpected or adventurous. While I'd like to think our reputations are in good shape, Maria and I are in the same boat as Bilbo. We are not the same people we were when we left Chicago. Although we've been empowered to chase new experiences, expand our comfort zones, and seek the truth behind assumptions, I find that the more we do this, the smaller I become. The more we experience, the more we travel, the more I feel the depth of a glorious creation, made deeper by its Creator.

"You don't really suppose, do you, that all your adventures and escapes were managed by mere luck, just for your sole benefit?" says Gandalf to Bilbo, long after their adventure is over. "You are a very fine person, Mr. Baggins, and I am very fond of you; but you are only quite a little fellow in a wide world after all!"

"Thank goodness," Bilbo replies.

Thank goodness indeed.

Hi there! Like what you just read? Please write a review on Amazon, Barnes & Noble, or Goodreads.

About the Author

Matthew Caracciolo is a travel writer who primarily focuses on South Korea, the Midwest, and his hometown of Columbus, Ohio. His work has appeared on *Amateurtraveler.com*, in the *Daegu Compass*, *Columbus Navigator*, *Columbus: A Book Project*, and his blog on matthewcaracciolo.com. *The Waygook Book: A Foreigner's Guide to South Korea* is his debut novel. He lives in Columbus with his wife and their son.

CPSIA information can be obtained
at www.ICGtesting.com
Printed in the USA
LVHW080203130219
607372LV00008B/25/P